Edited by Roy Ferguson, Alan Pence, and Carey Denholm

Professional Child and Youth Care
Second Edition

UBCPress / Vancouver

09 08 07 06 05 04   5 4 3

Printed in Canada on acid-free paper ∞

National Library of Canada Cataloguing in Publication Data

Main entry under title:
  Professional child and youth care

  Includes bibliographical references and index.
  ISBN 0-7748-0423-8

  1. Child care – Canada. 2. Child care services – Canada. I. Ferguson, Roy.
II. Pence, Alan R., 1948- III. Denholm, Carey J., 1951-

HV861.C2P76 1992   362.7'1'0971   C93-091096-6

Canadä

UBC Press gratefully acknowledges the financial support for our publishing program of the Government of Canada through the Book Publishing Industry Development Program (BPIDP), and of the Canada Council for the Arts, and the British Columbia Arts Council.

UBC Press
The University of British Columbia
2029 West Mall
Vancouver, BC V6T 1Z2
604-822-5959 / Fax: 604-822-6083
www.ubcpress.ca

To our children:
Alexander, Leah, Eliot,
Justin, and Andrea

Contents

Preface to the Second Edition

In the half-dozen years since we wrote the preface to the first edition of this book it has been exciting to observe how quickly change in the field has occurred. The broad definition of the child and youth care field that was presented as a Canadian perspective in the first edition has recently been adopted by educators and practitioners in the United States as well. This means that the field will have a more consistent appearance on both sides of the 49th parallel. Educational programs will develop curriculum that is more standardized, and the ability to share teaching resources will become a reality. Service programs throughout the scope of the field will place a greater emphasis on the generic aspects of providing care across practice settings so that a more universal voice for the interests of children, youth, and families will be heard across the continent. Increasing attention will be given in both educational and service programs to aspects of multiculturalism. It would appear that the child and youth care field has adapted to change quickly and effectively. It will be fascinating to see where the next six years will take us.

When the first edition of this volume was published, the editors were faced with a number of difficult issues relating to the development of the book. We thought that the child and youth care field desperately needed a text but were unsure as to whether it should reflect a North American or a Canadian point of view. After considerable discussion, we decided to adopt a Canadian perspective in the book. This was a hard decision to make because it could possibly be interpreted as a form of isolationism by our colleagues south of the 49th parallel and occurred at a time when we were actively developing closer child and youth care linkages between Canada and the United States. Obviously, there were also significant implications for the decision with regard to the potential market for the book. We thought, however, that the scope and functioning of the child and youth care field in Canada was somewhat different than that in the U.S., and that it was vitally important to capture the unique Canadian perspective. Fortunately, in subsequent discussions of the text with our American colleagues, our decision was strongly supported and encouraged. In fact, the first and last chapters of this text contain material which first appeared in an article by Ferguson and Anglin (1985) in *Child Care Quarterly*.[1] Following the first edition of this text, a volume entitled *Perspectives in Professional Child and Youth Care* (Anglin, Denholm, Ferguson, and Pence 1990) was produced, which included contributions from authors throughout North America.[2]

The next major planning issue to be confronted was that of representing the broad scope of child and youth care functions and settings across Canada. This was a difficult problem to solve, since, within the confines of one text, it was not possible to include chapters on all of the settings which constitute the child and youth care mosaic in Canada. Consequently, we have included chapters on the following eight areas within the child and youth care field: residential child and youth care, juvenile justice, school-based child and youth care, child life (medical settings), child day care, early intervention programs, community-based child and youth care, and parent education/support programs. These particular areas were selected to represent points along the child and youth care service continuum because they illustrated the diversity of child and youth care practice and settings and were key to the field from a developmental and historical perspective. In this second edition of the book, we have included two new chapters, on rehabilitation and recreation, that have added considerably to the richness of the child and youth care service continuum. Obviously, there are still many other programs and settings, such as mental health, additional early childhood programs, and respite care, which could have been outlined if space had permitted. However, the intention of the text was not to present an exhaustive description of the entire child and youth care field but to illustrate that, in spite of the tremendous diversity of functions and settings, the similarities across these areas were greater than the differences.

---

1 Ferguson, R.V. and Anglin, J.P. 1985. The child care profession: A vision for the future. *Child Care Quarterly* 14:85–102
2 Anglin, J., Denholm, C., Ferguson, R., and Pence, A. (eds.). 1990. *Perspectives in professional child and youth care*. New York: Haworth

Another major issue in the planning of this text was that of achieving a geographical representation of authors from across Canada. In order to illustrate the extent of the Canadian child and youth care network, authors and editorial board members were selected on the basis of both interest area and geographic location. Clearly, there are countless others who could have been included, but the resulting list of people involved in the production of this text represent many of the key figures in the child and youth care field across Canada.

Of course, a text composed of invited chapters creates the problem of maintaining continuity across the contributions of authors with different perspectives, experiences, and writing styles. One solution to this problem would have been to devise an extensive format for the authors to follow in writing their chapters. We decided against this option, however, because we thought that it might be too restricting and, in fact, create more problems than it solved. We felt that these differences across chapters could be considered a strength as well as a weakness, and that if there really were common elements across the broad field of child and youth care, the reader would recognize them in spite of this diversity. We hoped, also, that the lack of homogeneity across chapters would reflect the colour and vitality existing within the child and youth care field.

The last major planning issue we encountered was identifying the target audience for the text. Since this would be the first text of its type in the field, it was difficult to avoid the tendency to adopt a 'shotgun' approach with regard to the market. We decided on the generalist perspective and hoped that the material would be of interest to child and youth care practitioners, college and university students, and to members of allied professions such as psychology, social work, education, nursing, and others in the health and human services. There is always a danger in pitching a book at too broad a target audience, but we thought this decision was justified, because our intention was to present an overview of the child and youth care field rather than to go into great depth in any of the areas.

Time has shown that our decisions were sound. The first edition of the book has been well received and is used as a basic text in educational programs in various parts of Canada. There is considerable movement in the U.S. towards the adoption of a broader definition of the field of child and youth care, a definition similar to the one outlined in this book, so that a more homogeneous North American perspective is emerging. The second edition of the text contains updates on all of the chapters and has added, as noted earlier, two new ones on rehabilitation and recreation. It is surprising how much has happened in the field since the first edition appeared in 1987, and the authors of each chapter have attempted to capture the major issues that have arisen and to examine their impact on child and youth care. The editing of the second edition has been complicated by one of the editors (Denholm) now being located in Australia, but modern electronic communication systems have made a continued collaboration possible.

As we noted in the first edition, this book represents the joint efforts of many contributors and we believe this is one of its greatest assets. We have thoroughly enjoyed the collaboration with our colleagues from across the country in producing this book and we would like to offer it as a tribute to the Canadian child and youth care field.

Roy Ferguson
Alan Pence
Carey Denholm

Preface to the First Edition

In this book, the first of its kind, the contributors illustrate the broad scope of the child and youth care field in Canada and note some of the similarities, differences, and critical issues within selected practice areas. Where the field was once primarily defined within the context of residential care and child day care, it is now seen in Canada from a wider perspective, as will be outlined in the subsequent chapters. However broad the child and youth care field might be it is the essence of practice, with its unique blend of caring and professionalism, that binds it together.

We also identify some of the key persons and programs upon which the child and youth care field is built. In acknowledging the history of the child and youth care field, as well as its current state, it is our intention for the text to serve as a transition to the future. The future embodies change that can, in turn, be viewed as creating either threat or opportunity. It is hoped that this text will be useful in facilitating adaption within the field, so that the future of child and youth care across the country will continue to be filled with opportunity.

This book represents the joint efforts of many contributors; we believe this is one of its greatest assets. We have thoroughly enjoyed the collaboration with our colleagues from across the country in producing this book and we would like to offer it as a tribute to the Canadian child and youth care field.

Roy Ferguson
Carey Denholm
Alan Pence

Acknowledgments

The editors wish to acknowledge the dedication of those child and youth care workers within the many areas of practice who have laboured for years with high commitment and low social and financial reward so that the children and youth in their care would have a brighter and stronger future. Without them we would be a less caring society, and the foundation stones of the child and youth care profession, upon which this book is based, would not have developed. We also acknowledge the insights and strengths of those families and children who have participated with child and youth care workers in defining the roles and responsibilities of professional practice. Finally, we would like to acknowledge the support and participation of the editorial board members, who shared their expertise and enthusiasm to make this book possible.

Professional Child and Youth Care

1
The Scope of Child and Youth Care in Canada

Roy Ferguson, Alan Pence, and Carey Denholm

Introduction

This chapter looks at the current state of the field and some of the forces that are impinging upon it and then outlines the scope of professional child and youth care. The chapter concludes with an examination of the essence of child and youth care practice, which, it is suggested, is the mortar that holds the mosaic of the field together.

Forces Shaping the Child and Youth Care Field

The delivery of child and youth care services to children and their families throughout Canada is the result of an evolution that has been shaped by a combination of political, economic, historic, and social factors. Professional child and youth care in this country has moved away from being defined, essentially, through the two primary historical streams of residential care and day care towards a broad scope of interrelated but clearly identifiable areas of practice. Child and youth care professionals function in a variety of settings, which, together, constitute a wide continuum of services to children and families across Canada.

There are a number of factors within contemporary society that have had a direct influence upon the way in which professional child and youth care has evolved: the normalization principle, mainstreaming, the movement away from a psychopathological orientation, an emphasis on prevention and early intervention, and an emphasis on program accountability.

The emphasis on the normalization principle (Wolfensberger 1972) began to be manifest in the human service delivery mechanisms during the early 1970s. Simply stated, it advocates that developmentally handicapped persons should experience conditions of everyday life which are as close as possible to the norms and patterns of the mainstream of society. This ideological position has had a significant impact upon treatment philosophies and standards of care within the human services. One of the more obvious effects of the normalization principle was the movement, whenever possible, away from institutional care. There was a reluctance on the part of governments to build new institutions, and, in fact, many existing ones were closed down and the residents returned to their local communities, where alternate systems of care delivery were developed. This tendency still continues, with the vast majority of services being provided within a community context.

The effects of normalization were also felt within the education system. Mainstreaming, or integrating special needs children in regular community schools, began as an educational philosophy and continued to gain strength until it became a legislated position in many parts of the country. As more developmentally handicapped children moved out of special classes and into the regular school system, the need for professionals to attend to the non-educational needs of these children became increasingly evident.

Another philosophical shift within the delivery of human services has been the movement away from a psychopathological orientation. In programs for children and families, more emphasis is being placed upon the promotion of competence, with a focus on normal growth and development. This shift in orientation has changed the way in which programs are designed and has resulted in more key roles for child and youth care practitioners, who, by nature, tend to have a developmental perspective on care.

Early intervention and prevention is another force which has shaped professional child and youth care. Service agencies are now attempting to identify children and families with special needs and provide them with a program at the earliest possible point. The emergence of infant development programs in various provinces is a good example of the early intervention/prevention thrust. These programs are usually structured so that the provision of care is carried out by an interdisciplinary team working directly with the child and family in their own natural environment. Similarly, resources are being built into existing service structures, such as hospitals, schools, and day care systems, which are aimed at preventing problems before they occur. Although the effectiveness of prevention programs is difficult to evaluate, governments seem increasingly more assured that prevention should be a priority within the human services. The recent emphasis within federal and provincial health ministries on a health promotion perspective, for example, is very encouraging and represents a significant departure from the traditional way in which health care was conceptualized.

Another major societal influence on professional child and youth care is the continuing economic situation and the resultant emphasis on program accountability in terms of cost-effectiveness. As service demands are either maintained or increased while economic resources diminish, programs will be required either to demonstrate their effectiveness or to modify accordingly. Clinicians will need to be familiar with evaluation procedures in order to demonstrate the efficacy of their interventions. Program structures will change to include more care provided by professionals with a generalist orientation, while expensive specialists will be utilized primarily on a consultative basis. Further, during periods of fiscal restraint and diminishing resources, social programs become a primary target for cost cutting. A popular approach has been to 'privatize' government service delivery through purchase of service contracting. However, in the absence of a system of service delivery standards and an effective monitoring mechanism, a privatized service delivery model can become one that pays little attention to the quality of care being provided (Martin 1990).

Multiculturalism is a rapidly growing consideration in Canada as the ethnic diversity of the population increases. Consequently, child and youth care service programs are striving to provide more culturally-sensitive care, and educational programs are building an increasing amount of cross-cultural content into their curricula. Some of these developments will be reviewed in the last chapter.

These are some of the key societal forces that have influenced the evolution of the child and youth care field over the past decade. The effects of these forces will continue to be felt for some time to come, and, undoubtedly, new forces will emerge that will also impinge on the ways in which the field develops.

The Essence of Child and Youth Care Practice

A commitment to addressing the needs of families within a context of caring might characterize the essence of the child and youth care field and, perhaps, even distinguish it from other professions. Just as Maier (1979) sought to delineate the 'core of care,' we, as child and youth care professionals, need to explore and attempt to set out the essence of child and youth care practice. Ferguson and Anglin (1985) suggest four elements as being the essence of child and youth care.

(1) Child and youth care is primarily focused on the *growth and development of children and youth*. While families, communities, and organizations are important concerns for child and youth care professionals, they are viewed as contexts for the care of children. The development of children and youth is the core.

(2) Child and youth care is concerned with the *totality of child development and functioning*. The focus is on persons living through a certain portion of the human life cycle rather than with one facet of functioning, as is characteristic of most other human service disciplines. For example, physiotherapists are concerned primarily with physical health, psychiatrists with mental health, probation officers with criminal behaviour, teachers with education, and so on. Only the emerging field of gerontology appears to share child and youth care's concern with the life cycle as a totality.

(3) Child and youth care has developed within a *model of social competence* rather than within a model of pathology. Child and youth care workers view the behaviour of children and youth from a developmental perspective and design interventions that build on the existing strengths and abilities of the individual. *Therapeutic relationships* require a high level of personal/professional development on the part of the practitioner and require the integration of a complex constellation of knowledge, skills, and elements of self.

(4) Child and youth care is based on (but not restricted to) *direct, day to day work with children in their environment*. Unlike many other professionals, child and youth care practitioners do not operate in a single setting or on an interview or session-oriented basis. Children and youth are worked with in their own environments, whether they are residential centres, schools, hospitals, family homes, or the street. Although child and youth care workers also assume supporting roles such as supervising, directing, training, policy-making, and researching, they remain grounded in direct care work.

Caring and professionalism are not mutually exclusive entities, and the challenge to the child and youth care field is that of evolving in a manner which acknowledges both the human and technical aspects of professionalism and maintains a good balance between them.

The Scope of Professional Child and Youth Care

Child and youth care is conceptualized as a field with a broad scope and is reflected in a model which Denholm, Pence, and Ferguson (1983) have depicted as an umbrella (Figure 1.1). Each of the sections of the umbrella represents a different specialized area of service, and the handle indicates the range of educational and training opportunities.

Figure 1.1

Umbrella model

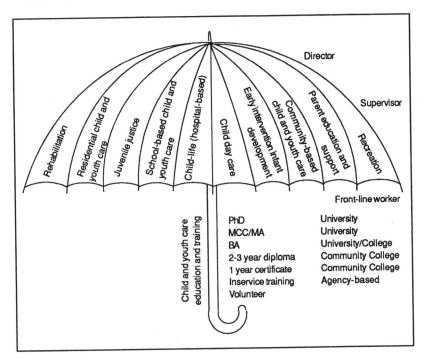

Just as the panels of an umbrella are interconnected, so are the various areas of child and youth care practice, and all these areas are necessary in order to provide a continuum of service to children and families. The generalist orientation and generic skills of the child and youth care professional provide continuity in the system as children and families seek services from various segments of the model.

Child and youth care education and training is seen as the handle in the umbrella model, with the divisions indicating the levels available to the practitioner. The interval between each level of training is representative of field experience, so that education, training, and practical experience interact within this sequential approach.

The handle on an umbrella is critical to its operation in the same way that education and training is central to the scope of the child and youth care field. Educational programs within this model must provide students with a broad, generic base of knowledge and skills applicable to all manifestations of child and youth care practice, so that they have maximum opportunity for vertical and horizontal mobility within the field. By implication, the higher up the handle, the greater the requirements placed on the standard of performance, level of independence, accountability, and responsibility. The model depicts the relationship between the levels of education/training and the opportunities for advancement within and across the various segments of the field.

The three divisions (front-line worker, supervisor, and director) indicated on the sections of the umbrella represent the major vertical levels of possible involvement in each of the ten major areas of practice identified throughout Canada today. The areas of practice demonstrate the broad scope of the child and youth care field as well as the diverse range of employment opportunities available to graduates from the different training levels.

Of particular importance is the notion of horizontal mobility across the various segments of the umbrella. It is generally recognized that all child and youth care employment areas have as their core a large number of similar knowledge and skill elements such as human development, interpersonal communications, problem solving skills, counselling skills, program development, and evaluation. It is important, then, that education/training programs prepare students in a manner which will allow them to function in various employment settings with children, youth, and families. The encompassing nature of the umbrella model of child and youth care represents a system of service delivery in which the preventive, primary, and tertiary levels of care for children, youth, and families are available regardless of setting or need.

The segments included in the umbrella model are not meant to indicate an exhaustive range of child and youth care areas of practice but, rather, to represent some of the major areas at present. Certainly, other segments, such as early childhood education, mental health, legal mediation, and work with gifted children, could easily be included within this spectrum of child and youth care services.

An Evolving Model of Child and Youth Care

Physical and conceptual models are used by a variety of professionals to help them to organize information, ideas, theories, and to facilitate planning. Models assist the user to better understand phenomena in both the past and the present as well as to see new patterns for the future.

The umbrella model outlined in Figure 1.1 has been useful for depicting the broad scope of the child and youth care field. It is an effective way to show the range of specialized practice settings where service to children, youth, and families are being provided. An extension of this model was made by Denholm (1990) to depict the higher education and career pathways available to the practitioner. However, the umbrella model does not include other variables, such as age/development of the target populations found in different practice settings, nor does it include the core, generic practice functions that exist across all age groups and all practice settings.

Ferguson (1991) extends the umbrella model into a cube model, depicting a three-dimensional interaction of practice setting, age/development of the target client population, and core practice functions. In this model, one vector, defining the cube, consists of the service settings contained in the umbrella and is shown interacting with the second vector, which is the age/development of the client. The interaction of these two vectors defines the practice differences across settings. For example, working with an infant in an intensive care unit of a hospital requires a different subset of knowledge and skills than does seeing an adolescent in a community mental health program.

The third vector in the cube model represents the core knowledge and skills that are generic to professional practice across all client age groups and all service settings. Examples of some functions that might be included in this vector are: assessment procedures, interpersonal communication, individual and group interventions, research/evaluation, and ethics. These are the elements that create the similarity between child and youth care practice across age and setting differences. While the cube model is an improvement on the earlier umbrella model in that it shows child and youth care practice as an interaction of setting, age, and function, it is still limited in that it does not include a context for this interaction.

The onion model (Ferguson 1991) is a third generation model that reflects an ecological perspective, wherein consideration is given to the reciprocal interactions between human development and the multiple environments in which it occurs. Bronfenbrenner (1979) suggests taking an integrative approach that examines the relationships between and among systems rather than just focusing on the characteristics of any one of them. (Various applications of an ecological perspective are outlined in a volume edited by Pence, 1988.) The interacting systems were portrayed by Bronfenbrenner as a series of concentric circles, and in adapting these to the new child and youth care model, they were given a three-dimensional perspective and depicted as the layers of an onion. In the onion model (see Figure 1.2) the cube is embedded in this sphere to show the interactions of the three vectors within and across a variety of systems that provide an ecological context.

Figure 1.2

Ecological onion model

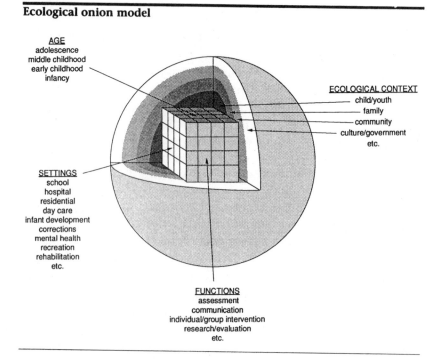

For example, in considering an intervention (function) with a preschooler (age) in a hospital (setting) we can consider an interaction of contextual variables such as the child's perception of hospitalization (individual context), the degree of family stress (family context), available social support/educational mechanisms (community context), prevailing beliefs about health care (cultural context), and existing health care policies (governmental context). Hence, the onion model is capable of considering a multitude of contextual variables that impinge on child and youth care practice across different age groups, functions, and settings.

The ecological onion model considers the various systems surrounding the client which must be successfully understood in order to provide quality care. This is significant because the ability to move easily within and across these systems is one of the unique characteristics of the child and youth care profession, as noted in the next section of this chapter. This ability to function in the client's natural environment and to move easily through various systems in the course of an intervention places child and youth care professionals in a strong position to coordinate and integrate service delivery to children, youth, and families.

In Public Report No. 22 (British Columbia 1990), it is noted that the coordination of care across systems is one of the major problems across child welfare, mental health, and youth corrections services. This is not surprising when one considers that most of the allied professionals have assumed specialist roles within the human service delivery system. Their focus is often on a fairly specific aspect of care, such as assessment, medication, protection, counselling, and probation. By contrast, the child and youth care practitioner usually assumes more of a generalist perspective, in which emphasis is placed on the interaction of all aspects of care. This generalist orientation, coupled with an ecological perspective, places child and youth care workers in a position to effectively function in an integrator role on the treatment team, pulling together and organizing information and input from a variety of sources. This would certainly lead to a more effective and efficient care delivery system characterized by better resource coordination, less duplication of services, and fewer cracks between systems.

The ecological onion model is a mechanism that evolved from the original umbrella model and is useful in depicting the complex interaction of age, setting, function, and system variables that define child and youth care practice. It is important to develop models and refine them because our thinking and our models are so closely intertwined. Our thinking shapes our models, which, in turn, shape our thinking.

Towards a Universal North American Perspective
The Child and Youth Care Education Consortium has been a key vehicle in bringing about a convergence of the Canadian and U.S. perspectives in the child and youth care field. The idea of an education consortium was first proposed at the Conference-Research Sequence in Child Care Education in 1981–2 at the University of Pittsburgh and was formally established at an organizational meeting at the University of Victoria in March 1990. The Child and Youth Care Education Consortium represents college and university child and youth care programs

across Canada and the United States, and its purpose is the advancement of postsecondary education for professional child and youth care. A second meeting of the consortium was held at Ryerson Polytechnic in Toronto in January 1992, and, at this meeting a description of the field was developed that recognized its broad scope and interaction with allied disciplines. The description of the field developed on 25 January 1992 is as follows:

> Professional Child and Youth Care practice focuses on the infant, child and adolescent, both normal and with special needs, within the context of the family, the community, and the life span. The developmental-ecological perspective emphasizes the interaction between persons and the physical and social environments, including cultural and political settings.
>
> Professional practitioners promote the optimal development of children, youth, and their families in a variety of settings such as early care and education, community-based child and youth development programs, parent education and family support, school-based programs, community mental health, group homes, residential centres, day and residential treatment, early intervention, home-based care and treatment, psychiatric centres, rehabilitation programs, pediatric health care and juvenile justice programs.
>
> Child and Youth Care practice includes skills in assessing client and program needs, designing and implementing programs and planned environments, integrating developmental, preventive, and therapeutic requirements into the life-space, contributing to the development of knowledge and practice, and participating in systems interventions through direct care, supervision, administration, teaching, research, consultation, and advocacy.

This description of the field of child and youth care, developed by educators throughout Canada and the United States, is significant in that it embraces the broad scope of the field that was depicted in the umbrella model developed by the school of child and youth care in the early 1980s. When the first edition of this book came out in 1987, there were still many persons who felt that the field should be restricted to the historic foundations that included child day care and residential care. In fact, there were some who felt that child and youth care should refer only to residential care for children with behavioural problems.

Fortunately, the notion of a broader description of the field prevailed and is moving rapidly to a more universal acceptance. This was clearly demonstrated when the above definition was reviewed in 1992 at the International Leadership Coalition for Professional Child and Youth Care held in Milwaukee, where it received strong support from educators, practitioners, researchers, and administrators. This broad description of the field no longer represents a primarily Canadian perspective but, increasingly, a North American view.

The next ten chapters will address different segments of the umbrella model of child and youth care presented earlier. The chapters are presented in a sequence which begins with child and youth care in institutional settings and which progresses towards community-based care with a greater emphasis on prevention and early intervention. The chapters are ordered to begin with residential care, since it was one of the major historical roots of the child and youth care field. The reader is encouraged to note how the four elements reflecting the essence of child and youth care (outlined earlier in this chapter) are manifest in the areas of practice described in each of these chapters. The final chapter will look to the future and consider some of the implications of an expanded scope for the child and youth care field.

References

British Columbia. Office of the Ombudsman. 1990. *Public services to children, youth and their families in British Columbia: The need for integration.* Public Report No. 22

Bronfenbrenner, U. 1979. *The ecology of human development: Experiments by nature and design.* Cambridge: Harvard University Press

Child and Youth Care Education Consortium. 1992. Minutes of meeting of 25 January 1992, Toronto

Denholm, C.J. 1990. 2000 and beyond: Future careers for child and youth care professionals. In J. Anglin, C. Denholm, R. Ferguson, and A. Pence (eds.), *Perspectives in professional child and youth care.* New York: Haworth

Denholm, C.J., Pence, A.R., and Ferguson, R.V. 1983. *The scope of professional child care in British Columbia.* In C. Denholm, A. Pence, and R. Ferguson (eds.), *The scope of professional child care in British Columbia.* Victoria: University of Victoria Press

Ferguson, R.V. 1991. Umbrellas to onions: The evolution of an interactive model for child and youth care education. *Journal of Child and Youth Care* 5:11–23

Ferguson, R.V. and Anglin, J.P. 1985. The child care profession: A vision for the future. *Child Care Quarterly* 14:85–102

Maier, H.W. 1979. The core of care: Essential ingredients for the development of children at home and away from home. *Child Care Quarterly* 8:161–73

Martin, R. 1990. Purchase of service contracting: The arms-length relationship. *Child and Youth Care Administrator* 1:29–34

Pence, A.R. (ed.). 1988. *Ecological research with children and families: From concepts to methodology.* New York: Teachers College Press

Wolfensberger, W. and Nirje, B. 1972. *The principles of normalization in human services.* National Institute of Mental Retardation, Toronto

2
Residential Child and Youth Care
Gerry Fewster and Thom Garfat

Introduction

Whatever the future might hold for the profession of child and youth care, its heritage has been firmly entrenched within the worlds of institutions, treatment centres, and group homes across Canada and throughout North America. In these settings, child and youth care workers must deal with the social and developmental needs of children and adolescents twenty-four hours a day, seven days a week. Serving as the consistent human element between the child and a frequently confusing world, child and youth care workers provide the essential mediating relationship through which the influences of parents, teachers, peers, siblings, and therapists take on meaning and relevance. No other profession has chosen to assume this breadth of perspective or level of personal and interpersonal responsibility. Beyond the time-tested theories and practices found in psychology, social work, education, or psychiatry, child and youth care has been founded upon the accumulation of experience through involvement in the daily lives of children and young people. This experience has already done much to humanize and energize residential programs; indeed, the knowledge gained in these settings is now being increasingly applied to child and youth care practices (see Hunter et al. 1982; Milner 1982; Trieschman et al. 1969.)

Since residential child and youth care covers a broad range of facilities, programs, practices, and populations, it is necessary to restrict the scope of the discussion presented in this chapter. The focus is upon residential treatment for children broadly described as being 'behaviourally and emotionally disturbed.' This viewpoint reflects the particular interests and experiences of the authors, although it is acknowledged that residential child and youth care workers are actively involved in hospitals, residential centres, and group homes serving physically and mentally handicapped, mentally ill, and learning disabled youngsters. In recent years there has been a significant shift in service delivery systems across North America, and many child and youth care workers now find themselves working as specialists in natural families and specialized foster homes. Within the 'behaviourally and emotionally disturbed' group, we would also include children considered to be chronically delinquent, depressed, anxious, aggressive, and developmentally delayed.

The Concept

Residential programs for 'troubled' children and adolescents continue to struggle for acceptance within service delivery systems across North America. These programs are vulnerable to changing community attitudes, professional preferences, and economic considerations, but different models of residential care and treatment have emerged and continue to develop. Proponents insist that, used appropriately, such programs can provide the most intensive and effective help for children and their families, while offering protection to both the resident and the community (Hoffman 1974; O'Keefe and Castaldo 1981). Opponents, on the other hand, argue that residential services provide intrusive, restrictive, and expensive environments, reflecting society's general intolerance of deviant behaviour.

An even more conclusive allegation is that residential programs simply 'don't work.' Conversely, proponents respond to this assertion by asking, 'What doesn't work?,' given that residential programs are infinitely varied in their philosophies, objective, and practices. The debate is endless, since it involves matters of opinion, dogma, and polemics that have never been tested for differential outcome effects. In this sense, residential treatment is no better and no worse than the field of psychotherapy in general (Deschner 1982; Eysenck 1965). Similarly, in the field of corrections, Martinson (1974), following an extensive review of programs throughout the United States, firmly concluded that 'nothing works.' A more cautious approach to the examination of residential care and treatment appears to call for carefully controlled research on the assumption that some things work, for some individuals, some of the time (Edwards et al. 1979; Hackler 1978).

Research evidence relating to the treatment of troubled children and adolescents remains distinctly equivocal. The residential centres are generally the first component within the service spectrum to be challenged in terms of excessive costs, levels of intrusion, and humanitarian considerations. This situation is unlikely to change until such programs establish clear, attainable goals, expose their practices to analytical scrutiny, and demonstrate cost-effectiveness. Meanwhile, the widespread abolition of residential programs attempted in Massachusetts and California does not seem to enhance the overall quality of services to children and young people and appears to be influenced more by political considerations (Chafel and Charney 1980). In the early 1990s these political issues have become entrenched in the realities of economic recession. During this time, most governments have been seeking ways to cut their social and health service costs and, as always, residential programs are a primary target. In the rush to dismantle the larger centres and create new, cheaper community alternatives, the anti-institutional movements have flourished.

Despite the lack of empirical evidence, the fact remains that child and youth care practitioners and other professionals working in residential settings believe that they definitely help the young people entrusted to their care. This belief appears to be maintained whether such practitioners work in large multi-faceted interdisciplinary centres (Herstein and Simon 1977) or small community-based group homes (Maloney et al. 1983). It is to be hoped that such beliefs will find increasing empirical support as child and youth care and its related professions become more systematic and research-oriented.

Residential Services for Children

Residential institutions, of one form or another, have flourished throughout history. Despite the varied nature of their activities, they can be characterized more by their similarities than by their differences (Wollins and Wozner 1982). From monastic retreats and English public schools on the one hand, to maximum security prisons and mental asylums on the other, residential institutions have served to remove particular individuals and groups from the mainstream of society in order to bring about control, enlightenment, change, and protection. Admission has frequently been involuntary, based upon coercion or forcible removal, and 'success' has been determined by the operating authority. More often than not, institutions of all types generate controversy, speculation, suspicion, and, at times, open hostility about what really goes on inside. Yet society continues to tolerate and develop institutional settings for a variety of purposes.

Residential environments for children and adolescents have generally received an 'institutional' label and have been subjected to the associated ambivalence, despite tremendous variations in programs, activities, and facilities. The harsh reality is that the residential setting is the only alternative for individuals, who, for one reason or another, cannot or will not function within the established norms of social and familial environments. As Wollins and Wozner (1982) suggest, the ultimate value of such settings is determined by whether, in the final analysis, they expand or restrict opportunities for their residents. From a societal perspective, the question is: are residential programs for children intended to expand opportunities or do they restrict such freedom in the interests of social control? As Thomas and Poole (1975) have suggested, this continues to be the most fundamental dilemma in establishing compatible goal structures within residential settings.

History of Residential Care and Treatment in Canada

In a review of the development of residential care and treatment programs in Canada, Pawson (1983) identifies three overlapping periods of influence. 'The Puritan Era' (1600–1800) insisted that the group care of children was primarily a regional responsibility. The regions, in turn, tended to pass this responsibility to either municipalities or religious and private charitable organizations. While the primary focus of residential programs at this time was on the provision of housing and basic care for homeless, orphaned, or impoverished children, the disturbed, or disturbing, were often housed with the insane, the socially deviant, the mentally handicapped, and other 'rejects' from an intolerant society.

'The Refuge Manager Era' (1750–1890) saw the beginning of the development of facilities created specifically for children. This period also witnessed the evolution of the concept of protection, as opposed to simply the provision of housing, for children. Canadian legislation both reflected and led this change in orientation (e.g., the Act for the Prevention of Cruelty to and Better Protection of Children (1893)).

'The Child Saving Era' (1850–1925) brought an increased emphasis on foster care for disturbed and delinquent children. This move towards deinstitutionalization and specialization can be seen as the point from which differential treatment programs for children and youth slowly began to emerge. For those who believe that the current rush to create community alternatives represents a brand new notion, history would suggest otherwise.

Throughout these periods, sponsorship for residential programs was generally provided by either penal or welfare interests, although medical and educational interests also promoted various forms of residential intervention. (In fact, the first Canadian hospital/school for retarded children was founded in Ontario in 1876.) For the most part, however, residential services in Canada from the turn of the century to the 1940s consisted of orphanages run by welfare organizations for the 'needy' and correctional programs designed to encourage children to change their anti-social ways through discipline and the learning of a trade. Many of these facilities were operated by religious organizations or other community groups, although there was a growing tendency for such organizations to seek some form of public subsidization. At the same time, legislation designed to protect children from various forms of abuse was gradually introduced into most provinces. Systems of public guardianship or wardship also developed, as did societies and organizations committed to protecting the well-being of children. During the 1930s and 1940s, there was a distinct swing away from institutional care for the 'dependent' child in favour of the surrogate family. The residual children were those who, for one reason or another, challenged the resources and tolerance of the community. While some of these children, through their anti-social behaviour, qualified for correctional programs, others were grouped according to specific problems, such as physical handicap, functional retardation, or mental defectiveness. The classification and treatment of children in accordance with the traditional concepts of mental illness is a relatively recent phenomenon (DSM III).

As residential programs began to specialize in the provision of services to particular populations, it became increasingly apparent that communities were seeking the removal of many children, who, because they could not be classified, were slipping through the institutional net. Such children, through their attitudes and behaviour, failed to conform to social expectations, frustrating families and exhausting the range of available community services. Since this behaviour appeared to be all they had in common, these children were given the generic label 'emotionally disturbed.' Assessed and tagged in this manner, they became candidates for various forms of social control, including residential treatment.

Since these children's problems were relatively undifferentiated, and nobody seemed to have a quick 'cure,' residential programs, looking for a sense of purpose (along with the necessary resources), sought to legitimize long-term residential treatment. This movement seemed more the product of an intolerant society than of any serious attempt to identify and meet the needs of these children. By 1971, 205,000 Canadian children under the age of 18 were not residing within the parental home. It was noted that 3.2 per cent of this group were in facilities for emotionally disturbed or delinquent youth. Although some organizations attempted to use the surrogate family model as the cornerstone of long-term developmental treatment, others began to refer to their front-line staff as 'child care workers' and charged them with the responsibility of meeting the day to day needs of the resident. In developing a new sense of identity, residential programs began to align themselves with particular therapeutic approaches, ranging from broad psychoanalytic orientations (Bettleheim 1949; Davids 1975) to more specific concepts, such as reality therapy (Glasser 1965) and behaviour modification (Patterson 1975).

These efforts attempted to combine individual treatment with strategic group care (Herstein and Simon 1977; Whittaker 1983) within the context of a total therapeutic living environment (Polsky 1962). The mandates of these programs were clearly influenced by the jurisdictional boundaries of provincial service delivery systems. Since most were either operated or funded by provincial governments, the jurisdictions involved were, most notably, hospitals and medical care, mental health, child welfare, and corrections and education. Regardless of mandate, however, 'treatment' had clearly become the name of the game from the psychiatric hospital to the Ontario Training School and, with this, came the specialization of roles and the creation of a differentiated class of 'experts,' in which child and youth care was to find its humble place. The task was seen as providing a total environment for residents that incorporated, or replaced, the influences of home, school, and community. With the professionalization of child and youth care, the use of family therapy, the swing towards 'normalization,' (Wolfensberger 1972) and the growing concern for escalating costs, this movement began to moderate during the mid-seventies. In an effort to retain community ties for children in residential care, 'progressive' agencies began to involve families, use community resources, and, wherever possible, move treatment practices beyond the residential milieu. In this regard, the residential centres had actively pursued a process of deinstitutionalization even before the term became popular in the late 1970s and 1980s.

Development of Residential Child and Youth Care

The professionalization of child and youth care emerged alongside the specialization in residential care and treatment. As the limitations of the surrogate family model became increasingly apparent, the responsibilities of child and youth care workers increased, and the role of the primary treatment agent emerged. The therapeutic value of child and youth care became increasingly apparent, and, even in traditional psychiatric settings, the value of these practices was acknowledged.

It was in the larger residential treatment centres, however, that child and youth care emerged as the fundamental staffing component. As Berube (1984) has demonstrated, professionalization could not occur without a stable work force with appropriate training. Many of the developmental and educational requirements were created through the resources of larger residential programs. Junior colleges across the country responded, as did the universities in Montreal and Victoria, in setting up programs designed specifically for child and youth care practitioners. These opportunities, along with the emergence of provincial child and youth care associations, reinforced a sense of professional identity and a platform for collective action.

In residential centres, some of these developments have created tensions within organizational and professional structures. With the movement towards more multimodal treatment designs, child and youth care practitioners tended to find themselves standing between the child and a confusing array of stimuli. Seemingly unaware of their unique role, many practitioners adopted a protective stance, assuming primary responsibility for the well-being of the child. In one large Canadian treatment facility, for example, the child and youth care staff refused en masse to accept directions given by senior clinical staff. In another institution, child and youth care workers were temporarily replaced by nursing staff and paramedics. Fortunately, many of these tensions are being ameliorated as child and youth care practitioners become fully contributing participants on multidisciplinary teams. The gradual incorporation of child and youth care into the therapeutic arena has contributed significantly to moving the focus of treatment from pathology to normality, competence, and growth (Durkin 1983).

During the late 1970s, child and youth care began to move out of its residential homestead into schools, communities, and homes. New models developed, based upon relationship concepts (Garfat 1984; Burns 1984), scientist-practitioner designs (Jung et al. 1984), family intervention (LeTulle 1979), and school-based services (Krueger 1977). Meanwhile, publications such as *Child Care Quarterly* and the *Journal of Child and Youth Care* moved the profession beyond oral tradition and into the area of systematic enquiry. The overall effect of these developments on residential care and treatment programs has already been profound; there is no reason to believe that the impact will diminish in the years ahead.

Contemporary Approaches

Moving into the 1980s, residential services continued to emphasize the role of the family and the community in the process of care and treatment. In the larger treatment centres, the movement was towards short-term treatment intervention (Hoffman 1974) combined with intensive community support (Fewster 1979; Nelson 1973). While treatment populations became increasingly specific (Clary 1975; Garrels 1984), approaches became increasingly multimodal (Pawson 1983; O'Keefe and Castaldo 1981). A predominant trend was towards small group settings in the community, serviced through a central resource organization (such as Thistletown in Ontario and Youth Horizons in Quebec). Other initiatives moved away from more traditional psychotherapeutic approaches to focus upon educational designs (Krueger 1977; Lewis 1980; Trieschman 1976) and family-centred models (Barker et al. 1978; LeTulle 1979). In other cases, residential centres, such as Dellcrest in Ontario and William Roper Hull Child and Family Services in Alberta, chose to focus on non-residential community initiatives such as home care and day treatment programs.

In Canada, most of the developments in residential treatment have occurred within child welfare rather that mental health jurisdictions. This somewhat incongruent state of affairs can be almost entirely attributed to a federal funding system that supports provincial welfare programs but offers no assistance whatsoever to mental health initiatives. In many provinces, this means that in order to have access to residential treatment, a child must first acquire some form of child welfare status. This can, of course, be distressing to both the child and the family, and they may resist or refuse what otherwise would be an appropriate placement. By the same token, providers of residential treatment services find themselves involved more in welfare and protection than in treatment.

In spite of these developments, residential care and treatment continues to maintain the traditional institutional image; it is considered by many observers and policymakers to be an undesirable form of intervention — a form to be used only when all else has failed. While this attitude may well have promoted the misuse of residential programs, it appears to satisfy the conflicting perspectives of both those who wish to remove disturbing individuals from society and those who believe that such programs are, by their very nature, restrictive and punitive (Martin et al. 1976). Similarly, residential programs also become useful pawns for politicians and policymakers who wish to demonstrate humanitarianism, hard line fundamentalism, or decisive cost control through symbolic gestures. New justifications have been created through a spate of widely publicized abuse. The Mount Cashel affair in Canada is a typical example of how the inner life of certain residential programs can shock the general population. On the other hand, the literature on child abuse clearly suggests that all forms of abusive behaviour have been prevalent in all sectors of our society for as long as we have records to be scrutinized. The chances are that this state of affairs will continue to exist until residential programs demonstrate that they operate in the best interests of children and families through the enhancement of options and personal autonomy. For this to occur, such programs need to articulate clear operational models that can be understood and evaluated in accordance with the identified needs of clients, service delivery systems, and the community at large.

Residential Models
For the residential worker, a particular program model or design offers both opportunities and constraints. Hence, the professional practitioner would be well advised to seek out those programs that provide the greatest opportunities for personal and professional growth. In reality, this turns out to be a highly idiosyncratic exercise, since no two residential programs and no two practitioners are identical. Models are based upon assumptions and beliefs about the nature of humanity, the nature of the social context, the causes of psychological disturbance, and the process of change. These assumptions are then translated into action through general objectives, goals, strategies, and specific activities. The closer the program and the individual practitioner are in relation to these issues, the greater the probability of achieving the desired outcomes. The further apart the program and the individual, the greater the potential for conflict, confusion, dissatisfaction, and failure. Clearly, where this unhappy state of affairs exists, the ultimate losers are the child and the family.

For residential care and treatment programs to occupy a legitimate position within the spectrum of child and family services, they must be matched to the needs of particular clients and service delivery systems. In this way, programs become accountable for what they do, and users become accountable for the choices they make. While much work needs to be done in this area, it is clear from the literature that many individual models have been emerging over the past few years (Fewster 1977; Harris 1983; O'Keefe and Castaldo 1981; Pawson 1983; and Trieschman 1976). From an information-evaluation perspective, the task is one of examining these models differently in terms of populations served, procedures used, costs involved, outcomes expected, and so forth. The first step in this direction might be the development of a broad typology within which the various designs can be conveniently grouped. The typology offered here is both speculative and tentative and is designed primarily to assist the reader in recognizing the various orientations towards residential care and treatment in North America.

The Mental Health Model

From this perspective, society is seen as a living organism requiring built-in mechanisms (or antibodies) to maintain optimal functioning. For individuals, the term mental health implies that the mind, like the body, may take on various states of well-being, ranging from exemplary fitness to debilitating disease and sickness. Terms such as treatment and therapy have been coined to define the task of producing a cure for the debilitating condition that will restore the organism to its state of wholeness and well-being. The process is, then, an event in which the practitioner must identify the particular malady, prescribe and implement a course of action, and assess the results of the intervention. For child and youth care workers, the question is whether they are treatment practitioners or just adjuncts to the process, dealing with the 'other twenty-three hours' (Trieschman et al. 1969) of the client's life.

Advantages of this model include: social and professional respectability; prescribed assessment and intervention methods; the security of time-tested tradition and established diagnostic definitions. Disadvantages include the possibility that: clients may perceive themselves to be 'sick'; clients may become dependent upon the practitioner for the cure; labels may become self-fulfilling prophesies; change may be attributed to the practitioner and not the client; practitioners who assume this responsibility may themselves become sick — or detached and arrogant.

The Social Behaviour Model

This design assumes that society is a vehicle for socialization in which individuals learn to adapt to environmental conditions. Problems arise when learning mechanisms break down through individual inadequacies or situational anomalies. The task of the program is, then, to establish a learning milieu in which individuals are taught to adapt behaviour through interpersonal and environmental contingencies. From this perspective, behaviour change is assumed to be a prerequisite for psychological development and personal growth. Child and youth care workers in these settings must be prepared to attend primarily to the overt behaviour of residents, applying the technology of cognitive behaviour modification.

Advantages of this model include: clearly articulated theoretical paradigms; well-developed and time-tested technology; specified and measurable outcome data and high competency feedback potential for practitioners and residents. Disadvantages include: a controlled and controlling environment; the lack of concern for non-behavioral aspects of client functioning; the reduction of the practitioner's status to that of technician; the lack of generalization of behavioural gains following discharge and the possibility that clients become dependent upon external contingencies.

The Psycho Education Model
In this model, learning is considered to be an active two-way process between the individual and the world. Individuals make choices based upon their interpretation of available information. When information is made available and understood, individuals can then be responsible for the choices they make. Problems arise when information is lacking or when the individual is unable to comprehend it. The task then becomes one of establishing an interactional treatment milieu that takes every event as a potential learning experience for both the client and the practitioner. Child and youth care workers in this type of environment have primary teaching responsibilities, attending to both the potential of the environment to provide and the potential of the individual resident to comprehend.

Advantages of this model include: attention focused upon the client in context; relative freedom for both resident and practitioner to interact; relatively clear teaching/practice models of education; de-emphasis of control functions. Disadvantages include: unclear outcome indicators; unpredictability of events; questionable professional and public legitimacy; lack of standardized criteria for either admission or discharge.

The Systems Model

The systems orientation has gained popularity in recent years, particularly in the area of family intervention. The basic assumption is that all events, including behavioural events, can be best understood in terms of the systems they represent. In physics, these systems are part of the physical universe. In the behavioural sciences, such systems are assumed to exist within individuals and in the social milieu. Hence, to understand the behaviour of a child, a practitioner must understand the context in which the behaviour occurs. This is not the same as responding simply to environmental cues, since the environment has an on-going life of its own, and this organization is internalized within individual perception and cognition. The treatment task involves understanding how the systems work and using intervention strategies to bring about changes or modifications. Where the family therapist must come to terms with the family system, the child and youth care worker must understand all the various systems that impinge upon the life of a child and how these various systems might interact.

Advantages of this model include: practitioners acknowledge the complexity of human behaviour; residents are not detached from the social world of home, school, and community; the child is not perceived as the ultimate cause of the problem; the system of the residential environment is subject to on-going scrutiny and analysis. Disadvantages include: treatment models are complex and vague; operational models are weak and indicators ambiguous; individual responsibility may be transferred to the system; systems are never 'known' but are assumed from individual behaviour.

The Correctional Model

The classical correctional model is based upon one aspect of learning theory: the function of negative sanctions. The basic assumption is that society must effectively inhibit anti-social or deviant behaviour through punishment or the withholding of awards. Hence, the correctional oriented program attempts to teach the resident the error of his or her ways through the imposition of sanctions — particularly the restriction of personal liberty. Child and youth care workers in these settings usually find themselves in a highly controlled environment, teaching moral and social values to a highly resistant population of youngsters.

Advantages of this model include: clearly defined expectations and procedures; emphasis on personal responsibility; clear delegation of responsibility and authority; environmental predictability. Disadvantages include: limited opportunities for practitioners and residents; conflicts between treatment and control functions; routinized environments; inadequate attention to differential treatment.

The Diversionary Model

Diversionary models may contain a whole range of assumptions about the nature of society and humanity. Their basic premise, however, is that there are certain essential pursuits that will divert an individual from debilitating problems through the acquisition of particular values, the enhancement of esteem, and the building of competency. Such programs might focus upon religious teaching, survival in the wilderness, learning a trade, working on a farm, or contributing to a closed community. Child and youth care workers in these programs must accept their underlying values and be prepared to exemplify their characteristics.

Advantages of these approaches include: commonality of staff commitment; uncomplicated expectations; rejection of pathology notions; focus upon individual responsibility. Disadvantages include: simplicity; propensity for cultism; restricted opportunities for staff and residents; inadequate identification and generalization of outcomes.

The above categories are not necessarily exhaustive or mutually exclusive. Many programs might contain aspects drawn from a number of the models identified here. In this case, we would encourage the designers to articulate their model clearly and perhaps add to or modify it. Nor is it suggested that the model types described here necessarily reflect particular service delivery jurisdictions. It is possible, for example, for a program operating within a mental health jurisdiction to adopt any of the identified orientations. What is being proposed is that residential programs need to articulate their model and beliefs and make them available for professional and community scrutiny (Mordock 1979). The development of typologies should enhance consumer discrimination and empirical evaluation (Witkin and Cannon 1971). It is further suggested that such efforts also serve to promote a more appropriate use of residential programs within the service spectrum, since such strategies are being increasingly designed to perform specialized functions like short-term stabilization (Cohen 1984; Perry 1985) and preparation for adoption (Powers and Powell 1983).

Current Issues in Residential Care and Treatment

In developing specific methods for residential programs, it must be recognized that residential strategies differ from other forms of intervention in a variety of ways. Many issues are peculiar to this field. In this section, we have chosen to highlight a few of these issues based upon their perennial presence and the expressed concerns of service users, practitioners, and providers.

Withdrawal of Funding

The vulnerability of residential programs to financial cutbacks, political postures, and philosophical swings has already been identified in this chapter. It must be stressed, however, that this vulnerability is one of the most critical issues affecting service delivery. If, in fact, there are children and adolescents who require residential services in our communities, the closure of residential programs can have a number of very undesirable consequences. By continuing to test the tolerance and understanding of families and communities, these young people may well be caught up in escalating patterns of rejection and alienation (Martin et al. 1976). Some children undoubtedly end up in other forms of institutional care, such as adult mental hospitals (Chafel and Charney 1980). Others, in need of treatment, eventually find themselves in conflict with the law and incarcerated within the penal system. It is interesting to note that, in the late 1980s, following a lengthy purge of residential treatment facilities, the province of Ontario announced the development of a number of new correctional facilities for youth. Similarly, in 1990, an Ontario provincial conference of mental health workers paid tribute to a particular psychiatrist for her decision to admit children to the adult psychiatric wards. From the perspective of the practitioner and the service provider, the effect of this pervasive vulnerability is the withholding of legitimation, security, and support. Caught in this situation, it is not surprising that residential programs frequently resort to secrecy, gimmickry, unattainable aspirations, and false claims. Such a climate is hardly conducive to systematic planning, evaluation, and development.

The Decision to Refer

Admission to a residential program may remove a child completely from a familiar living environment and place him or her in a totally foreign milieu in the company of other children, who may demonstrate bizarre or disturbing behaviours. The program is staffed by strangers and infused with policies, procedures, and rules designed to affect the child's behaviour, both directly and indirectly. This change may induce the trauma of separation, the fear of loss, and the powerful spectre of the unknown. It provokes fear and uncertainty, creates confusion, and invokes in the child tremendous questions about self and society. For these reasons, the decision to place a child in a residential program must be taken with great care and consideration for the impact upon the individual, the family, and the community.

While it would be comforting to consider such decisions as being made 'in the best interests of the child and family,' our experience suggests that such decisions are more determined by the attitudes and values of the community, the tolerance of the family and the community to deviant behaviour, and the particular beliefs held by the professional community about the desirability of particular intervention options. Hence, assessed needs and background information are frequently biased towards the preferred strategy. In communities that place high value upon the maintenance of the nuclear family, the intervention choice may well be community rather than residentially based. In communities such as those in northern Canada, removal is often seen as a form of banishment from the communal order and is considered only as a last resort.

The imposition of such values may or may not be in the best interests of the child and family. In Canada, for example, we are not particularly accepting of behaviours that differ from the community norm. For this reason, we tend to see residential placement as a means of removing a deviant person from society rather than as a way of providing the most effective form of treatment. In general, the greater the tolerance of the community for deviance, the less the use of residential treatment. For this reason, the planning for residential placement must consider the particular needs of the child and family and the availability of a residential environment capable of meeting those needs. Unfortunately, we continue to use residential treatment based upon the level of disturbance that a child is creating for a community rather than on the value of the residential environment. In many cases, the *status* of the child becomes a critical variable. Since residential centres are generally funded through child welfare programs, access to those services is limited to those children who have some formalized welfare status. This situation increases the likelihood that certain children will be placed in residential centres, while other, perhaps more appropriate, candidates will be denied access.

The racial status of a child may also be a significant determining factor. As Pawson (1983) pointed out, Native children constituted 39 per cent of the total number of children in care in British Columbia, 40 per cent in Alberta, 50 per cent in Saskatchewan, and 60 per cent in Manitoba. A high proportion of Native children are placed in residential treatment programs operated by members of the dominant culture. Despite increasing attempts to respond to these cultural differences (Stuart 1970), the problem continues to be monumental. Fortunately, with the development of new information and assessment techniques, residential centres are more able to make a clear statement about the possibility of a child benefiting from placement in their facilities. Such developments have made it easier to match a child's needs with the characteristics of a particular residential environment. Again, this requires that residential centres be more explicit in terms of their particular operational model.

The Focus of Intervention

The residential treatment environment provides program planning for a child on a twenty-four-hour-a-day basis. While this affords a unique opportunity for involvement in a child's life, it also produces a very special set of concerns for child and youth care practitioners. In *The Other Twenty-Three Hours* (1969), Albert Trieschman and his colleagues dramatically highlight the importance of considering the total day in planning for the treatment of children in residential centres. Since children and practitioners interact at all points of the day, any event might become a significant entry point for treatment intervention. The focus, therefore, of intervention in residential treatment differs dramatically from the focus of intervention in more community-based forms of treatment. The child and youth care team, operating within its own model of treatment, must determine how such common activities as waking up, going to bed, eating meals, self-hygiene, interacting with peers, or even reading a book figure in the overall treatment of the individual. Consequently, the focus of treatment is extremely broad; planning must take into account all aspects of the child's daily life. With the development of multi-model therapy approaches, the emergence of professional child and youth care has done much to convert traditional linear treatment approaches into interactional designs that encourage the child and the family to become active participants in the treatment process.

Group Work in Residential Care

The fact that children in residential care must live together in a group makes the group context one of the most natural areas for intervention and treatment planning. Such groups can become powerful forces in the promotion of positive change, or they can become equally powerful forces in resisting change or even promoting regression. Thus, planning for an individual in residential care must take into account both the impact of the group on the individual and the impact of the individual upon the group.

The potential for negative group influence is one of the most regular concerns expressed about residential care and treatment strategies (Schaefer 1980). In an environment where other individuals exhibit disturbed behaviour, a child might express disturbance more clearly or feel an obligation to be as disturbed as the rest of the individuals in the group. Additionally, group norms may be more powerful than adult expectations in situations where clearly developed treatment designs are lacking. It is also frequently the case that an increase in disturbance is a manifestation of a child's resistance to being in the environment in the first place. Behavioural deterioration or regression, however, cannot be simply attributed to negative group effects. In some cases, it may indicate that the child, perceiving him- or herself to have found security and protection, finally displays signs of disturbance which had been successfully controlled or concealed in former, less secure, environments.

On the positive side, natural groupings of children in residential centres can lead to therapeutically meaningful activities and outcomes. The development of such designs as 'positive peer culture' (Herstein and Simon 1977) establishes the climate for this type of approach. As Whittaker and Garbarino (1983) indicated, however, such group work does not necessarily have to follow traditional group therapy models. It may be tailored towards the specific needs of individual participants and programs. The potential here probably reflects one of the most exciting challenges in residential child and youth care: the challenge of working with a group that actually lives together on a daily basis. These groups develop more rapidly than do traditional therapy groups, as they are not necessarily paced by the group facilitator. In residential groups, the interaction of group members occurs continuously, as opposed to being restricted to a fixed period of group interaction.

Differential Treatment and the Group Context

While many people perceive residential treatment to be primarily a group process, children are placed in such programs because of individual needs concerning growth and development. As a result, a residential child and youth care worker must become skilled in the provision of individual treatment within the group context. While maintaining, supporting, and leading the group with one hand, the worker must be supplying individual analysis, treatment, and caring with the other.

Some residential centres have chosen to meet this need for individualized treatment through the use of professionals who support the child and youth care team. In some situations, child and youth care practitioners focus upon individual needs, while other clinical staff emphasize group intervention. Still other models of treatment call for the individual needs of the child to be met within the context of a specialized group therapy conducted within the residential centre (Van Scoy 1976). Clearly, these options will be determined by the particular model adopted by the centre in question. In the final analysis, the residential treatment program must attend to individual needs on a differential basis, and this cannot be achieved merely through the introduction of periodic sessions of individual counselling or psychotherapy. Individual assessment, treatment planning, and intervention must be an integral part of the system through which the residential centre mobilizes its wealth of resources.

Normalization

The apparent artificiality of residential environments has been the focal point of considerable concern (Wolfensberger 1972). While there is considerable variation in the degree to which residential treatment environments approximate life in the community, the chances are that the more intensive the program design, the less 'normal' the environment. For children requiring intensive treatment, this may not be such a tragedy, since their regular environments have apparently failed to encourage 'normal' development. The real problems begin to emerge when a child spends an inordinate amount of time in a residential treatment milieu. Obviously, this type of setting is no place for a child to experience 'normal' developmental processes or the influences of socialization. In this regard, residential treatment centres are faced with a dilemma. By attempting to expose a child to all of the 'normal' social and environmental influences, treatment resources can become diffused, and the time spent in treatment can be extended. On the other hand, most centres are expected to accomplish specific treatment goals as quickly as possible and move the child back into the so-called normalized world. As Davids and Salvadore (1975) have shown, pressures to reduce the duration of treatment can have a detrimental effect on post-discharge adjustment. It is quite possible, however, for a residential setting to provide an enriching, nurturing environment (Goldberg 1982). As a concept within the child development field, then, normalization represents a useful notion. But applied to intensive residential treatment, it requires considerable caution in terms of intent and application.

Control versus Treatment

Since most children in residential centres are involuntary participants, their perceptions and experiences of treatment are markedly different from those of the voluntary client (Oxley 1977). They frequently perceive themselves to be controlled; and, in testing out this hypothesis, they effectively coerce the residential staff into establishing controlling structures and imposing authority (Dahms 1978). Since many children in residential programs appear to have external loci of control orientation to begin with (Friedman et al. 1985; Nicholson 1979) the inherent dangers of a controlled environment are self-evident. Experience suggests that programs that strive primarily to control behaviour tend to induce the dreaded state known as institutionalization; they foster mechanistic child and youth care approaches that leave little scope for personal development and autonomy. Additionally, the pressure to control the behaviour of children is often imposed from external community sources (Mayer and Peterson 1975), particularly where delinquency is assumed to be a primary area of concern.

Paradoxically, it is in this arena that child and youth care has faced one of its greatest challenges and, perhaps, made one of its greatest contributions. The primary task of the residential worker is to create in each child a belief in personal efficacy and autonomy. More than any other single factor, this appears to be the key to successful treatment in a residential setting. In our experience, it has taken the growth of professional child and youth care to help to realize that this can be accomplished within a residential environment, since the pathway to freedom is, in fact, a transition from control to autonomy.

Termination of Treatment

The discharge of a young person from a residential centre is markedly different from the termination of treatment from community-based programs (Hirschberg 1970). Just as the entry into treatment is a traumatic experience, so the termination of treatment can be anxiety provoking. The individual emerging from the residential program, typically, has been living in a very self-contained, psychologically closed community where interaction with, and the demands of, the outside world have been greatly limited. Returning to the community, therefore, means renewing relationships with a world that was experienced as hostile, depreciating, and rejecting. Leaving residential care also involves the severing of relationships with a large number of individuals, both children and staff, some of whom may have been extremely close and significant. Acceptance and success within the program may well be measured against the possibility of rejection and failure within the community.

Given all that is occurring at the point of discharge, it is hardly surprising that many children exhibit severe regression when they near the termination of treatment. Process and timing are critical treatment/discharge variables. In order for the discharge or transfer to be successful, the resident team, in conjunction with the child and family, must be preparing for termination of treatment long before it occurs. As the date for discharge comes closer, the treatment team must help the child to take small, experiential steps towards living back with her/his family and in the community. In this process, the child must have the opportunity to experiment with newly learned behaviours and attitudes in an environment which, previously, had held different expectations. Preparing the family, or the alternative placement, is a task that must be undertaken by the residential staff, since only they understand the experiences of the child and know what needs to be done. Fortunately, in most modern residential centres, the family is actively involved throughout the entire treatment process, making it possible for discharge planning to begin almost from the point of admission.

The timing of discharge from residential treatment is generally considered to be a grey area, demanding considerable expertise and clinical judgment. In this regard, the child's state of readiness must be related to that of the family, school, and community. Although the present trend is towards short-term treatment (Hoffman 1974), premature discharge can significantly undermine treatment in the long run (Davids and Salvadore 1976). Along with the state of readiness of the child and family, decision-makers must also consider the availability of support resources and follow-up services.

Cost of Residential Treatment
The late 1980s and early 1990s have been marked by widespread economic recession. During such times of constraint, the financial costs of

residential care and treatment become particularly salient to those who wish to curtail social program expenditures. While it is true that residential treatment has become an increasingly costly proposition, so have other components within the service delivery system. One problem is that the costs of operating a residential facility cannot be hidden or disguised; all of the necessary resources are on site and are contained within a single budget. The modern residential program provides a wide range of highly specialized resources and services twenty-four hours a day. Providing such services at a community level, on a far less intensive basis, would undoubtedly cost far more in financial terms. The fact is that, from an economic perspective, residential child and youth care can be a viable proposition. Total care is provided to the child with support and treatment for the family. The twenty-four-hour-a-day operation means that resources are seldom left idle. Services are immediately available and resources are redirected to meet the changing needs of clients. Economics of scale reduce significantly the overhead costs of service delivery. Efficiency can be maximized through the establishment of financial and administrative controls.

On the other hand, the only way of resolving the cost issue is to compare, over time, the real costs of not using residential treatment for children and families who actually require such a service. This means a differential analysis of career costs for disturbed children and dysfunctional families. What needs to be assessed is whether or not effective residential treatment does, or can, reduce the overall costs of service delivery. Until this occurs, residential centres will continue to be the target for those who wish to withdraw finances from the system.

Effectiveness of Residential Treatment
Considering that residential treatment centres tend to cater to the most disturbed youngsters, it is probably safe to say that they do not work miracles; but outcome research on all forms of psychotherapy with children has produced little that is either convincing or compelling (Abramowitz 1976). Ultimately, this critical question will not be adequately addressed until residential programs clearly state their goals and define their treatment strategies. Meanwhile, there is growing evidence to suggest that differential treatment effects can be identified (Davids and Salvadore 1976; Deschner 1980; Matsushima 1979). Despite the equivocal nature of the evidence, it is clear that residential programs can be analyzed and evaluated; adequate empirical designs for this purpose are becoming increasingly available (Brubakken 1974;

Millman and Pancost 1977; Mordock 1979). However, there are still many conceptual problems to resolve. Knowledge of the goals of particular organizations must be related to populations, time frames, and specific indicators of success. As Nelson (1973) has suggested, an adequate evaluation of residential care and treatment must involve analysis of the family, the community, and the service delivery system. Until the task of evaluation is taken seriously, outcome information regarding residential services will continue to be tailored to meet the particular needs of the information provider.

Future Directions

Despite the economic conditions and the perennial objections and challenges, residential treatment programs for 'troubled' children and their families continue to adapt to changing conditions and to contribute to service delivery systems across North America. Without widespread popularity or acclaim, they somehow manage to maintain a developmental pattern that stands in sharp contrast to many of the revolutionary alternatives that come and go with changing fads and fashions. If nothing else, they continue to provide some security to the service spectrum, and, should they go the way of the dinosaur, some things will undoubtedly be lost (in much the same way as health care systems would suffer with the abolition of intensive care units). In this final section, we attempt to highlight those aspects of residential care and treatment that appear to represent the most significant recent developments and future challenges.

Deinstitutionalization

From our perspective, the term deinstitutionalization describes the movement away from remote residential facilities that hover in the murky chasm somewhere between society and oblivion. It represents a process through which residential programs become increasingly responsive to the individual needs of their clients, as members of families and communities. This cannot take place, however, with restricted funds or mandates. On the contrary, it calls for a renewed commitment and a re-mobilization of resources that expand the scope of residential care and treatment within the community (Bachrach 1976). It requires the support and encouragement of funding bodies looking for rational service development rather than the traditional 'quick fix.'

Despite insecurities and uncertainties, many residential developmental agencies in the last decade have managed to set a rational, developmental course towards deinstitutionalization. These efforts represent some of the most exciting prospects for the future. In Canada, agencies such as Thistletown in Ontario, Youth Horizons and Shawbridge in Quebec, and the Ranch Ehrlo Society in Saskatchewan have been able to decentralize their resources and to develop small, community-based facilities catering to the particular needs of the client population. The critical administrative issue in these developments is that the specialized clinical, educational, and social expertise and resources have not been decimated but have been re-mobilized to promote independent living for the service recipients. Other agencies, such as William Roper Hull Child and Family Services in Alberta and Dellcrest in Ontario, have developed extensive community-based programs that serve as extensions of, and alternatives to, the primary residential facility. Again, the apparent success of these initiatives has been built upon the concentration of expertise and resources developed through the operation of the central residential facility.

Where they have been allowed to occur, these developments in deinstitutionalization have provided a vehicle for the diversification and specialization of professional child and youth care. Practitioners are becoming increasingly capable of moving freely between the residential centres and the community, as needs and events occur. Hence, we find child and youth care professionals operating in schools, homes, and local communities, bringing new knowledge and skills to the professional domain. With the demise of the larger centres, many of these practitioners find themselves working without the same quantity or quality of support resources. On the positive side, however, we have seen the emergence of new approaches and technologies that strengthen the autonomy and competence of the front-line worker. As increasing numbers of children are maintained in communities, the variety of specialities continues to increase. In this regard the proliferation of 'homebuilder' and 'specialized foster-care' programs represents interesting prospects for the future (Bernfeld, Blase, and Fixsen 1990).

The primary restriction on all of these initiatives is financial: those who pay for residential services insist on getting residential services; those who do not are often predisposed simply to withdraw funding. An additional problem arises from current provincial trends to decentralize services. The smaller local regions are often unable to support the extensive multidisciplinary agencies required for effective residential strategies (O'Keefe and Castaldo 1981). The solution for such dilemmas is for agencies and funding bodies to review carefully the mandates of effective residential agencies and to develop creative funding mechanisms that permit resources to be mobilized efficiently in accordance with the needs of the target populations.

Privatization

The tendency for governments to privatize social and health services has been pervasive throughout North America for a number of years. Predicated upon a belief that this will inspire community initiatives, reduce service costs, and reduce direct government responsibilities, the popularity of privatization seems to be escalating across Canada. While it is too early to assess the overall effects of this movement on the provision of residential services, we would offer some cautionary words to its proponents. First, community initiatives will not reflect community needs unless such needs are carefully assessed by some independent authority. Second, short-term cost reductions may be quickly lost when private operators establish a firm hold on particular segments of the market. Third, a reduction of direct government responsibility may be accompanied by an associated loss of control over the expenditure of public funds. Our greatest concern, however, is for the quality of care and treatment. Unless standards are carefully articulated and stringently monitored, the programs considered the most successful could well be the cheapest rather than the best. In the quest to reduce costs, child and youth care would probably be the first to suffer, since the profession is generally less protected and regulated than are its counterparts. In the final analysis, the client would be the ultimate loser.

Legislative Changes

While many Canadian provinces are currently examining or changing their child welfare and mental health statutes, national trends are more likely to be influenced by changes in federal legislation. In this regard, the Canadian Constitution (1982) and the Young Offenders Act (1985) are probably the most critical.

The potential impact of the new Canadian constitution on residential services has yet to be fully examined. When a school principal in Alberta can be charged for giving a 14-year-old a detention, however, the implications become apparent. Those who work in residential and treatment facilities are becoming increasingly aware that most events occurring on a daily basis contain elements that could be challenged in accordance with the constitutional rights of residents. The flood gates have yet to open, but it is possible that program operators and practitioners will be called into question as individual Canadians become more conscious of their legal rights. However, this does not necessarily spell doom and disaster. It should, at least, encourage professionals to examine their existing practices and to develop creative ways of meeting the needs of children and families without using overly restrictive and coercive devices. In fact, it is probably true that most residential programs have less to fear than do most other programs, since they have traditionally been open to scrutiny and surveillance. In our view, the application of constitutional principles could be one more step in bringing residential care and treatment out of the proverbial closet.

Family Participation

The incorporation of family therapy into children's residential services across Canada dates back to the early 1960s. Even before this time, many residential facilities maintained on-going contact with families, frequently involving them in the treatment process. Over the last decade, however, natural and surrogate families have become critical elements in the residential mosaic, serving to preserve the developmental integrity of the child while changing their own styles towards enhanced individual and collective growth (LeTulle 1979).

Because most residential centres deal with poorly motivated or resistant families, the problem of engagement becomes a critical issue. Residential workers have had to become particularly adept in the art of restoring the faith of family members disenchanted with both the child and the service delivery. Traditional family therapy approaches have been modified to incorporate a range of specific interventions based upon the concepts of self-help, group support, and parent training. Of particular significance are developments like the 'Teaching Family Model' (Bernfeld, Blase, and Fixsen 1990), which can be applied to natural, foster, and specialized-foster families. The real point of interest is that many such approaches and technologies were born and nurtured in the more traditional residential programs.

These developments in the areas of residential/family approaches have made it necessary for child and youth care practitioners to resolve one of their most fundamental dilemmas: that is, who is actually responsible for the parenting role? By incorporating the family into the treatment program, residential workers have come to see themselves as professionals rather than as surrogate parents. The challenge for the future is for child and youth care workers to extend their unique areas of knowledge and expertise into the family context, thereby creating one

more link in the process of deinstitutionalization and the range of professional family-focused services.

Accountability and Evaluation

With the emergence of clear operational models, the stage will be set
for residential centres to become increasingly definitive about what
they do, why they do it, and how well they achieve their stated objectives. With the advent of multi-modal approaches, the task of systematic evaluation is necessarily complex, but, as Feist et al. (1985) have
suggested, residential environments can be analyzed and differential
outcomes can be identified (Davids and Salvadore 1976). Modern computerized methods of data collection and analysis are already well established in the technology of many residential centres. In this regard,
behaviour-oriented programs appear to have the initial advantage
(Wilson and Lyman 1983), but it can be confidently expected that the
technology will be effectively applied across a wide range of settings
and program designs. It is to be hoped that this trend will not serve to
transform human beings into 'dependent variables,' and that the hu-
manization of residential care and treatment will continue to be a major emphasis in all future developments.

Summary

In this chapter we have attempted to outline the past, present, and
future of residential care and treatment, albeit from an idiosyncratic
perspective. We have suggested that residential programs should continue to be viewed as an integral part of the continuum of services to
troubled youngsters and their families. For this to occur, such programs
must take a leap of faith by coming forward and letting their intentions, practices, and outcomes be known. Despite the current trends towards 'normalization' and 'communitization' of service delivery systems, residential programs can continue to play a vital role not only as
a placement of 'choice' for certain youngsters but as a training and
practice arena that can continue to generate new knowledge skills and
experiences from which children, families, communities, professionals, and community programs can benefit. For this to occur, governments and other funding bodies will need to establish the necessary
mechanisms and resources to provide a secure base for new initiatives
and long-term development. In all of this, we see on-going development of professional child and youth care as a critical factor in the evolution of child-centred services across North America in general and in
Canada in particular.

References
Abramowitz, C.V. 1976. The effectiveness of group psychotherapy with children. *Archives of General Psychiatry* 33:320-6
Bachrach, L.L. 1976. *Deinstitutionalization: An analytical review and sociological perspective.* Rockyville, MD: National Institute of Mental Health
Barker, P., Buffe, C., and Zaretski, R. 1978. Providing a family alternative for the disturbed child. *Child Welfare* 57:373-9
Bernfeld, G.A., Blase, K.A., and Fixsen, D.L. 1990. Toward a unified perspective on human service delivery systems: Applications of the teaching family model. In R.J. McMahon and R. DeV Peters (eds.), *Behavior disorders of adolescence.* New York: Plenum
Berube, P. 1984. Professionalization of child care: A Canadian example. *Journal of Child Care* 2:1-11
Bettleheim, B. 1949. A psychiatric school. *Quarterly Journal of Child Behaviour* 1:86-95
Brubakken, D. 1974. Assessing parent training utilizing a behavioural index of parent-child interactions. Paper presented at the annual convention of the American Psychological Association, New Orleans
Burns, M. 1984. Rapport and relationships: The basis of child care. *Journal of Child Care* 1:47-56
Chafel, J. and Charney, J. 1980. Deinstitutionalization: Dollars and sense. Paper presented at conference of the Council for Exceptional Children, Minneapolis
Clary, S. 1975. Diagnosis and prescriptions for L.D.: Problems of E.D. adolescents in a residential treatment centre. Paper presented at the International Federation of Learning Disabilities, Brussels
Cohen, Y. 1984. Residential treatment as a holding environment. *Residential Group Care and Treatment* 2:33-44
Dahms, W.R. 1978. Authority versus relationship. *Child Care Quarterly* 7:336-44
Davids, A. 1975. Therapeutic approaches to children in residential treatment. *American Psychologist* 36:809-14
Davids, A. and Salvadore, P.D. 1976. Treatment of disturbed children and adequacy of their subsequent adjustment: A follow-up study. *American Journal of Orthopsychiatry* 46:62-73
Deschner, J.P. 1980. Critical aspects of institutional programs for youths. *Children & Youth Services Review* 2:271-86
Durkin, R. 1983. The crisis in children's services: The dangers and opportunities for child care workers. *Journal of Child Care* 1:1-14
Edwards, D.W., Zingale, H.C., Mueller, D.P., Yarvis, R.M., and Boverman, H. 1979. Child therapy outcomes in a community mental health centre. *Children & Youth Services Review* 1:215-24
Eysenck, H.J. 1965. The effects of psychotherapy. *International Journal of Psychiatry* 1:97-144
Feist, J.R., Slowiak, C.A., and Colligan, R.C. 1985. Beyond good intentions: Applying scientific methods to the art of milieu therapy. *Residential Group Care and Treatment* 3:13-31
Fewster, G.D. 1977. *The social agency.* Alberta: WRHH Publication
–. 1979. Canada: Residential Adolescent Treatment. In C. Payne and K. White

(eds.), *Caring for deprived children*. London: Croom Helm

Freidman, R., Goodrich, W., and Fullerton, C. 1985. Locus of control and severity of psychiatric illness in the residential treatment of adolescents. *Residential Group Care and Treatment* 3:3–13

Garfat, T. 1984. Entre nous: Between us. Introduction to the Fourth National Child Care Workers Conference, Montreal

Garrels, D. 1984. Autism, the ultimate learning disability: A case management approach. *Journal of Child Care* 1:23–36

Glasser, W. 1965. *Reality Therapy*. New York: Harper & Row

Goldberg, B. 1982. Institutional care versus home care. *Journal of Child Care* 1:21–33

Hackler, J.K. 1978. *The great stumble forward*. Toronto: Methuen

Harris, N. 1983. Renaissance House summary report. *Journal of Child Care* 1:15–19

Herstein, N. and Simon, N. 1977. A group model for residential treatment. *Child Welfare* 56:601–12

Hirschberg, J.C. 1970. Termination of residential treatment of children. *Child Welfare* 49:443–7

Hoffman, A. 1974. Indicated undergirdings of mastery learning. Unpublished study conducted at Adlar Center, Champaign, Illinois

Hunter, D., Webster, C., Konstantareas, M., and Sloman, L. 1982. Children in day treatment. *Journal of Child Care* 1:45–59

Jung, C.H., Bernfeld, G.A., Coneybeare, S., and Fernandes, L.V. 1984. Toward a scientist-practitioner model of child care. *Journal of Child Care* 2:13–26

Krueger, M.A. 1977. The 'program day' as school day in residential treatment. *Child Welfare* 51:271–8

LeTulle, L.J. 1979. Family therapy in residential treatment of children. *Social Work* 24:49–51

Lewis, W.W. 1980. Tennessee Re Ed: From innovation to establishment. Paper presented at CEC Conference on the Severely Emotionally Disturbed, Toronto

Maloney, D.M., Fixsen, D.L., Surber, R.R., Thomas, D.L., and Phillips, E.L. 1983. A systems approach to professional child care. *Journal of Child Care* 1:55–71

Martin, L.H., Pozdnjakoff, I., and Wilding, J. 1976. The use of residential care. *Child Welfare* 55:267–78

Martinson, R. 1974. What works — Questions and answers about prison reform. *The Public Interest* 35:22

Matsushima, J. 1979. Outcomes of residential treatment: Designing accountability protocols. *Child Welfare* 58:303–18

Mayer, G. and Peterson, J.C. 1975. Social control in the treatment of adolescents in residential care. *Child Welfare* 54:246–56

Millman, H.L. and Pancost, R.O. 1977. Program evaluation in a residential treatment centre. *Behavioural Disorders* 2:66–75

Milner, R. 1982. If you need my help just say the word. *Journal of Child Care* 1:11–26

Mordock, J.B. 1979. Evaluation in residential treatment: The conceptual dilemmas. *Child Welfare* 58:293–302

Nelson, R.H. 1973. Community considerations in the evaluation of a children's residential treatment centre. Paper presented at the annual meeting of the American Psychological Association, Montreal, Quebec

Nicholson, L. 1979. Locus of control in a residential treatment centre. Unpublished manuscript, William Roper Hull Home, Alberta

O'Keefe, E.J. and Castaldo, C.J. 1981. A multimodal approach to treatment in a child care agency. *Child Care Quarterly* 10:103–12

Oxley, G.B. 1977. Involuntary client's response to a treatment experience. *Social Casework* 58:607–14

Patterson, G. 1975–82. *A social learning approach to family intervention.* Vols. 1–3. Eugene, OR: Castallia

Pawson, G.L. 1983. *Residential group-care and treatment programs.* Social Work Papers 17. Los Angeles: University of Southern California

Perry, P. 1985. Woods Christian Homes stabilization unit. Unpublished program design. Calgary: Woods Christian Homes

Polsky, H.W. 1962. *Cottage 6: The social system of delinquent boys in residential treatment.* New York: Russell Sage

Powers, D. and Powell, J. 1983. A role for residential treatment in preparation for adoption. *Residential Group Care and Treatment* 2:31–69

Schaefer, C. 1980. The impact of peer culture in the residential treatment of youth. *Adolescence* 15:831–45

Stuart, R.B. 1970. *Trick or treatment.* Chicago: Research

Thomas, C.W. and Poole, E.D. 1975. The consequences of incompatible goal structures in correctional settings. *International Journal of Criminology and Penology* 3:27–42

Trieschman, A.E. 1976. The Walker School: An education-based model. *Child Care Quarterly* 5:123–35

Trieschman, A.E., Whittaker, J.K., and Brendtro, L.K. 1969. *The other twenty-three hours.* Chicago: Aldine

Van Scoy, H. 1976. The child care worker as an activity group co-therapist. *Child Care Quarterly* 5:221–8

Whittaker, J.K. and Garbarino, J. 1983. *Social support networks: Informal helping in the human services.* New York: Aldine

Wilson, D.R. and Lyman, R.D. 1983. Computer assisted behavioural assessment in residential treatment. *Residential Group Care & Treatment* 1:25–31

Witkin, M.J. and Cannon, M.S. 1971. *Residential centres for emotionally disturbed children.* Washington, DC: National Institute of Mental Health Publications

Wolfensberger, W. and Nirje, B. 1972. *The Principles of Normalization in Human Services.* Toronto: National Institute of Mental Retardation

Wollins, M. and Wozner, Y. 1982. *Revitalizing residential settings.* San Francisco: Jossey-Bass

3
Child and Youth Care and the Canadian Youth Justice System
Del Phillips and Barbara Maslowsky

Child and youth care professionals who work with young offenders need to know the law as it relates to youth, understand the way the youth justice system functions and its relationship to other components of the child welfare system, and possess the necessary skills for working with adolescents. Statistics Canada estimates that 37,657 young Canadians under the age of eighteen years appeared before youth courts during 1990–1, and 29,661 young persons were found guilty of at least one offence. Of the 117,692 charges heard by youth courts, 74,973 resulted in guilty findings. The courts heard 45,051 cases (excluding Ontario) in which at least one of the charges before the court resulted in a guilty finding (Canadian Centre for Justice Statistics 1991a).[1]

The youth court's dispositions, where guilt was established, ranged from secure custody to absolute discharge. In approximately 12 per cent of the cases the youth was placed in secure custody, with open custody accounting for 13 per cent, probation 48 per cent, and all other dispositions 26 per cent (Canadian Centre for Justice Statistics 1991b). Of particular concern is the disproportionate number of aboriginal youth who are in custody facilities. Kenewell, Bala, and Colfer reported that in Ontario 'aboriginal youths are in custody at four times their rate in the population' (Barnhorst and Johnson 1991:160).

The media are quick to bring more serious youth offences to the public's attention. The problem of youth crime is large, and the public has acquired a strong perception of its importance. It has also recently captured the attention of Canadian legislators, who have passed the Young Offenders Act (YOA 1984).

This chapter is primarily about the YOA; it is intended for child and youth care workers who work with young persons who have come into conflict with the law. It is divided into three sections: the young offender and relevant aspects of the YOA; organizational/structural aspects of the youth justice system and where it fits in the broader context of child welfare; and, finally, information about the responsibilities youth workers will encounter when working with young offenders.

The Young Offender

Headlines in the neighbourhood newspaper often contain lead stories such as, 'Elderly Grocer in Hospital Following Robbery Attempt by Two Youths.' The story might describe how the youths, aged 14 and 15, entered a grocery store run by an elderly gentleman and demanded money. When he resisted, he was attacked and badly beaten. The youths were arrested several blocks away with the money, candy bars, and cigarettes stolen from the store.

The young offender comes into the youth justice system because of what he/she has done, not who he/she is. The youths in this vignette have become part of the youth justice system: although they are not representative of average offenders, they do attract the most publicity. According to Statistics Canada, violent offences accounted for only 10.9 per cent of all charges heard by Youth Courts (Youth Court Statistics 1991) and 10 per cent of all convictions (p. 29). Convictions for violent offences included murder (26), attempted murder (6), sexual assault (721), assault (4,536), robbery (890), weapons/firearms/explosives (1006), and other (331), with females accounting for 16.8 per cent of the convictions.

There were 46,332 convictions for property offences, including 15,014 for break and enter and 13,605 for theft under $1000.00. In this category males accounted for 90 per cent of the charges with guilty findings. Given this information, the child care professional may well ask if the behaviour of a young offender is substantially different from that of any other adolescent. Most adolescents test limits, conflict with adults, and face increasing societal expectations at a time when the struggle for independence, freedom, and recognition from both peers and adults is uppermost. Most live by the norms and laws of society, participating in institutions established by adults for children (such as schools, organized sports, community activities, and family activities). Although many so-called 'normal kids' break the law at one time or another, few are ever arrested; of those arrested, most are 'diverted' from the youth justice system by the police or court. Thus, repeat offenders or youths having committed serious crimes are the individuals most likely to become the clients of child care professionals.

Juvenile Delinquency

Although this chapter focuses on systemic issues related to the involvement of child and youth care professionals with young offenders, theories about why youths become offenders deserve some consideration. Much has been written to attempt to explain why young persons come into conflict with the law. For example, child abuse may be a significant factor in subsequent delinquent behaviour (Garbarino, Schellenbach, Sebes, and Associates 1986). Theories reflect physiological, sociological, and psychological biases (Gold and Petronio 1980). Newman and Newman (1986) describe five identifiable groups of delinquents. They are: (1) the psychopathic delinquent, described as having personality characteristics that include 'impulsiveness, defiance, absence of guilt feelings, inability to learn from experience, and the inability to maintain close social relationships'; (2) the neurotic delinquent, where 'delinquent behaviour is thought to arise from psychological conflict and anxiety'; (3) the psychotic delinquent, reflecting an inability to test reality, control personal impulses, and utilize good judgment; (4) the organic delinquent, resulting from mental retardation and/or brain damage; and (5) the gang delinquent, whose membership in a group meets the delinquent's need for 'status, resources, and relationship.' Holin (1990) provides an overview of some of the theories of offending and presents a position supporting a 'cognitive-behavioural' model. Although theories about delinquency exist, none are definitive.

Young offenders often initially resist adult intrusion and control in their lives. When charged with an offence, the youth has been placed by a person in authority (police officer, judge) under the control of another authority figure, such as a child care professional. The involuntary nature of this relationship requires patience, skill, and knowledge on the part of the youth care worker in order to overcome the resistance and hostility that the youth may experience. Recognition of this sense of powerlessness is, therefore, essential in dealing with the behaviours that the youth worker encounters — behaviours that range from subtle cries for help to overt hostility. One aspect of the work with young offenders requires that workers be familiar with relevant legislation and procedures within the youth justice system.

The Young Offenders Act

The YOA is federal legislation enacted in 1984 by the Canadian Parliament. To understand the relationship between federal and provincial legislation, it is essential to outline the relationship between the powers of the federal Parliament and the provincial governments.

The Constitution Act (1982) (formerly the British North America Act (1867)) sets out the division of powers between the federal and provincial governments. This is done in a way that subjects every person to the laws of two authorities, the Parliament of Canada and the legislatures of the provinces. As Hogg (1985) states, 'the central authority and the regional authorities are "coordinate," that is to say, neither is subordinate to the other' (p. 30). Under the Constitution Act, one authority does not have the power to enact legislation in 'classes of subjects' assigned to the other. Section 91 of the act enables the national parliament to enact laws for the 'Peace, Order and good Government of Canada.' Under the 'classes of subjects' are, for example, 'Unemployment Insurance' and 'the Criminal Law.' Section 92 lists the 'classes of subjects' which the Constitution Act assigns exclusively to the provinces. These include 'the Administration of Justice in the Province including the Constitution, Maintenance and Organization of Provincial Courts, both the Civil and of Criminal Jurisdiction.'

The federal government enacts the criminal law (the criminal code) and is responsible for making laws establishing the procedure to be followed in criminal matters (such as the YOA). The provinces, on the other hand, are responsible for passing laws with respect to 'the administration of Justice in the Provinces,' and for the purpose of establishing, maintaining, and managing the provincial courts. The provinces establish the court procedures in civil matters; the federal government defines procedure in relation to criminal matters. In addition to the administration of justice through the court system, provincial governments are responsible for general policing and services to young offenders. Procedural legislation determines the function of the other three components of the system: the police, the courts, and the services to youths who have come into conflict with the law.

Offence legislation sets out what behaviour is unlawful and enables the system to intervene in the life of a youth. Thus, it is the youth who is the first, and key, component of the youth justice system. The relationships between procedural and offence legislation under the federal and provincial governments and their effect on the four components of the youth justice system are presented in Figure 3.1.

Figure 3.1

**Relationship between various aspects
of the legislation and the young offender**

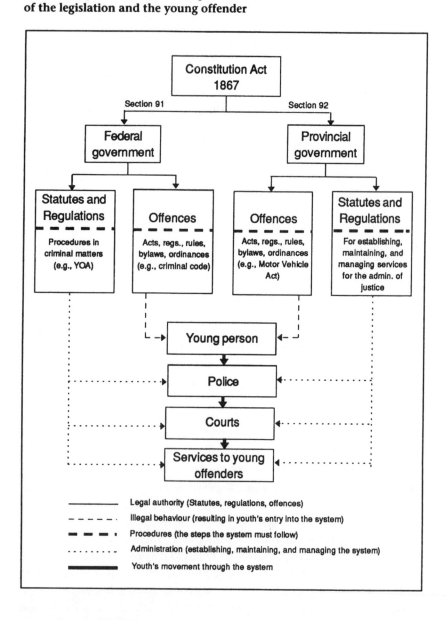

Legal authority (Statutes, regulations, offences)

Illegal behaviour (resulting in youth's entry into the system)

Procedures (the steps the system must follow)

Administration (establishing, maintaining, and managing the system)

Youth's movement through the system

Operation of the YOA

Like most other pieces of legislation, the YOA defines, empowers, and limits actions and behaviours. It is referred to as a 'procedural statute.'[2]

However, no longer do we speak of 'juveniles,' 'juvenile delinquents,' 'juvenile court,' or 'industrial schools.' The Juvenile Delinquents Act (1908), embodying the fundamental principles of the 'child saving movement,' provided for a separate court and special court procedures for young people charged with committing 'delinquencies' as well as for the development of a probation service.[3] For seventy-six years, this act had a pervasive effect on shaping youth corrections in this country. The YOA, which replaced it, was the result of twenty years of public debate, undergoing many revisions in response to changes within society.

Under the YOA, a young person is anyone between 12 and 18 years of age. Previously, considerable age variation existed among provinces; in some provinces, persons aged 16 or 17 years were governed by adult criminal law. As children under age 12 cannot be prosecuted for committing an offence, they cannot be held criminally responsible.

For a young person to appear in 'youth court' under the YOA, he or she must be charged with a violation of a federal statute, such as the Criminal Code, Narcotic Control Act, or Food and Drug Act. Other crimes not included in federal statutes include truancy, driving, and liquor offences. Each province has its own legislation and penalties for these offences; all are tried in youth courts. The following is a summary of the main aspects of the YOA.

Philosophy and Intent

The Declaration of Principle clearly sets out the philosophy and intent of the YOA (Sec. 3) and provides basic principles for interpretation and application. One such principle is that the young person is seen as having the same rights and protection under the law as do adults. However, no longer does the court act in the role of a kindly parent in a relatively informal setting. Youth courts, like adult courts, are open to the public, which allows for public scrutiny and awareness of matters relating to young offenders. There are some instances where young persons are given special protection. For instance, names of young persons charged with or convicted of offences cannot be published (Sec. 38(1)).

According to the Declaration of Principle, young persons have the right to be informed (Sec. 3(1)(g)), to be heard in court, and to participate in the processes leading to decisions that affect them. Responsibilities in this area fall to police, judges, staff of detention and custody facilities, probation officers, child welfare workers, and all other persons and agencies who are involved in the youth justice system. Sections 11 and 12 of the YOA ensure that a young person must be informed upon arrest, at all court appearances, and on court documents of his/her right to be represented by counsel. Section 56 requires that police officers take special steps to inform a young person of his/her rights prior to taking a statement.

The YOA also guarantees counsel for the young person. This provision might be used, for example, in situations where the young person and his/her parents are not in agreement. The YOA provides for copies of court reports, such as dispositional reports and medical/psychological reports, to be given to the young person. However, the judge may decide to exclude the youth from receiving all or part of the report if it is considered injurious. In addition to the range of court dispositions available, the YOA reflects concern for minimal intervention through other provisions, such as alternative measures.[4] Thus, there has been a movement from a preoccupation with the young offender's needs to a focus on the nature of the young person's offending behaviour.

Responsibility and Accountability

The notion of 'mitigated accountability,' or lessened accountability, is reflected in the maximum length of disposition available under the YOA: two years for a probation order or two or five years for a custody order, depending on the seriousness of the offence (Sec. 20). Also, provisions for community service and personal service provide an opportunity for the young person to work off his/her debt to the community in general or to the victim. This is a departure from the Juvenile Delinquents Act, wherein the juvenile was depicted as a 'misguided, misdirected youth.'

Special Needs

Although the act focuses on the nature and seriousness of deeds, the Declaration of Principle states that both the needs of the young person and the interests of his/her family should also be taken into consideration at the time of disposition. While the Declaration of Principle refers to the youth's family, many youths who come before the courts under the YOA are in the care of the state. The youth's 'family' may be foster parents or other significant adults in the youth's life, and the youth's parents may have little or no involvement with him or her.

Removal from the home can have a dramatic effect on the youth, as it separates the youth from his/her support system. It may also affect the youth's parents or care givers and other members of the youth's family, including siblings. Child and youth care professionals need to be aware of the effects of separation on the youth and his/her family (Steinhauer 1991).

The negative effects of institutionalization must be weighed against society's need for protection. Recognition of the special needs of the young person reflects a major distinction between the youth justice and adult corrections systems. These needs arise out of the young person's state of dependence and his maturity. The act not only recognizes that young offenders require 'supervision, discipline and control' but also underlines the need for 'guidance and assistance' (Sec. 3(1)(c)).

There is a considerable amount of flexibility in the YOA, facilitating the assistance of young persons with special needs through the wide range of dispositional alternatives, including treatment orders. The provision for various predispositional and medical/psychological reports affords the opportunity to take into account the opinions of social work, child care, psychological, and psychiatric professionals. This provides the youth court judge with information about the personal profile of the young person. In this way, the disposition of the court, following a finding of guilt, is able to balance the seriousness of the offence with the needs of the young person.

Parental Rights and Responsibilities

Parents or guardians are considered responsible for the care and supervision of their children; for this reason, young persons should be removed from parental supervision 'only when measures that provide for continuing parental supervision are inappropriate' (Sec. 3 (1)(b)). Parents receive notice of all court proceedings and copies of reports prepared for the youth court. Parents who attend proceedings under the YOA are not parties to the proceedings, but they are assured an opportunity to be heard. Furthermore, the courts can compel a parent to attend proceedings. In some cases, parents may reject the child because of embarrassment experienced as a result of the child's behaviour. This sense of failure may also show through in their relationships with professional staff. It is also important to note that an order to detain a young person for treatment cannot be made without the consent of the parent where the parent is taking an active interest. This encourages the involvement of parents in decision-making.

Child and youth care professionals working in treatment programs may have to account to the parents for what they do with the child. This may be seen by the professional as interference in the treatment process rather than constructive involvement by the parent. At minimum, parents may wish to become informed of the intended outcome of a particular program before they involve their child.

Rights of Society

The YOA also articulates that society has a right to be protected from illegal behaviour. For the first time, legislation has concerned itself with the victims of youth crime. Although not essential, there is provision in the act for the results of an interview with the victim to be attached in predispositional reports that go before the court. When an order is made that the young person must make compensation in kind to the victim (known as 'personal service order'), the victim must be aware of and agree to the terms. Not only does this 'repay' the victim for the damage done, but it also makes the youth more aware of the impact of his/her behaviour on another person.

Dispositions

Section 20 of the YOA sets out all of the dispositional options available to the youth court judge, including maximum limits pertaining to each disposition. The range of dispositions can be grouped in two categories: community dispositions (including detention for treatment) and custody dispositions.

Within the range of community dispositions, there is provision for orders involving financial payment and compensation or return of property. For instance, the YOA allows for a fine of up to $1,000 to be paid 'at such times and on such terms as the court may fix' (Sec. 20(1)(b)). There is also provision for orders involving service to the community (community service) and service to the victim (personal service). Probation is another community disposition under the YOA and is limited to a maximum period of two years. The role of the 'youth worker,' as defined by the YOA, is to supervise the young person in complying with the conditions of a probation order and to assist him/her until the disposition has been completed. The youth court may also order that a young person be detained for in-patient treatment. This disposition must be preceded by a medical/psychological report recommending that the young person undergo treatment for any of the following conditions: a physical illness or disorder, a mental illness or disorder, a psychological disorder, an emotional disturbance, a learning disability, or mental retardation. One example is the treatment of adolescent sex offenders. In recent years concern has been growing about the increasing incidence of sexual offences in the adolescent population. Placing youths in a specialized treatment program is one option available in jurisdictions where such programs exist (Canadian Child Welfare 1989).

The range of custody dispositions reflects two types of custody, open and secure. Like community dispositions, all custody dispositions are prescribed for a definite period of time. Generally, custody dispositions are not to exceed two years in length. However, custody dispositions may be for periods of up to five years for murder. Amendments to the YOA in 1992 raised the maximum disposition for murder from three years to five years less a day. The five years comprises of three years of custody followed by two years of community supervision, unless the court orders that the youth, at the end of the three-year period, remain in custody for the balance of the sentence (Sec. 26.1(1)). Whether we speak of open or secure custody, the YOA requires that the young person be held separate and apart from any adult charged or convicted of an offence. Section 24(1) defines open custody as a community residential centre, group home, child care institution, or wilderness camp. Secure custody, on the other hand, is defined as a 'place of secure containment or restraint.' Each province has made its own policy decisions regarding the designation of open and secure custody.

Professionals involved with young offenders in custody settings should also be familiar with the provisions regarding 'temporary release' from custody (Sec. 35). Releases may be granted for medical, compassionate or humanitarian grounds, rehabilitation, reintegration into the community, education, or employment (for periods not exceeding fifteen days). Under this section the young person may be released with or without escort.

Transfers to Ordinary Court

There is provision for transfer to ordinary adult court if the person was fourteen years of age or over when the alleged offence was committed. The transfer hearing is not a trial. Rather, it is a hearing to determine whether the interests of society might better be served if this matter went to trial in an adult court. If the matter is transferred to adult court, the sanctions of the adult law apply.

Reviews

The act details the grounds for reviews, defines who is eligible to apply and when, and delineates the possible outcomes. It is particularly important that child care professionals working with young persons in custody settings or on probation orders be aware of the purpose, mechanics, and implications of reviews. These professionals are often assisted by representatives from the local probation office or from the local Crown's office, who detail the provisions, policies, and procedures relative to reviews.

Figure 3.2 provides an operation description of the YOA by identifying the process through which the young offender passes. It includes the various stages, decision points, and alternatives from the occurrence of an alleged offence through to the court's final disposition. This also describes the 'activities' that take place in the youth justice system and the relationships of the various components. As this is an overview, slight variations may be seen between provinces, depending on the youth justice model adopted.

In summary, marked alteration in the treatment of young persons before and under the law have occurred. Proclamation of the YOA has resulted in a number of changes to the youth justice system; these are reflected in terminology, attitude, theme, and philosophy. In addition to the young offender, new procedures, including ongoing changes to the YOA, affect all persons involved in the youth justice system.

Youth Justice and the Child Welfare System

The Young Offenders Act describes the roles, responsibilities, and relationships of various aspects of the youth justice system. As referred to previously, it has four primary components. Programs may be provided directly by provincial governments or through private or non-profit agencies funded by contracts, grants, or fee for service arrangements. Custody programs are generally provided as a direct service of government and tend to be the best known aspect of youth programming. However, there are a range of programs providing care, treatment, custody, and control for young persons charged with or found guilty of an offence. The most common include secure and open custody, institutional and community treatment, probation, counselling, education, and work experience. As noted earlier, Canada's constitution requires that YOA programs and other services to children and youth be delivered through provincial governments. Many provincial government services to youth, including young offenders, have evolved through circumstance, tradition, or political expedience without the benefit of a comprehensive planning process that maximizes the quality and effectiveness of the service delivered, making the best possible use of limited financial resources. A significant proportion of young offenders

Figure 3.2

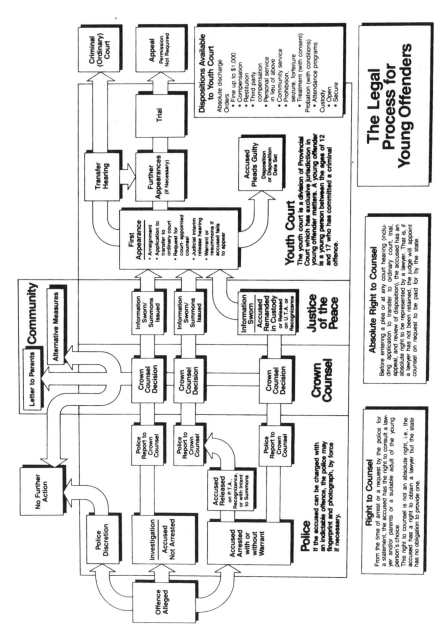

The Legal Process for Young Offenders

Community

No Further Action

Letter to Parents

Alternative Measures

Criminal (Ordinary) Court

Appeal
Permission Not Required

Trial

Transfer Hearing

Further Appearances (If Necessary)

First Appearance
• Arraignment
• Application to transfer to ordinary court
• Request for court-appointed counsel
• Judicial interim release hearing
• Warrant or resummons if accused fails to appear

Accused Pleads Guilty
Disposition or Disposition Date Set

Dispositions Available to Youth Court
Absolute discharge
Orders
  • Fine up to $1,000
  • Compensation
  • Restitution
  • Third party compensation
  • Personal service in lieu of above
  • Community service
  • Prohibition, seizure, forfeiture
  • Treatment (with consent)
Probation (with conditions)
  • Attendance programs
Custody
  • Open
  • Secure

Youth Court
The youth court is a division of Provincial Court which has exclusive jurisdiction in young offender matters. A young offender is a young person between the ages of 12 and 17 who has committed a criminal offence.

Information Sworn/ Summons Issued

Information Sworn/ Summons Issued

Information Sworn
Accused Remanded in Custody or Released on U.T.A. or Recognizance

Justice of the Peace

Crown Counsel Decision

Crown Counsel Decision

Crown Counsel Decision

Crown Counsel

Police Report to Crown Counsel

Police Report to Crown Counsel

Police Report to Crown Counsel

Police Discretion

Investigation
Accused Not Arrested

Accused Released on P.T.A., Recognizance, or with Intent to Summons

Accused Arrested with or without Warrant

Offence Alleged

Police
If the accused can be charged with an indictable offence, the police may fingerprint and photograph, by force if necessary.

Right to Counsel
From the time of arrest or a request by the police for a statement, the accused has the right to consult a lawyer and/or parents or a suitable adult of the young person's choice.
This right to counsel is not an absolute right, i.e., the accused has a right to obtain a lawyer but the state has no obligation to provide one.

Absolute Right to Counsel
Before entering a plea or at any court hearing (including application to transfer to ordinary court, trial, appeal, and review of disposition), the accused has an absolute right to be represented by a lawyer. That is, if a lawyer has not been retained, the judge will appoint counsel on request to be paid for by the state.

Courtesy Legal Services Society of BC

are also clients of service streams such as child welfare, children's mental health, and youth alcohol and drug programs. The special educational and health needs of many young offenders are also well known to professionals in this field. Figure 3.3 provides an example of the array of services provided to youth by one provincial government. Although each province is unique in the way services are delivered, most provinces have a similar range of programs.

The Integrated Model
In this structure, services to young offenders are included as part of a single service delivery system such as a children and family ministry; resources for children and their families are administered under one broad organizational structure. Ontario, the Northwest Territories, and the Yukon have adopted aspects of this model in which child welfare, youth correctional programs, and health services to young offenders all fall within the same administrative structure, although Ontario is currently providing services to 16- and 17-year-old offenders under the Ministry of Correctional Services (adult corrections).

The Social Welfare Model
Services to young offenders in this model are included under the department or ministry providing adult social or welfare services. An example may be seen in Quebec, where the youth justice system is included under the Ministry of Social Services. Other provinces to adopt this approach are Manitoba, Newfoundland, Nova Scotia, and Saskatchewan.

The Corrections Model
All correctional services for both young offenders and adults are provided under a corrections ministry, department, or branch of government. For example, in British Columbia all services to young offenders are provided under the Corrections Branch, a department of the Ministry of the Attorney General. Youth corrections, therefore, is within the same structure that administers adult corrections. Alberta, New Brunswick, and Prince Edward Island have also adopted a similar model.

Advantages and Disadvantages of these Models
The integrated model offers a single organizational structure providing all services to a particular youth. Its advantages include the following.

Figure 3.3

Major child, youth, and family programs in BC by administrative authority

(Dotted line indicates funding relationship)

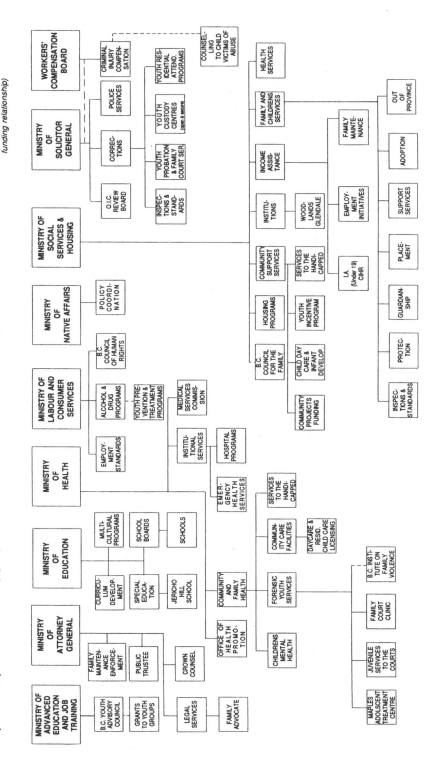

(1) More effective planning and coordination of youth services. The mandate to provide effective services is spread across a single authority, minimizing the gaps and overlaps which can occur between the 'mandates' of separate authorities. Geographical boundaries are standardized so that one authority is responsible for all services to children and youth within its particular area or locality. This simplified system provides greater opportunity for the local citizenry to comprehend and participate in planning and developing services in their community. Understanding the system will enhance the public's awareness of the issues and may contribute to increased public support for child and youth initiatives. The integrated model also brings together the various professions and disciplines under one administrative structure, providing the opportunity for improved communication as well as sharing knowledge and skills in planning and delivering services.

(2) Improved service delivery. The tools for quality control, including standards of care, professional practice standards, and organizational policies and procedures, can be standardized to permit the effective supervision and evaluation of services to children and youth. A single authority improves access to service and could offer a simplified single point of entry to all services at the local community level. In addition, professionals working within an integrated system may be able to take a more holistic view of the youth's needs in relation to the need of the community to be protected. For example, many children in young offender facilities are themselves victims of emotional, physical, and sexual abuse. They require the care and skill of well trained professionals to assist them in coming to terms with the trauma they have been subjected to, and this has to take place in the context of society's need to be protected from further offences.

(3) More effective problem-solving. A single organizational structure has within it the authority to resolve problems quickly. When a problem crosses ministry or departmental boundaries, the process for resolving the issue can be slow and cumbersome.

(4) Less disruptive transition between programs. The various programs within the integrated system tend to flow more smoothly from one to another: transitions can be carried out in a planned way with minimum disruption. The youth is less likely to become lost in the gaps between the programs in which he/she is participating.

(5) Improved information-sharing. Information is shared through a formal structure rather than informally between systems.

(6) Better funding. The allocation of financial resources determines the quality and quantity of programs and services provided. This decision is to some extent based on the strength of the ministries' representation at the political level. It could be argued that it is politically more acceptable to lobby for children's programs in general than for programs for young offenders who are part of a larger corrections ministry.

(7) Improved fiscal management. The integrated model can reduce gaps and overlaps in program funding and can offer a more efficient organizational structure. Other models have multiple bureaucracies, each with its own attending support system for operating and/or funding services.

Although Ontario had adopted some of the features of an integrated model, serious concerns about organizational, resource, and justice issues were identified in the report of the Advisory Committee on Children's Services. Ontario's *Children First* report (Ontario 1990) stated that

> some critics argue that justice is not applied equally across social groups. They contend that children from poor and native families are more likely to end up in court, while middle-class children are more likely to be diverted into mental health treatment programs.
>
> Presentations made to the Committee indicated a system that is overloaded, and within which the mental health needs of the youth are not well met. The courts are crowded with a backlog of cases, and the treatment services that now exist for young offenders are overloaded ...
>
> Many of these youth have serious behavioural and emotional problems; their appearance in the juvenile justice system instead of the treatment system is almost a matter of chance. Yet once they are in this system, the youth are labelled 'young offenders' and this makes it even less likely that they will get the intervention they need in the future ... Service providers are frustrated ... They feel unable to make significant progress using case-by-case approaches to service, yet they have limited capacity to organize a more systemic response incorporating prevention and early intervention. (p. 46)

The economic climate in Canada, and the federal government's decision to cap transfer payments to the provinces, suggests that additional resources for child, youth, and family services will be scarce. There is, however, some evidence to suggest that significant improvements in effectiveness and efficiency could be achieved by provinces through the restructuring of the child, youth, and family service system to ensure more integrated approaches similar to those suggested in the Ontario and BC reports.

The integrated model has at least one major disadvantage. If a particular service is not part of its mandate, there may be no other system available to provide it. For example, if alternative educational programs for behaviourally disturbed youths are not available within a family and child services ministry, and this ministry is responsible for young offenders, then young offenders may not receive this service. The criteria for gaining entry to many programs may disqualify youths who exhibit disruptive behaviour. Alternatively, professionals working with youths may prefer those who are more amenable to treatment. This process may result in a greater number of young offenders being placed in institutions rather than in community programs.

The social welfare model provides services to young offenders under the umbrella of a social welfare ministry or department. Health services, for example, are not usually included under this ministry. Although not as wide-ranging in scope as is the integrated system, it provides services to a broader range of clients than does the corrections model. The social welfare model may provide foster programs, child welfare, and services to children, families, and young offenders. Because a social services system generally provides a wide range of services, it may be able to respond more effectively to the needs of the child than may the narrower focus of the corrections model.

The corrections model, sometimes referred to as the justice or responsibility model, provides services to young offenders in terms of custody and control. This model often involves placing young offenders under the administrative umbrella of adult corrections where there is reduced emphasis on the needs of the child and the prevention of offending behaviour, and increased emphasis on the protection of society. However, programs developed within the corrections system specifically for young offenders are more likely to focus on aggressive behaviour. In this system, the special needs of youth for health care (physical and psychological) and social services, such as release planning, are provided through ministries, departments, or agencies outside the corrections system. This approach relies to some extent on goodwill between the various components of the system rather than on a formal organizational structure. One of the difficulties with this approach is that the relationships between the various interrelated systems and all the professionals involved with the youth become so complex that even those most familiar with the system become confused by it. Figure 3.3 provides an example of the many youth and family programs within one provincial jurisdiction . Although most provinces provide a similar range of programs, each province has a different organizational structure for delivering services.

An advantage of the corrections model is that the role of youth justice is defined in more narrow and clear terms. There is less likelihood that corrections will become the broad net catching youths who are experiencing behaviour problems but are not a danger to the community. However, with this approach there may be a tendency to minimize the importance of services intended to contribute to the emotional, social, and psychological development of the youth. Consequently, services could become more control oriented.

Although various levels of coordination and integration are incorporated into the models described above, the fundamental issues of organizational structure require further analysis. Several major studies have identified the need for an integrated continuum of comprehensive, responsive, and accessible cross-disciplinary services to youth with special needs and their families. In 1970, the Commission on Emotional and Learning Disorders in Children (CELDIC) Report took a three-year look at Canada through the eyes of a child. The commissioners stated:

> If we were asked to put into a single word what distressed us most we would say divisions ... We divide our services: health, education, welfare, corrections. We provide these through different levels of government ... and through public and private endeavour. The people who provide services are divided ... There are many different professions, and they all speak different languages. Their tribal jargon serves to separate professions from each other and from other potential helpers. No single factor has caused us more concern than the picture of different professions struggling to establish their own power base, distrustful of each other, refusing to share their so-called 'confidential' information and in this division frequently foiling the child. (p. 1)

More than twenty years later, Rix Rogers, special adviser on child sexual abuse to Canada's minister of health and welfare, released the report *Reaching for Solutions* (1990). This report, based on meetings with over 1,600 people from across Canada, described problems of jurisdictional and professional competition, and the crucial need for improved coordination of government and nongovernment services focused on solving problems at the community level. As a result of Rogers' report and Canada's support of the United Nations Convention on the Rights of the Child, the federal government established a Children's Bureau to coordinate national efforts on behalf of children and youth.

At the provincial level, major reports from Ontario and BC have raised concerns about the serious fragmentation of services provided to children, youth, and families. Ontario's Report of the Advisory Committee on Children's Services, *Children First* (Ontario 1990), found that

> the system we now have for serving children in this province is made up of several provincial ministries, hundreds of local authorities, and over a thousand agencies. They all have their own mandates, catchment areas, resources, and accountabilities. Providers of services, whether branches of provincial ministries, voluntary-sector agencies or local governments, endeavour to meet their own responsibilities and their own agendas. But there is no governing framework to pull the network together. There is no real system for children. (p. 107)

This report recommended the establishment of 'locally elected children's authorities to have responsibility for planning, systems management and resource allocation for social, educational, correctional, health and recreational services for children' (p. 121). The provincial government was also urged to 'establish a provincial children's authority that integrates responsibility for all major legislation, strategic planning, policy and program development, and funding of services for children ... [to] incorporate, at a minimum, ministerial responsibilities for children now lodged in the Ministries of Community and Social Services, Education, Correctional Services, Health, and Tourism and Recreation' (p. 118).

In November 1990, following the tragic death of a youth in a contracted facility in British Columbia, the provincial ombudsman found that child welfare, children's mental health, and youth corrections services were seriously fragmented and that standards were not being uniformly applied or monitored (British Columbia 1990).

The report's first recommendation called upon the provincial government to seek more effective ways to empower communities and to establish 'a single authority within government ... with a formal mandate, executive powers and an adequate resource base to ensure uniform, integrated and client-centred provincial approaches to policy setting, planning and administration of publicly funded services to children, youth and their families' (p. 12).

The state of Hawaii has also conducted a comprehensive review of services to 'at risk' youth which recommends developing an Office of Youth Services (National Child Welfare Resource Center for Management and Administration 1991). At the time of writing, none of the provincial governments had adopted the organizational changes required to implement the recommendations outlined above.

Trends within Society and the Work of the Child and Youth Care Worker

The YOA has shifted the emphasis away from preoccupation with rehabilitation towards concern for the protection of the public. Inherent in this is the danger that provinces may interpret this shift as justification for moving away from a developmental approach (that is, treatment and rehabilitation) towards a custodial stand (control, containment, and lockup). In practical terms, this approach is cost-effective (at least in the short-term), is easily understood, and avoids viewing corrections as rehabilitation. This position is consistent with Martinson, who stated, 'with few and isolated exceptions, the rehabilitative efforts that have been reported so far have had no appreciable effect on recidivism' (Martinson 1974). In a later publication, Martinson (1976) commented that 'correctional treatment is about nine-tenths pageantry, rumination, and rubbish' (p. 180). Although this 'nothing works' debate has centred largely on adult corrections, such thinking has also permeated youth corrections. However, many administrators and the majority of professionals working with young offenders believe that young people have particular needs which require special care. Administrators and professionals must continue to assert that the system has as one of its objectives the growth and development of Canada's youth.

The role of the child and youth care professional will naturally be affected by the philosophy of the organization in which the professional is employed. If the agency or ministry providing the services stresses the needs of the youth, then much of the training that child and youth care professionals receive will be compatible with the goals of the system. However, if the organization sees its role primarily as protection for society through the control of the youth's behaviour for the duration of the judicial order, then child and youth care professionals will be required to function in an environment which may conflict with their training and orientation.

Child and youth care professionals working with young offenders must come to terms with a number of expectations from society, government, senior administration, colleagues, and academics. They are summarized below.

Rehabilitation

This has as its objective the behaviour change of the youth so that future offences will not be committed. If the youth does not commit further offences, then it can be assumed that 'rehabilitation' has occurred. Child and youth care professionals may enter this system with the assumption that if the young offender is brought before the court and sentenced to probation or institutional confinement, it is the responsibility of both the system and the professional to elicit this change.

Retribution

This objective assumes that, as the young offender has broken the law, he/she must be punished. In contract, programs that have as their objective the 'treatment' of the offender may be seen as too soft or even pleasant. However, the acceptance of punishment as an objective leaves open the possibility for allegations of staff abuse. The YOA states that 'while young persons should not in all instances be held accountable in the same manner or suffer the same consequences for their behaviour as adults, young persons who commit offences should nonetheless bear responsibility for their contraventions' (Sec. 3(1)(a)). The act further states that 'young persons who commit offences require supervision, discipline and control' (Sec. 3(1)(c)). Accountability and punishment are not synonymous, nor does the act suggest that the objective of a disposition, whether custodial or non-custodial, is punishment. Similarly, discipline and control do not give staff in a custodial setting licence to exercise power in a way that is inhumane or otherwise punitive. Although the term discipline may be closely aligned with punishment, it more generally refers to the rules governing conduct. Its use in the act does not appear to refer to the imposition of punishment for breaking the law.

Control

This differs from rehabilitation in that the control exercised is supposed to prevent further delinquencies from occurring during the period of the disposition. Emphasis is placed on protecting society by removing the youth from the community. The proponents of the control approach look to the section of the act that states, 'society must ... be afforded the necessary protection from illegal behaviour' (Sec. 3(1)(b)). This section of the act, taken out of context and not applied in relation to the needs of the youth, may result in the propagation of an expectation prominent in adult correctional circles. This refers to the 'warehousing' of the offender for the duration of the sentence with minimal involvement by others, other than the provision of food, shelter, and basic activities such as work and education.

Normalization

The fourth expectation is that the young offender will be provided with a humane environment with the same general conditions and services that would be available in the community. The only limitation should be the degree of restriction on the young person's freedom — restriction required to protect society from illegal behaviour. This meets both the requirement of YOA and one of the underlying tenets of the child and youth care profession; it emphasizes the importance of meeting the special needs of youth in an effort to maximize the individual's potential.

Regardless of the exact youth justice model adopted by the province or the expectations placed on the child and youth care professional, youths have rights guaranteed by the Canadian Charter of Rights and Freedoms (1982) and the Canadian Bill of Rights (1960) and, most recently, the UN Convention on the Rights of the Child (1990). Child and youth care professionals working with young offenders need to have some understanding of issues involving these rights. Coughlin (1973) identifies the following three rights. First, there is 'a moral power in virtue of which human beings may make just claims to certain things' (p. 8). An example is the right of a six-year-old to claim the candy which he/she is holding and not be forced to give it up. Second, there are natural or human rights, which belong to a person 'by reason of his very existence as a human person, and therefore [are] not conferred upon him by parents or church or state or any other individual or community of men' (p. 8). These unconditional rights include the right to 'life, food, drink, shelter and certain level of physical, emotional, intellectual, and spiritual growth' (p. 9). Third, there are civil rights, which are based 'on natural rights and are the state's explicit enunciation of rights that it guarantees to every citizen' (p. 9). The Canadian Charter of Rights and Freedoms and the Canadian Bill of Rights outline civil rights, as does the United Nations Convention on the Rights of the Child. Other declarations of rights that have been adopted by the United Nations, including the Declaration of Rights of the Child (1959), Standard Minimum Rules for the Treatment of Prisoners (1955), and the Universal Declaration of Human Rights (1948). Although these declarations do not have the force of law, they stress the importance of ensuring that the rights of the individual are maintained. On 11 December 1991, Canada formally ratified the UN Convention on the Rights of the Child. The UN Convention is an especially important document in that it sets standards for the care of children and requires the participation of children in decision-making that affects them. Except for the reservation placed by the federal government when it ratified the Convention to give it authority to transfer children to adult court (YOA, Sec. 16(1)), the federal and provincial governments must comply with all other provisions. The Convention guarantees the child's right to be heard in decisions that affect him/her. Article 12 states:

(1) Parties shall assure to the child who is capable of forming his or her own views the right to express those views freely in all matters affecting the child, the views of the child being given due weight in accordance with the age and maturity of the child.
(2) For this purpose, the child shall in particular be provided the opportunity to be heard in any judicial and administrative proceedings affecting the child, either directly, or through a representative or an appropriate body, in a manner consistent with the procedural rules of national law.

In addition, under the terms of the Convention, professionals are required to place the child's best interest ahead of other considerations. It states that 'in all actions concerning children, whether undertaken by public or private social welfare institutions, courts of law, administrative authorities or legislative bodies, the best interests of the child shall be a primary consideration' (Article 3).

As reflected in the Convention on the Rights of the Child, there is a growing international and national consensus about the rights of children and youth. Child and youth care professionals working within the youth justice system will be confronted with the issue of children's rights balanced against the conditions within restrictive environments. The youth is an involuntary participant in the system and can only be released into the community if certain conditions are met. Limitations on freedom are imposed in order to maintain the care, custody, and security of the resident and the protection of staff. Control is required to maintain the rights of the other residents and the staff and provide a reasonable living environment. Not only does the YOA state that young offenders have the 'right to be heard and included in the decisions affecting them' (Sec. 3(1)(3)), but the also have the right 'to the least possible interference with freedom bearing in mind the needs of young persons and the interest of their families' (Sec. 3(1)(f)). Within policy regulations and rules, there still remains some discretion in decision-making by staff working with young offenders.

The principles of administrative fairness must apply to all decisions made by a child and youth care worker supervising young persons, whether on probation, in community programs, or in secure institutions. Criteria can be applied to all decisions to determine level of fairness. Fairness is determined by whether the decision is contrary to law, unjust, oppressive, discriminatory, arbitrary, unreasonable, or is not explained appropriately. Two important elements come together to ensure that a decision affecting a child is made fairly and is in the child's best interests. This involves 'advocacy' coupled with an authority that has a legislated mandate to investigate and monitor decisions affecting children.

James Lardie, in discussing advocacy for children with serious emotional problems, states child advocacy was defined as 'intervention on behalf of children into the systems and institutions which impinge on their rights' (Kahn, Kamerman, and McGowan 1972). More basically, a child advocate is a person who questions, 'If that child were my child, would she be where she is? Or treated as she is?' And if the answer is NO!, then the child advocate takes positive action about it NOW (Friedman, Duchnowski, and Henderson 1989). The advocacy principles outlined by Lardie are equally applicable to young offenders, many of whom have serious emotional problems.

The second area involves investigating and monitoring decisions made by the state that affect the child. In several provinces the Office of the Ombudsman fulfils this responsibility (Drever 1991; Phillips 1991).

Two of the basic features of the institution of ombudsman, as described by Verhellen (1990), include being a fully independent instrument of the legislative authority with unlimited investigative power, having access to any document related to a case and being directly available to the individual to have a matter investigated, with a broader option of giving opinions on any government action.

In summary, the youth justice system exists because of society's perceived need to be protected from the illegal behaviour of young people. Thus, laws representing these interests are enacted to enable society to deal with illegal behaviour. The law requires a system for young offenders that is separate from the adult criminal justice system, and the YOA provides the basis for dealing with offences committed by youth in Canada.

The Relationship between the Child and Youth Care Professional and the Young Offender

The third component of working with young offenders involves the professional skills and abilities of the child and youth care practitioner and the type of relationship he or she has with the young offender. Positions within the youth justice system may range from counselling in a diversion program to working in a secure custody centre. In most cases, the practitioner has two equally important but divergent roles. He/she must ensure that the youth is abiding by the court order, yet he/she must also provide the youth with support, direction, and guidance. Although these goals are often in conflict, and the time available to spend with the youth may be minimal, the relationship between youth and worker can be rewarding as well as productive. Success depends upon the worker's skill at non-judgmental listening, involving the youth in making decisions, and ensuring that expectations are clearly defined. The initial contact with the worker will be affected by the emotional state and attitude of the youth. The message to the youth must be: 'I accept you as a person even if your behaviour is unacceptable.'

With a progression through the system from lesser degrees of control (such as alternative measures) towards greater control (such as custody), the role of the child and youth care professional becomes more intrusive in the life of the youth. In most larger urban communities, a wide range of services are established and available to young offenders. Community service, restitution, diversionary counselling, and other programs are provided. Dispositional options ordered by the court include community programs, probation supervision, treatment, and open and secure custody. However, in many of the more remote or rural areas, there may be few programs for youths. Subsequently, individualized programs need to be developed to accommodate dispositions and the need for care and control.

Often there is a definite increase in the level of control imposed on the young offender when the intervention is court-ordered. The consequences for violating a court-ordered disposition are serious, and the court can impose heavy restrictions on the freedom of the youth. Youths in secure custody have often 'run the gamut' of available problems, having had numerous court appearances and perhaps having committed serious crimes such as robbery or murder. This environment generally provides minimal freedom, all staff represent total control, and all doors to the outside are locked. The routine is regimented and opportunities for youths to make decisions are severely curtailed. Rigid behaviour control, peer pressure, the multiplicity of interactions between staff and residents, the lack of privacy, and the loss of freedom often combine to make the institution a dehumanizing and destructive place. However, secure custody is sometimes the only way of protecting society from aggressive or violent behaviour. It is the single most restrictive disposition available to the youth court under the YOA and is intended for a minority of offenders for whom there is no other option.

In a recent discussion with residents in a secure custody facility, one of the authors asked a number of youths to describe the most effective staff member. The 'best' staff member was described as follows:

Every youth stated that the staff member really cared about him. There was also a perception that the staff member 'liked kids' in general.

Each youth made some reference to fair discipline and treatment; that is, when asking the child to do something the staff member explained why it should be done.

Most youths commented on the staff member's availability and willingness to listen when they had a problem. This is reflected by one youth, who added, 'he seemed to know when something was bothering me and we would talk about it.'

The staff member did extra things outside working hours. For example, one youth had been taken by an off-duty staff member into the community for a family visit. He commented that the staff member realized how important it was to visit with family and trusted that he would not run away.

The same youths were also asked to describe the worst staff member. Comments included: 'doesn't like kids,' 'only comes to work for the pay,' 'plays head games,' 'sits in the office,' 'pokes fun at me,' and 'calls me down in front of everybody.' This information suggests that any worker in this setting is under close scrutiny. These comments by youths concerning the 'best' and 'worst' staff members are supported by Gold and Petronio (1980), who identify two themes of effective interventions: the support of warm, accepting relationships with adults, and the enhancement of adolescents' self-images as autonomous and effective individuals in the present and future (p. 523).

The relationship between workers and youths within these settings may be limited by time, routines, the dynamics of the existing peer group, and the degree to which meaningful relationships have been established in the past. Each worker, for example, has acquired a range of knowledge gained through education, training, and past experience. Knowledge from the youth justice field includes restrictions imposed by law, decisions handed down by the courts, policies, procedures, and verbal instructions from supervisors, youth assessments and reports, and ideas from the youth's family, the victim, and other professionals. However, a critical component in the transition of this knowledge to action involves the values of the worker. Like the physical properties of a prism that refract and disperse the sun's rays into a spectrum of colour, the actions of the individual worker in relation to the client are focused, filtered, and diffused during this transition.

Similarly, the young offender will see and interpret the decisions, actions, and intentions of the child and youth care professional through the prism of his/her own value system. This information will, in part, be translated into behaviour. This behaviour, in turn, provides clues for the worker to incorporate into his/her repertoire of experience, thus completing the cycle. Finally, it should be understood that the application of various procedures in this setting may take on some degree of flexibility. The same policy applied by different staff members may initiate differing reactions in youths, from compliance, resistance, and hesitation to anger.

The following describes one application of professional skills, knowledge, and attitudes within a closed custody setting.

It's 6:45 a.m. You arrive at the institution and an on-duty staff member unlocks the door and lets you in. Upon arrival you are assigned to a unit. On the unit you are briefed by the off-going staff as to problems or noteworthy events occurring during night shift. You receive your keys and check each room, counting the number of youths in care and their condition. At 7:30 a.m. you wake the residents and ask them to shower. After showers, breakfast is served and after breakfast the group must be prepared for school. Prior to school, residents are expected to tidy their rooms and make their beds. The schedule follows through lunch and the afternoon activities, and at 3:00 p.m. the next shift comes on duty.

This work involves the constant supervision of the activities and behaviour of the youths. Consequently, the potential for conflict is very high. Some youths are cheerful in the morning, but for some it's the most difficult part of the day. For those not in school there are work programs or other activities. Workers are involved in the continual process of balancing the demands of the organization (that is, getting him/her to school on time) against the needs of the youth (for example, 'I didn't get much sleep last night because I'm worried about something that's happening at home and I want to deal with it right now'). The worker can take a moment to talk with the youth about his/her problem or can react under the pressure of the moment and use authority to impose control. The latter approach will probably result in a struggle for power. Mismanaged conflict often results in escalating tension, beginning with defiance, then shouting, and finally either a voluntary retreat by the youth to his/her room or a physical demonstration. If the youth becomes physically aggressive, staff may need to be summoned. If the youth is not intimidated into submission by the show of force, he/she may be restrained and physically placed in a secure room. This is a 'no-win' outcome, as the resident ends up missing school and the staff member has not accomplished the objective of getting him/her there.

Sometimes there are no alternatives to physical control. Child and youth care professionals working in settings where physical control may be required should keep in mind five basic tests to be applied when use of force is required.[5]

(1) The objectives must be lawful. There must be an act or regulation that permits the use of force to obtain compliance or control. The legal authority for use of force should be reflected in agency policy.

(2) The resistance to the attainment of the lawful objective must be evident. The degree of force required must be linked to the resistance. Resistance may be either verbal or physical.

(3) Reasonable alternatives to the use of force must be either unavailable or have been tried and proven unsuccessful. Force should be used as a last resort and then only to the extent necessary to effect control. The resident should be given 'space' and time to 'cool off' in an effort to avoid the use of physical force. If force is required, the resident should be advised in advance that force will be used.

(4) The force used must be minimal (that is, no more force than is re-

quired to overcome the resistance or to effect control). Force may be incrementally escalated as the resistance by the resident increases. The force used involves 'restraint'; not strikes, blows, arm-bending, headlocks, or other methods of inflicting pain. Inflicting pain is not an acceptable means of control or restraint for youth. It increases anger and hostility and makes physically hurting others an acceptable practice.

(5) The force used must be directly related or limited to the attainment of the lawful objective. For example, if staff are moving a resident to a secure room because he/she is destroying the furniture, once in the secure room he/she must be free to move about. Physically restraining him/her for an additional period of time to 'get the point across' is not acceptable (Hawaii 1983:63–5).

When a youth reports that he/she was subjected to excessive force or abuse, it is the responsibility of the ethical professional to report it. Durkin (1982) states that 'the experience (of reporting) is difficult and lonely, particularly when it threatens job security and future employment.' Durkin goes on to state that 'it is the further responsibility of professionals to improve the overall quality of services and to change the conditions that lead to institutional child abuse' (Hanson 1982:13).

It is often when staff perceive minor issues as serious that hostile and aggressive incidents result. Such incidents are unlikely to occur when the staff member is non-judgmental, capable of handling minor frustrations, and able to open channels of communication, allowing problems to be resolved in a mature and constructive manner. Patience, sensitivity, a sense of humour, and the ability not to feel threatened when challenged can make working with young offenders an enjoyable, productive, and rewarding experience.

It is very important that the child care professionals working with young offenders acknowledge the dignity and self-worth of every youth. In addition, it is the professional's responsibility to do his or her part to ensure that the institutional landscape is dominated by the intention to provide the most humane and caring environment possible within what can otherwise become a coercive, restrictive, and dehumanizing existence for both residents and staff.

Guiding Principles for Child and Youth Care Professionals in Youth Justice

Child and youth care professionals have a key role to play in ensuring that the needs of children and youth in the Canadian youth justice system are effectively met and their rights protected. Several funda- mental principles are essential in achieving this end. These include the following.

(1) Placing children and youth at the top of the political agenda with the view that resource allocation to this population is an investment rather than an expenditure.

(2) Developing consolidated child, youth, and family legislation which defines the rights and entitlements of children and youth. Nova Scotia's Children and Family Services Act (1990) is one example of this approach.

(3) Establishing child-centred, culturally sensitive organizational structures that (a) recruit professional staff who are sensitive to the needs of particular groups of youth who tend to be over-represented in YOA and child welfare systems, including aboriginal, refugee, new immigrant, developmentally disabled, and poor children, and to provide appropriate training to this end; (b) integrate child and youth programs at the policy, planning, research, and resource allocation levels of government, and ensure effective coordination and case management with related service sectors such as income security, housing, police, and hospitals;[6] (c) empower the local community to take the initiative in developing and delivering services that are relevant, easily understood, and accessible; (d) set and monitor standards of service, provided through public, private and non-profit organizations, and standards of care and conduct for the staff within these organizations (Charles and McIntyre 1991); (e) ensure that there is a continuum of conflict resolution mechanisms available, including advocacy, mediation, internal review, external appeal, and, where appropriate, access to the courts to provide safeguards when problems arise involving children and youth; and (f) provide for a general research strategy and the required funding to assess the effectiveness of the YOA in meeting the principles it embraces, the effectiveness of programs delivered under its authority and the cost-effectiveness of early intervention in providing services which may prevent criminal behaviour, and other recommended research objectives (see Hudson et al. 1988:180–2).

Summary

This chapter has provided an overview of three basic components essential to practising in the youth justice field. These are: (1) knowledge of the Young Offenders Act and how it affects the young offender, the system, and the child care profession; (2) knowledge of how the various components of the system, such as the youth, family, police, courts, and services, interact; and (3) discussion of the skills and approaches required by child care professionals within settings in which young offenders are placed.

It is important that the child and youth care professional, working closely with young offenders, separates who he/she is from what he/she does. By recognizing and respecting the power and authority vested in this position, the professional is less likely to become embroiled in power struggles with youths and, consequently, is less likely to become involved in destructive or abusive relationships. The rejection, rule-breaking, and inappropriate behaviour of a youth can have significant impact on the emotions of the professional worker.

The Young Offenders Act, like any new legislation, will undergo interpretation over a number of years. The adoption of the Canadian Charter of Rights and Freedoms has also had an impact on the development and interpretation of the Young Offenders Act, as will the UN Convention on the Rights of the Child. The youth justice system in Canada is experiencing a significant period of transition. As changes have taken place in the system, the child care profession has gained recognition and status. Skilled practitioners are being recruited in ever-increasing numbers. This provides child and youth care professionals with the opportunity both to influence and impact youth justice in Canada.

Notes

1 Ontario's data were not included as information was not available for the full 1990–1 fiscal year. The Canadian Centre for Justice Statistics states that, as there were difficulties in the reporting process, 'the published information based on these data must be interpreted as indicators of caseload and case characteristics rather than precise measures' (Youth Court Statistics 1991).

2 *Black's Law Dictionary* describes the difference between procedural and substantive laws: 'As a general rule, laws which fix duties, establish rights and responsibilities among and for persons, natural or otherwise, are "substantive laws" in character, while those which merely prescribe the manner in which such rights and responsibilities may be exercised and enforced are "procedural laws" ' (Black 1979: 1,083).

3 In 1857 Upper and Lower Canada passed legislation, taking a preliminary but important step in recognizing that children charged with offences should not be treated in the same way as adults. This legislation allowed magistrates to 'deal summarily with children' where the penalties for conviction were less severe than under criminal law (Archambault 1983). In 1894 Canada amended

the criminal code, making it mandatory that persons under sixteen years of age be tried separately from other accused persons and without publicity. Although tried separately, young offenders were subject to court processes and procedures applied to adults (McGrath 1965).

4 Alternative measures are measures other than judicial proceedings used to deal with a young person alleged to have committed an offence under the Young Offenders Act. In a sense, YOA legislates a concept of 'diversion.' However, not all diversion programs are to be considered alternative measures programs. Many diversion programs do not comply with the rigid legislative provisions which apply to alternative measures programs. For a program to be considered an alternative measure program, it must be formally designated as such by provincial authorities. The YOA allows each province to determine whether it wishes to implement alternative measures programs and provides flexibility for the development of different types of programs in response to needs, interests, and resources. The reader is advised to contact local provincial authorities to determine the status and scope of alternative measure programs in his or her province.

5 These five points were originally taken from documents from the Office of the Ombudsman (Hawaii 1983).

6 Prevention and the commitment of resources intended to support families before, or as soon as, problems arise also requires an integrated approach between the universal child-serving systems, such as public health and schools, and other services such as child welfare, youth corrections, and children's mental health. This continuum of flexible and responsive services must respect the child's dignity and need for stable and loving relationships.

References
Archambault, O. 1983. Young offenders act: Philosophy and principles. *Provincial Judges Journal* 7:1
Bala, N. and Lilles, H. 1982. *Young offenders act annotated*. Solicitor General of Canada
Barnhorst, R. and Johnson, L. (eds.). 1991. *The state of the child in Ontario*. Toronto: Oxford University Press
Black, H.C. 1979. *Black's law dictionary* (5th ed.). St. Paul: West Publishing
British Columbia. Office of the Ombudsman. 1985. *The Willingdon case*. Public Report No. 13
–. 1990. *Public services to children, youth and their families in British Columbia: The need for integration*. Public Report No. 22
Canadian Centre for Justice Statistics. 1991a. *Juristat Service Bulletin* 11(14), Pub. No. 85–002
–. 1991b. *Juristat Service Bulletin* 11(18), Pub. No. 85–002
Charles, G. and McIntyre, S. (eds.). 1991. *The best of care: Recommendations for the future of residential services for troubled and troubling young people in Canada*. Ottawa: Canadian Child Welfare Association
Commission on Emotional and Learning Disorders in Children (CELDIC). 1970. *One million children: The CELDIC report*. Toronto: Leonard Crainford

Coughlin, B. 1973. The rights of children. In A. Wilderson (ed.), *The rights of children: Emergent concepts in law and society*. Philadelphia: Temple University Press

Drever, D. 1991. The role of Manitoba's ombudsman in the child welfare system. *Journal of Child and Youth Care* 6:67–71

Durkin R. 1982. Institutional abuse from a family systems perspective: A working paper. *Child and Youth Services* 4:15–22

Friedman, R.M., Duchnowski, A.J., and Henderson, E.L. 1989. *Advocacy on behalf of children with serious emotional problems*. Springfield, IL: Charles C. Thomas

Garbarino, J., Schellenbach, C., Sebes, J., and Associates 1986. *Troubled youth, troubled families*. New York: Aldine De Gruyter

Gold, M., and Petronio, R.J. 1980. Delinquent behavior in adolescents. In J. Adelson (ed.), *Handbook of adolescent psychology*. New York: Wiley

Hanson, R. (ed.). 1982. *Institutional abuse of children and youth*. New York: Haworth

Hawaii. Office of the Ombudsman. 1983. *Investigation of allegations of the use of unreasonable force against inmates during the shakedown of the Oahu Community Correctional Center for December 14th through December 18th, 1981*. Honolulu: Office of the Ombudsman

Hogg, P.W. 1985. *Constitutional law of Canada*. Toronto: Carswell

Holin, C.R. 1990. *Cognitive-behavioural interventions with young offenders*. Toronto: Pergamon

Hudson, J., Hornick, J., and Burrows, B. (eds.). 1988. *Justice and the young offender in Canada*. Toronto: Wall and Thompson

Kahn, A., Kamerman, S.B., and McGowan, B.G., (eds.). 1972. *Child advocacy: Report on a national baseline study*. New York: Columbia University School of Social Work

McGrath, W.T. (ed.). 1965. *Crime and its treatment in Canada*. Toronto: Macmillan

McNeill P. (ed.). 1989. *Adolescent sex offenders: Prevention, treatment and management*. In conference proceedings, 6–8 November 1989. Joint National Conference. Ottawa: Canadian Child Welfare Association

Martinson, R. 1974. What works? Questions and answers about prison reform. *Public Interest* 35:22–54

–. 1976. California research at the crossroads. *Crime and Delinquency* 22:180–91

National Child Welfare Resource Center for Management and Administration. 1991. *Strategic plan for the office of youth services in Hawaii*. Portland, Maine: University of Southern Maine

Newman, B.M. and Newman, P.R. 1986. *Adolescent development*. Ohio: Merrill

Ontario. 1990. *Children first*. Report of Advisory Committee on Children's Services. Ministry of Community and Social Services. Toronto: Queen's Printer

Phillips, D. 1991. Administrative fairness with children and youth: The B.C. Ombudsman model. *Journal of Child and Youth Care* 6:67–71 and 73–7

Rogers, Rix. 1990. *Reaching for solutions*. Report by the Special Advisor on Child Sexual Abuse to Canada's Minister of Health and Welfare. Ottawa: Ministry of Supply and Services

Steinhauer, P. 1991. *The least detrimental alternative: A systematic guide to case planning and decision making for children in care.* Toronto: University of Toronto Press

Verhellen, E. 1990. Ombudswork: An effective tool toward the implementation by NGOs of the Convention on the Rights of the Child — A framework for discussion. Paper presented at Forum '90, *Working for children in a changing world.* The NGO-Summit on Child Welfare, IFCW, Cologne, Federal Republic of Germany, 26–9 August

Youth Court Statistics. 1991. *Preliminary data, 1990–91.* Ottawa: Statistics Canada

Legislation

Canadian Bill of Rights. Reprinted in the Revised Statutes of Canada 1985, Appendix 3, c. 44

Canadian Charter of Rights and Freedoms. Part I of the Constitution Act 1982, being Schedule B of the Canada Act 1982 (UK), 1982, c. 11

Children and Family Services Act. Statutes of Nova Scotia, 1990, c. 5

Constitution Act 1867 (UK). 30 and 31 Vict., c. 3, Sec. 91 (formerly the British North America Act 1867)

Criminal Code of Canada. Revised Statutes of Canada, 1985, c. C-46

Juvenile Delinquents Act. Revised Statutes of Canada, 1970, c. J-3

United Nations. 1948. Universal declaration of human rights. United Nations Document No. A/811

–. 1955. Standard minimum rules for treatment of prisoners. Geneva A conf. 6 Li7. First United Nations Congress on the Prevention of Crime and the Treatment of Offenders

–. 1959. Declaration of the rights of the child. Official records of the General Assembly, Fourteenth Session, Supplement No. 16, 1960, p. 19. General Assembly Resolution 1386 (viv)

Young Offenders Act. Revised Statutes of Canada, 1985, c. Y-1 (originally proclaimed 2 April 1984)

Additional Readings

Bala, N., Lilles, H., and Thomson G.M. 1982. *Canadian children's law: Cases, notes and materials.* Toronto: Butterworth

Bartollas, C., Miller, S., and Dinitz, S. 1976. *Juvenile victimization: The institutional paradox.* Toronto: Wiley

Brownlie, I. (ed.). 1981. *Basic documents on human rights* (2nd ed.). Oxford: Clarendon

Corrada, R.R., LeBlanc, M., and Trepanier, J. (eds.). 1983. *Current issues in juvenile justice.* Toronto: Butterworth

Hackler, J. 1978. *The prevention of youthful crime: The great stumble forward.* Toronto: Methuen

Hudson, J., Hornick, P., and Burrows, B (eds.). 1988. *Justice and the young offender in Canada.* Toronto: Wall and Thompson

Jenkins, R.L., Heidemann, P.H., and Caputo, J.H. 1958. *No single cause: Juvenile delinquency and the search for effective treatment*. Maryland and Virginia: Maryland Correctional Association

Leon, J.S. 1977. The development of Canadian juvenile justice: A background for reform. *U Grad Hall Law Journal* 15:71

Leyton, E. 1979. *The myths of delinquency: An anatomy of juvenile delinquency*. New York: Oxford University Press

Lundman, R. 1984. *Prevention and control of juvenile delinquency*. New York: Oxford University Press

Millar, L. 1986. *The young offenders act*. Toronto: Guidance and Counselling, Guidance Centre, University of Toronto Press

Parker, G. 1976. The juvenile court movement. *University of Toronto Law Journal* 26:40

Paul, J., Neufeld, G., and Pelosi, J. (eds.). 1977. *Child advocacy within the system*. Syracuse: Syracuse University Press

Platt, A.M. 1969. *The child savers: The invention of delinquency*. Chicago: University of Chicago Press

Reid, S. and Reitsma-Street, M. 1984. Assumptions and implications of new Canadian legislation for young offenders. *Canadian Criminology Forum* 7:1–19

Solnit, A.J., Mordhaus, B.F., and Lord, R. 1992. *When home is no haven*. New Haven and London: Yale University Press

Steinhauer, P.D. 1991. *A systematic guide to case planning and decision making for children in care*. Toronto, Buffalo, and London: University of Toronto Press

West, W.G. 1984. *Young offenders and the state: A Canadian perspective on delinquency*. Toronto: Butterworth

Wilson, L.C. 1982. *Juvenile courts in Canada*. Toronto: Carswell

4

Canadian School-based Child and Youth Care

Carey Denholm and David Watkins

Introduction

During the past thirty years, the development of Canadian school-based child and youth care has neither followed a carefully scripted master plan nor has it emerged as a result of intentional national legislation. What is termed 'Canadian school-based child and youth care' refers to a myriad of programs containing individual histories, emphases, and therapeutic and educational aims supported by differing structural and administrative frameworks, all occurring within a variety of educational environments. Although the area of school-based child and youth care is now only receiving limited attention in professional child and youth care journals[1] and texts,[2] this work in Canadian schools is extensive and well established.[3]

Originally, the impetus for the development of many of these programs may have been in response to a heartfelt community need, an act of desperation on the part of a school principal, an administrative directive, or as components of expanded attention being given to a range of educational needs of children and youth. The rapid involvement of community-based agencies in the arena of privatization has stimulated the development and expansion of many of the school-based child and youth care positions, yet has also altered their philosophical and theoretical fabric. Thus, it is understandable that, as many of these programs have now developed their own long and unique history, comparison between programs and within provinces becomes difficult. Certainly, any attempt to establish a national perspective tends to become fragmented and somewhat disparate. Nevertheless, a number of interrelated yet separate trends have occurred throughout this time and may be seen as critical to the gradual evolution of child and youth care services within the Canadian education system.

Key Influences within Canadian Education

The CELDIC Report

Clearly the most influential document produced in recent years was the report by the Commission on Emotional and Learning Disorders in Children (CELDIC) (1970). Entitled *One Million Children*, this report focused attention on the urgency of developing new approaches to meet the 'special needs' of children and youth. Of specific relevance to the emergence of school-based child and youth care programs was the stated need to develop methods 'to provide continuity of care and immediate help ... by people close to the child in his home, school and community' (Lazure and Roberts 1970:8). The report continues:

> We were frequently distressed by the isolation of the school from other sources of help in the community. This provides an example of the division that we saw between many of the services and the helping professions, who were all working separately to aid children. We are convinced that these divisions are intolerable. They lead to a partial, fragmented effort when a total coordinated drive is required. (p. 4)

Prior to this particular document, the trend to acknowledge the multidimensional needs of children and youth can be seen in other reports. For example the Hall-Dennis Report (1968), commissioned by the Ontario Ministry of Education, stressed that 'there no longer be a distinction between one type of student and another; that education for an individual should progress along a continuum with the choices of experiences and rate of progress depending respectively on student's needs, interests and his/her own rate of maturing' (p. 150). Subsequently, two fundamental principles for governing school education in the province of Ontario were made. These were: (1) the right of every individual to have equal access to the learning experience best suited to his/her needs and (2) the responsibility of every school authority to provide a child-centred learning continuum that invites learning by individual discovery and inquiry (p. 150).

One example of the impact of the CELDIC Report is recorded by Haberlin (1976), who outlines the initial beginnings of the Kitsilano Elementary Child Care Program in Vancouver. In 1974, the Vancouver Resources Board made a decision to follow one of the recommendations of the CELDIC Report by placing three child care workers into three elementary schools. This program was in response to the needs of a very visible group of pre-delinquent boys, who were causing havoc in their school. By 1977, grants were approved to place six workers in six elementary schools. According to Neil (1981), the concept of placing social services-oriented counsellors in schools was also strongly supported by a report by the Educational Research Institute of British Columbia (Laycock and Findlay 1971). The primary role of the elementary school child care worker was to focus on specific social functioning and school-related behaviours which were affecting academic learning.

The CELDIC Report provided the philosophical 'groundwork' for a review of educational services for Canadian children, youth, and their families and for the legitimization of child and youth care services in schools. Two central implications emerged from this review. The first questioned whether or not the school should assume responsibility for the emotional and/or associated learning problems of all children; the second questioned the type and quality of service needed for exceptional students (Klassen 1981).

Normalization and Integration

'Normalization' is a broad principle of human management initially outlined in the Scandinavian literature in the late 1960s. It is defined as: 'utilization of means which are as culturally normative as possible, in order to establish and/or maintain personal behaviors and characteristics which are as culturally normative as possible' (Wolfensberger 1972:28). One of the major adaptations of this principle in North America involved the examination of the philosophical tenets and types of programs in which mentally handicapped children and adults were being placed. One related effect of this movement was the shift away from the institutional care of handicapped children in large residential centres to supportive care within their home environment. Subsequently, a vast body of approaches relating to the management of handicapped children at home (Porter and Coleman 1978; Wolfensberger 1983), provision of parent support (Standifer 1964; Wolfensberger and Menolascino 1970), and societal implications (Wolfensberger 1980; Wolfensberger and Thomas 1980) was developed.

When U.S. president Gerald Ford signed the Education for All Handicapped Children Act PL94-142 (Education of Handicapped Children 1977), an educational trend within the United States received federal sanction (Strain and Kerr 1981). In essence, the principle was to 'educate handicapped children in the least restrictive environment, as close as possible to their non-handicapped peers' (Kameen 1979). The 'least restrictive environment' is explained as follows:

(1) That to the maximum extent appropriate, handicapped children, including children in public or private institutions or other care facilities, are educated with children who are not handicapped, and

(2) that special classes, separate schooling or other removal of handicapped children from the regular educational environment occurs only when the nature or severity of the handicap is such that education in regular classes with the use of supplementary aids and services cannot be achieved satisfactorily. (Education of Handicapped Children 1977:42,497)

Subsequently, as Allan (1980) comments, many school board administrators in the United States and Canada 'leaped on the bandwagon without providing adequate teacher support or inservice training and without thoroughly examining the concept' (p. 15). Acceptance of both the philosophy and implications of normalization had a direct impact on local schools, often forcing untrained staff to learn to cope with severely handicapped children and adolescents within the normal school setting. Thus, the opportunity for community agencies and boards to establish and manage child and youth care services in these educational programs commenced. This opened a new avenue for the introduction of the child and youth care role to administrators, teachers, and parents.

Climate of Social and Educational Change

During the late 1960s, Canadian provinces experienced an increase in the number of training programs offered and taken by school counsellors, learning assistants, special education teachers, and child and youth care workers. Community and parent groups continued the trend established in the United States for involvement and active participation in public education. In response, 'experimental' educational programs grew more acceptable, if not fashionable. This developed into a plethora of 'alternate' education programs, attempting to expand learning options within the public school system. What emerged then were: (1) 'integrated' programs, designed to integrate subject areas within the regular school; (2) 'enriched' programs, emphasizing community spirit and enriched classroom learning; (3) 'alternate' schools, with a humanistic orientation and heavy involvement in student decision-making; and (4) 'rehabilitation' programs, aimed at potential or actual 'dropouts.'

Those programs classified as 'alternate' and 'rehabilitative' were more likely to have child and youth care professionals (usually funded by other non-education ministries) as part of the staff complement. As stated in the British Columbia GAIN Act of 1978, one reason for their involvement was 'to enable children or youth who are experiencing great difficulty at school for social and/or emotional reasons or who have dropped out of school, to acquire basic skills which will make it possible for them to re-enter the school system or proceed to further training or employment' (Sec. 2:183).

A range of school programs catering to the individual learning needs of students began to emerge; within many of these programs, positions for child and youth care workers were created. The establishment and solidification of these programs came about as part of the trend towards a more humanistic, child-centred approach and the establishment of divergent educational programs. Also, what must not be overlooked are the separate yet interwoven effects such things as the incidence of youth crime, unemployment, pregnancy, suicide and violence, immigration and learning difficulties had upon schools. In response to these largely non-academic needs, a different type of practitioner was being sought — a practitioner who could work beyond the usual confines of the classroom in new and unusual ways, who could cope with a range of demanding circumstances, and who could comfortably work alongside a range of professionals and families. It may be noted that, about the same time, the thrust for higher education and the general recognition of rehabilitation practitioners (who are employed to assist the integration of developmentally handicapped individuals within society) took place. As will be evident from the chapter included in this text, many of the central functions of the child and youth care worker and the rehabilitation practitioner are similar. In fact, some of the recently developed models of vocational training, social education, home living, and leisure time for handicapped young adults (Brown and Hughson 1980; DuRand and Newfeldt 1975; Marlett and Hughson 1979) may be applied to a wide variety of child and youth care work.

In summary, a number of events occurred during the 1960s and 1970s: the trend to decentralize large institutions and the evolution of more community-based programs; the impact of integration and parental demand for quality care of handicapped children; increased

training and educational opportunities for child and youth care professionals; the attention of the media on the need to develop more meaningful educational programs for children; the impact within the education system of the works of Neill (1960) and Holt (1974); and the
relative prosperity of provincial governments. Although many of these
factors can be examined separately, it should be seen that the interplay
has been dramatic and pervasive, contributing to the establishment of
varying types of child and youth care programs within this system.

Models of Canadian School-based Programs
The following is an outline of eight major types or models of Canadian
child and youth care programs. Variations within provinces are evident
in terms of location, student population size, staff complement, and
funding structure and mandate; hence its title may not indicate the
category into which a particular program may fall or its underlying
structure. For example, the authors have met child and youth care
workers from programs having the following names: Storefront Alternative, Eastside, Multiple Choice, New Dimensions, Total Education,
Options for Pregnant Teenagers, UpTown, Girls Alternative Program,
Outreach, Bridge, 8J9J, and Sunrise East. The following models illustrate the central differences between programs employing child and
youth care professionals. It should be noted that this list is not exhaustive and that local variations will be evident.

Model No. 1
In this model, one child and youth care worker is assigned to either a
regular elementary, junior secondary, or secondary school, with the
primary responsibility of working with non-handicapped children and
their parents (Neil 1981; Klassen 1981). The worker may be supervised
directly by the school principal or by a person external to the school.
She/he may be expected to perform a variety of functions, work during
non-school hours, have her/his own office, and be responsible for administering her/his own budget for materials and equipment. This is
similar to the position of the homeschool liaison worker in Ontario.

Model No. 2
The only difference between this and Model No. 1 is that the child and
youth care worker is assigned one or several handicapped children
throughout the entire day. These workers are often attached to special

education classes or classes for the mentally handicapped. Specific functions may include transportation, teaching and supporting the student throughout the day, conducting parent counselling, and designing the student's individual learning plan. This is similar to the position of the rehabilitation practitioner in Alberta.

Model No. 3

This model involves one or more child and youth care workers assigned to several schools. Again, these may be regular elementary, junior secondary, or secondary schools, with the principal or the sponsoring agency supervising and implementing the program (McMorran 1981; Hubbard and Phillips 1981). The worker may be called a youth counsellor, adolescent care worker, or child care worker and may also be required to monitor attendance and help irregular attenders increase their involvement and participation.

Model No. 4

Child and youth care workers also become involved within the school system on an itinerant basis. In this situation, the worker is hired by a community agency or board to provide child services to families within a designated area. Contact must be made with the school principal, relevant teachers, and school counsellors concerning referred clients, and the school may provide counselling facilities for the worker (Klassen 1981). The child and youth care worker seen as one of many external consultants and resource personnel within the network of student services at a community school is presented in Figure 4.1 (Nordstrom and Denholm 1986). In this particular situation, the worker maintains an indirect relationship with the school and is contracted on a request or referral basis.

Model No. 5

The 'alternate' program setting has a number of variations, but in most cases it occurs in one specific location. In this model the building and program are attached to an existing junior or senior secondary school. The staff are directly responsible to the school principal. Students for the program (primarily adolescents) come from within this school population. The child and youth care staff may or may not be direct employees of the school district (Denholm, Chrest, and Pylypa 1991).

Figure 4.1

Structure of student support services at Shoreline Community School

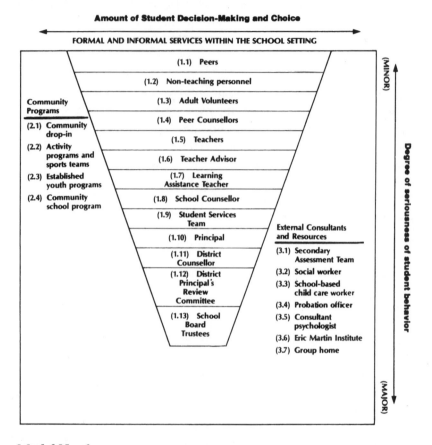

Model No. 6

A variation on the previous model uses the same staffing arrangement, but the building is physically separate from the 'parent' school; in some cases it is up to five miles away. The students are usually referred from specific neighbouring schools.

Model No. 7

In this particular type, building and program are autonomous; the education staff are employees of the school district, and the child and youth care staff are responsible to a community agency or board of directors. The teachers and academic program are the responsibility of a supervising principal appointed by the school district. Child and youth care supervision is established jointly by a personnel committee comprised of board members or representatives from the relevant ministry responsible for the funding (Figure 4.2). Students may apply to attend from any school and admission screening takes place internally.

Figure 4.2

Organizational and funding structure of alternate program

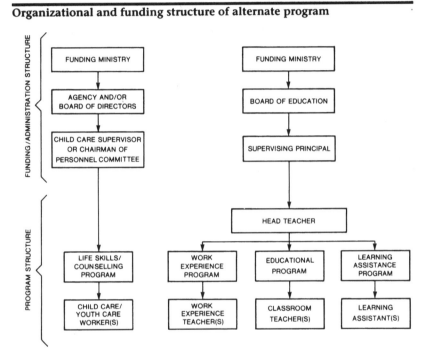

Model No. 8

This variation is to be found within the day clinic or centre, where children and/or adolescents are placed for short-term intervention and later returned to their regular school program. This is generally a non-residential program; child and youth care intervention may involve family counselling and support, child assessment, and teacher education. The demonstration of effective intervention techniques from a clearly articulated theoretical base may also be required of staff.

In summary, a number of models of program organization may be identified which differ in description, mandate, and staffing structure. It should also be noted that although programs may appear to be similar to a particular model identified here, in practice they may not be as easily identified. For example, variations will be found in terms of size of student body, historical development, style, and educational goals.

Functions of School-based Child and Youth Care Workers

What exactly do child and youth care workers do in schools? One sample response which may serve as a starting point for discussion is as follows: *The primary role of the child and youth care worker within the educational setting is to promote behavioural change and personal growth in children and adolescents who are having difficulties coping within this setting as a result of social, emotional, and physical problems and to assist in their academic success.* Single sentence definitions, however, only assist in providing direction, not substance. For example, it would be difficult to establish a full-time, accountable, school-based child and youth care position on the basis of this definition alone. In order to provide a more definitive response and to discover exactly what school-based child and youth care workers are doing, a compilation was made. This was extracted from published works (Anglin 1983; Denholm 1981a, 1983, 1988; Houndle and Ricks 1981; Klassen 1981; McMorran 1981; Neil 1981), from established guidelines in provincial education ministry and school district policy handbooks,[4] from various program documents,[5] and from personal discussions and consultations with school-based child and youth care workers over the past fifteen years.

Variations in the functions of workers were seen. These were related to the size of the program, type of structure, setting and funding arrangements, length of time established, type of student service, and educational level of the child and youth care worker. One clear trend emerged: the higher the educational level of the worker, the more clearly documented and specific were the established functions. It should be noted that these functions are not grouped into categories as in Anglin (1983), nor are they listed in order of significance. In addition, no one child and youth care worker position ever encompassed this complete list of functions. Only those that were consistently mentioned have been included; they will almost certainly occur within the majority of educational programs employing Canadian school-based child and youth care workers. They are classified into five main areas.

(1) School-related Functions

(a) Working in the classroom with the primary objectives of behavioural change, improvement of self-concept, and the development of social skills in individual students or the entire class. Also included may be the demonstration of individual and group management techniques to teachers and parents, the modelling of specific approaches with problem students, and the presentation of programs which focus on affective and social skills education.

(b) Assisting individual teachers in the preparation of recommendations on individuals or groups of students (or their families) for case conferences. Depending on any subsequent recommendations, this assistance may continue during the implementation and/or the evaluation phases referred to later in this chapter.

(c) Collecting information for school staff on classroom environments and the student population. Activities include the preparation of such information as the socioeconomic and geographic make-up of the community, the availability and limitations of community resources, relevant coming events, and position papers on research supporting a particular therapeutic approach. In response to the expressed needs of teachers concerning information on the social and emotional development of children or adolescents, the workers may also be requested to make the necessary arrangements for guest presentations, films, and the circulation of relevant literature.

(d) Coordinating case consultation and team meetings. In cooperation with the school principal, who may assume responsibility for conducting the meeting, the school-based child and youth care worker often organizes times, informs parents and other appropriate members about the conference, and ensures that all relevant information and reports are ready.

(e) Participating in school-related meetings. These include regular staff meetings, consultations with administration, school-based child and youth care team meetings, representations to government officials, professional workshops, school-initiated parent consultations, and membership in ad hoc committees such as curriculum planning and school discipline.

(2) Individual Student Functions

(a) Identifying and providing a suitably in-depth assessment of individual children and adolescents. This may involve planned observations within the classroom, school, and home environment, using formal assessment tools, conducting individual sessions with identified students, preparing confidential reports (including practical in-class suggestions), and communicating recommendations

to teachers, the school principal, and students (if appropriate).
(b) Designing, implementing, and evaluating interventions to assist students (and, if necessary, families) in dealing with specific school-related issues. The implementation stage may require brief counselling or a series of planned interventions. For example, the integration of handicapped students, organization of new student admissions, or assistance for students experiencing a death in the family may all require both counselling and intervention strategies.
(c) Referring students and their families to relevant social service agencies and medical personnel. This requires that the worker act as student advocate to ensure prompt attention and adequate delivery of services.
(d) Placing students in community-based programs and organizations. The intent is to enhance student self-esteem in relation to newly acquired physical, social, and living skills. Follow-up support is also conducted with those who require more intensive care to facilitate the successful bridge between the existing program and these resources.
(e) Participating in the existing work experience program. This may be conducted in cooperation with the work experience teacher through assisting students to meet set objectives, assessing the individual needs of students, and developing individual programs for students within specific work settings.
(f) Attending to the overall integration of one or several disabled students to whom they are assigned for the entire school day. This includes the supervision and/or provision of physical care such as feeding, tending to toiletry, and maintaining general physical comfort. Invariably, the worker becomes involved in the education of teachers and fellow students concerning the strengths, limitations, and developmental needs of the student and may also have to become proficient in the language used by the student (e.g., Bliss symbolics, sign language, Braille, and computerized language systems).

(3) Group Intervention Functions
(a) Assessing and preparing students for short-term group counselling, with the focus on the development of social skills. Involved in the establishment of specific groups (such as those dealing with anger management, relaxation training, or problem solving) is the responsibility to conduct these groups and to evaluate individual progress.

(b) Assessing, preparing, intervening, and evaluating 'identified' students for long-term group counselling. Topics may include life skills training, self-esteem development, peer counselling, and support for students with a disability or a chronic illness.

(c) Initiating and involving groups in recreational and other activities. These may include athletics, games, crafts, camping, and outdoor education, with the emphasis on self-reliance and socialization.

(d) Developing programs in response to student request or assessed need with both 'normal' and 'special needs' students in order to promote the integration of these children. An example would be the involvement of children having disabilities in regular sports and general age-appropriate activities with their non-disabled peers.

(4) Family-related Functions

(a) Conducting parent education programs. Examples include Parent Effectiveness Training (Gordon 1975), Systematic Training for Effective Parenting (Dinkmeyer and McKay 1976), and Systematic Training for Effective Parenting of Teenagers (Dinkmeyer and McKay 1983).

(b) Providing long- and short-term support to families. Examples may include providing information concerning financial problems or helping change a difficult living situation. This function is not as intense as family therapy but serves to facilitate family interpersonal communication and problem-solving skills.

(c) Referring parents who are in need of long-term counselling and support to a social service agency.

(d) Coordinating parent and family activity nights. The focus would be on assisting potentially isolated families (that is, immigrants, recent arrivals, parents of disabled students) to make contact with other families in order to promote family growth and development.

(5) Community Functions

(a) Consulting with other professionals in the community. This may involve being a board member of a community program, being involved with community centres, community care teams, and other social service agencies, and cooperating and consulting with officials from services such as health and police departments. Also included is liaison with residential care workers in an effort to maintain a consistent child management model across environments.

(b) Promoting interagency cooperation within the community. This would, primarily, be in response to specific situations which may affect the management and organization of the school.

Implications for Current Practice

One immediate implication addresses all college and university child and youth care training programs. It is vital that workers have adequate preparatory knowledge and skill in the areas of individual and group assessment, intervention and evaluation, counselling, recreational leadership, program planning, and professional consultation. In addition, it would be advisable for the student intending to seek employment in this environment to have had a minimum of two supervised practica, with school-based child and youth care workers, in different school settings.

During that time the student should have had the opportunity to work with a number of teachers in different programs, deal with students exhibiting a range of problems, be involved in report writing and case consultations, and accompany the worker on home visits. With special emphasis and skills in the areas of child and family development, child and youth care workers offer a range of non-educational functions within the school setting. Their role is to meet the student's behavioural needs, thereby enhancing the student's ability to benefit from the educational program. One of the many strengths of this role is that professional child and youth care workers have a conceptual and theoretical background coupled with a pragmatic understanding of the various systems which may affect the student or family. These competencies allow workers to move across the boundaries of government ministries in order to coordinate the total care system for the student.

Information on several Canadian programs involved in the preparation of school-based personnel is described elsewhere (Brown and Hughson 1980; Denholm 1986). Regardless of a list of clearly defined functions, an effective child and youth care presence within any school and school district comes about only through careful planning, preparation, and on-going support. Hence, the successful maintenance of this service requires that school personnel and child and youth care workers maintain an open and equal relationship.

In order to facilitate the acceptance and potential support for this type of intervention in schools, child and youth care workers need to: (1) know and understand the academic experience of teachers; (2) be aware of the special demands and stresses placed on teachers by the education system; and (3) understand how intervention and management techniques must be modified in order to suit the classroom and school environment. Alternately, teachers and other school personnel need to: (1) know and understand the academic and practical experience of child and youth care workers; (2) be aware of the special demands and stresses placed on these personnel by parents, students, the school system, and external supervisors and boards; and (3) be willing to listen and openly discuss child and youth care perspectives and approaches in relation to parents, students, and the school system (Denholm 1989).

Putting Theory into Practice
Knowing what Canadian school-based child and youth care workers do is only the first step. Several vital and related aspects involving the actual implementation of these theories must be addressed. Acceptance of the child and youth care presence within any school does not come about simply through a written job description, although a clear outline of what the worker is able to do and expected to perform is a prerequisite for success. It is equally important that the actual process of introducing a child and youth care worker into a school is attempted only with prior planning, organization, and diplomacy. For, as will be indicated, loss of support and alienation by staff are real hazards.

Perhaps the effectiveness of this role will depend on the degree to which the presence of the child and youth care worker is accepted personally and professionally by the staff as well as the on the degree to which the role is accepted by the parents and the school administration. The following five-phase approach may serve as a focal point for those practitioners who are contemplating working within this system. Although a number of issues relate to all workers entering schools, this approach is primarily designed for full-time, school-based child and youth care workers. It is also noted that this process is not considered prescriptive; adaptations will need to be made in relation to individual program needs.

Phase 1: Orientation or 'Earning the Right to Help'
Many of the functions described in this chapter have, as their common element, involvement with people (students, teachers, parents, community resource personnel). Therefore, the first step in beginning a child and youth care program in a school involves getting to know the people and establishing a productive working relationship (Hughes

and Lougheed 1991). Furthermore, it is suggested that this relationship must be earned (Parsons and Meyers 1984). Earning the right to help means the child and youth care worker must accept the stated goals of the school and be an active participant in helping students and teachers achieve these goals. The practitioner's orientation to students and to the school, then, must be clearly demonstrated as one of service. Although the school and the worker are allies and share many common objectives, approaches to the provision of 'service' to students may differ. In order to understand and work effectively with this potential conflict, the worker may function as if the school and student body are potential clients. Implied here is the need to begin serving the school and individuals in practical ways. This should be done in areas in which there is a visible need and the activity can be considered nonthreatening to the roles and tasks of others. The following are examples of service/helping activities appropriate to this orientation phase.

(1) Your school is hosting a basketball tournament this weekend. You offer to help paint posters welcoming visiting teams.

(2) During a meeting of the student government, you notice that the treasurer is having trouble keeping the statement of accounts in order. You offer to assist.

(3) Litter has collected at the back of the school and you organize a group of students to clean it up.

During this phase, the focus is on the functions of the child and youth care worker as a professional who works with people in visible ways and who is serious about making a commitment to service within the school — to both staff and students. It should be noted that this phase has no specific time period. That is, many of these activities should occur on a regular basis after the right to help has been earned. It is the child and youth care worker who needs to seize the opportunity to remain visible within this setting and who must continue to make a positive statement concerning the degree to which he or she is committed to the school.

Phase 2: Data Gathering or 'Determining What is Needed'

The functions of the child and youth care worker encompass a range of activities beyond the abilities of any one person. It is unrealistic to expect one individual to attend to them all with any degree of effectiveness. To avoid a haphazard selection, the functions relevant to each school should be identified in the form of a cluster of manageable tasks. Those relevant function statements should be related to the needs of the students within the setting and should be in harmony with the established guidelines and philosophy of their particular school (Denholm 1989). In an attempt to place the most relevant functions into a comprehensive job description, the worker should gather data to determine which functions reflect the greatest need. Data can be compiled in a variety of ways, including the administration of carefully designed questionnaires, interviews with former workers and allied professionals (such as the nurse or psychologist), informal discussions with teachers, counsellors, and administrators, and feedback from parents. Regardless of the degree of formality and the time taken for data collection, all results should be documented accurately and presented in a professional manner to the principal. This documentation should then form the basis for the next step: prioritization.

Workers should also prepare an outline of the activities in which they consider themselves competent. Included in this document might be relevant past experiences, special skills, preferred method of counselling and intervention, and a copy of any written material (personal or from their professional association) which might further explain their potential role. Publications assisting in understanding the change process within school (Apter 1982) and human service settings (Egan 1985), theoretical bases for behavioural change (Kanfer and Goldstein 1984), and practical applications within the classroom (Cartledge and Milburn 1980; Diekmeier 1991; Jarrett and Klassen 1986) would serve as appropriate sources and could be purchased to form a part of the child and youth care worker's professional library.

Phase 3: Planning and Prioritization or 'Who Needs Help First?'
Using the data relating to role definition and service delivery tasks within this system, child and youth care functions need to be put into a hierarchical order. This could involve the development of lists of daily, weekly, or monthly tasks. When potentially conflicting demands and expectations arise, the lists may be useful in assisting the worker to determine appropriate time allocation. It is stressed that the process of data gathering, followed by planning and prioritization, must be carried out in consultation with the school administrative personnel and other staff (such as school counsellors). The possibilities for success in this position will be enhanced when effective communication with these individuals has been established and they demonstrate understanding, agreement, and commitment to each of the child care worker's prioritized functions.

Phase 4: Implementation or 'Doing It'

With the role, functions, and priorities clearly established and supported, the child and youth care worker is now in a position to become 'fully operational.' That is, the theoretical descriptions of these functions can now be translated into practice. At this point, a number of suggestions can be made which might further facilitate the implementation phase and enhance the credibility of the worker within this system. For example, it is suggested that the worker (1) become familiar with the provincial legislation, policies, and regulations relating to her/his particular school district, school routine, and procedures and note the laws and regulations concerning such matters as the transportation of students; (2) clearly describe the referral process for students, staff, and parents for child and youth care services; (3) be sensitive to those matters which may create tension between themselves and students or staff members (such as flexible work schedule, dress code, having an office and telephone); (4) keep the staff informed about their work load and timetable (it is suggested that beginning workers offer an introductory workshop for teachers on the theory and practice of child and youth care, develop a brochure clearly describing the role, attend staff meetings to give brief reports and answer questions, and learn about the operation of the school); (5) always give teachers advance notice about any activities which may affect their teaching duties or schedule; (6) familiarize themselves with other school-based programs and their mode of operation; (7) keep a copy of a daily diary (placed with the school secretary) indicating the location and phone number of various appointments.

Phase 5: Evaluation or 'Where Was I Least and Most Effective?'

An important task is the establishment of criteria for success both in relation to the role description and to individual and group interventions. Self-report as well as external evaluation procedures should be completed on a regular basis. Included within the evaluation file should be teacher evaluations of presentations, copies of written parent feedback, and supervisory notes. A self-evaluation component is necessary for two reasons. First, feedback is the link between past and future performance, enabling the worker to adjust, correct, and improve the quality of service. Second, evaluation measures provide an excellent source of data with which to establish a level of accountability (Jarrett 1991).

Workers should expect that documented evidence of satisfactory performance will be required at some point. The child and youth care worker, in consultation with school administration, will need to consider carefully the characteristics of the setting in which this service will be provided and make appropriate decisions concerning these phases. Such decisions would concern the needs within each phase and the amount of time allotted to each. For example, the first phase might be successfully achieved within several weeks, depending on the particular setting. It may also be an ongoing process in some situations, as the worker is repeatedly required to reorient him- or herself and re-earn the right to help. Another consideration is that the child and youth care worker may be involved with more than one school, requiring the application of different approaches to service delivery within each.

Critical Issues in Canadian School-based Child Care
School-based child and youth care work brings with it a variety of interesting daily, weekly, and annual issues (Denholm 1991). Included are the articulation of the role of child and youth care in relation to the purpose or 'mission' of the school and responses to the emergence of child and youth care within this system. This section briefly describes several current issues frequently discussed in educational settings.

Issue 1: Financial or 'Who Pays the Piper?'
Who should bear the financial responsibility for the provision of child and youth care services? One perspective maintains that child and youth care is supplementary to the instructional component of the education process. Continuing with this position, the primary purpose for this service is to be supportive of the delivery of educational services. Therefore, as a supportive service (as distinct from a service providing 'a direct educational benefit' to students), the cost of this service is not a proper charge to the educational budget. The cost of such supportive services, it is argued, cannot be borne by the educational tax dollar.

It is here that the issue of financial constraints and education 'cutbacks' becomes a factor. The funding formula applied to schools is often tied to school size. With declining populations, services seen as additional to classroom teaching (such as librarian, learning assistance, child and youth care) are often reduced. Thus, practitioners need to maintain an active, visible, and accountable role within the school and community in order to combat this trend. Perhaps the recent unionization of non-teaching assistants at a number of boards of education in

Ontario is one way of developing some level of career attractiveness and permanent status.

Alternately, when child and youth care is seen as integral to the school system, the functions of the worker become a necessary extension of activities and experiences designed to benefit the 'whole' child. The activities of child and youth care professionals are seen not as supportive to teachers but as a specialized component of teaching. Therefore, the provision of these services in a school setting is a legitimate and proper expenditure of educational dollars. These perspectives have differing implications for school-based practitioners. In the former, the role may be one of separation from school staff, whereas in the latter, the role brings with it a potentially closer relationship with educational and administrative staff.

Issue 2: Supervision or 'Who Calls the Tune?'

When funding for a child and youth care position originates from another government department outside the education system, the host funding agency will typically establish guidelines relating to terms and conditions of employment. These guidelines will also be found when the funding source provides money through an intermediary agency such as a local board or non-profit society. Included within this document is the child and youth care job description, the decision-making process determining the policies and regulations governing the activities of the worker, and, possibly, the limitations on activities such as outdoor education experiences.

The management model within which the child and youth care worker must work may be more complex than that applied to teachers. For example, it is not unusual that permission must be obtained from two or three 'levels' in order to undertake a project or activity. These levels might include the school principal, the society or board administering the funds, and representatives from the relevant government department. In these circumstances, considerable effort must be taken to obtain clarification and agreements concerning management and decision-making issues. Some examples of these issues can be suggested as a series of questions.

(1) Who is responsible for supervising the day to day activities of the child and youth care worker?

(2) Other than the child and youth care worker, who is responsible and accountable for the activities of the child and youth care worker and the success of this program?

(3) How are decisions concerning the child and youth care worker's role, duties, and activities made?

(4) How does the child and youth care position fit into the normal organization of the school?

The experience of working in a school and having supervision and management external to this system may be cumbersome and may serve to inhibit the implementation of various programs (Robinson 1991). On the other hand, with these types of external review procedures, the worker does have additional support and guidance.

Issue 3: Employment or 'Who Wants to Dance?'

The introduction of child and youth care services into the school setting will raise a variety of personal and professional issues. These are matters which practitioners contemplating work in this system should consider. For those with community college training and certification as a child care worker, the issue of professionalization and the gaining of status in a 'B.A./B.Ed.-crazed world' may prove taxing. This, it would seem, is one of those issues which refuses to go away. With the development of more Canadian university child and youth care programs, perhaps this issue will reduce in intensity.

A related component is the issue of increased lobbying of support within universities for more generous transfer credit for college training, thus increasing opportunities for 'horizontal' academic advancement within the profession (Ferguson, Martin, and Wilson 1989). Regardless of the educational preparation, it would seem a constant that Canadian child and youth care workers are paid less than teachers and yet work equal hours and have an equal number of expectations placed upon them. The following questions are representative of areas that school-based child and youth care professionals may need to address.

(1) What are the financial rewards — are they going to be adequate and acceptable?

(2) What opportunities exist for promotion and advancement?

(3) Will the work be interesting, challenging, and satisfying?

(4) What will be the sources of frustration?

(5) What status does this position have, and is status of concern to me?

(6) What is the future security in the position?

(7) What benefits, such as pension and medical plans, are typically available?

(8) Will I be able to handle the personal stress and professional demands of this position?

Child and youth care workers who select the school system as their primary employment setting need to become aware of the range of issues and questions needing daily and weekly attention. With accurate information and understanding of the public nature of the task, school-based practitioners will be able to work towards support, encouragement, long-term survival, and, ultimately, effective practice within this setting. Furthermore, one's responses to these and other issues may indicate one's personal suitability and actual desire to be involved as a school-based child care worker.

Summary

This chapter has described Canadian school-based child and youth care work as, presently, consisting of a diverse series of unique and largely unconnected programs. In comparison, child and youth care professionals in schools in the United States have traditionally worked within residential facilities for emotionally disturbed children (Alwon 1979; Goocher 1975; Meisels 1975; Trieschman 1976). This role usually involves dealing with crisis-oriented situations within activity programs and during after-school hours. The reader will be aware that within Canadian schools, the child and youth care task may range from crisis work to preventive care, requiring wide-ranging individual and group approaches within a variety of settings. Although an overview of the current situation can be established at one moment, change and expansion continues to alter the character of this work. This fact alone may offer the allure, intrigue, and professional challenge required for successful school-based child and youth care.

In this chapter and other recent publications devoted to school-based work, a number of issues are mentioned repeatedly as keys to successful employment in these settings. These include the need for practitioners to demonstrate: (1) clarity of philosophy, role, and function; (2) planned, intentional, and measurable intervention; (3) knowledge of education and learning strategies within classrooms; (4) an engaging and attractive personality and high level of self awareness; (5) a cadre of intervention, evaluation, consultation, and parent education skills; (6) availability, openness, flexibility, humour, and the ability to be politically sensitive; and (7) attention to recent trends from research.

In addition is the call for a more educated, more politically astute, more cohesive and unified professional body of practitioners. No reluctance is spared in stating that this work is stressful, demanding, fraught with potential 'mine-fields,' and has, at this point in time, little job security, prestige, or opportunity for promotion within the education hierarchy. On balance, a visit to a school-based placement will reveal innovation, creativity, caring, structured and planned leadership, energy, vision, and commitment. The 'pathway' may be indeed long and strewn with 'boulders,' but it need not be barren.

That a selected group of school students desperately need the kind of support, perspective, and expertise offered by qualified child and youth care practitioners in order to cope within this system is not in question. However, some pressing needs remain: for those school-based practitioners who are now inadequately educated to make the sacrifice to seek further education; for those who need to write about their work to commence writing; and for those who need to propose new programs, re-design job descriptions, implement evaluation procedures, support beginning practitioners, or speak out for the psychosocial and behavioural needs of students to step forward and assume a level of leadership among their peers.

Notes

1 From a review of the four journals most heavily influencing the child and youth care profession in North America (*Child and Youth Care Administrator, Child and Youth Care Quarterly, Child Welfare,* and *Journal of Child and Youth Care*), few articles focus exclusively on the work of the school-based child and youth care professional.
2 Most major texts used in child and youth care education and training programs and considered pivotal to the field (Klein 1975; Krueger 1980; Mayer 1958; Trieschman, Whittaker, and Brendtro 1969; Whittaker 1979) fail to isolate and discuss this area of child and youth care work.
3 For example, in British Columbia, 142 programs were listed in 1979, 180 in 1982, and 185 in 1990 in the Directory of British Columbia Alternative Rehabilitative Programs, Victoria, BC. This would suggest that in this province there are between 300 and 500 child and youth care professionals associated on a full- or part-time basis in educational settings.
4 School District Policy from the Ministry of Education (British Columbia), Calgary Board of Education Special Education Handbook (1981), *Medicine Hat Public School Policy Handbook* (1983), Ontario Ministry of Community and Social Services, and Ontario Ministry of Education Administrative Guidelines (1981).
5 Papers and informal notes from the archives of the Ministry of Human Resources, Region 2 (Vancouver); Nanaimo Family Life Association; Victoria Girls' Alternative Program; Edwin Parr Community School, Athabasca; and visits to programs in Quebec, Ontario, Nova Scotia, Alberta, and British Columbia.

References

Allan, J. 1980. Integration and mainstreaming in the elementary schools: Facts, problems and solutions. *British Columbia Counsellor* 2:15–27

Alwon, B. 1979. An after school activity program. *Child Care Quarterly* 8:266–78

Anglin, J. 1983. Setting the sights: An assessment of child care job functions and training needs in British Columbia. In C. Denholm, R. Ferguson, and A. Pence (eds.), *The scope of professional child care in British Columbia*. Victoria: University of Victoria

Apter, S. 1982. *Troubled children: Troubled systems*. New York: Pergamon

Brown, R.I. and Hughson, E.A. 1980. *Training the developmentally handicapped adult*. Illinois: Thomas

Cartledge, G. and Milburn, J.F. (eds.). 1980. *Teaching social skills to children*. New York: Pergamon

Denholm, C. (ed.). 1981a. *Canadian trends in school-based child care*. Victoria: Fotoprint

–. 1981b. School-based child care in British Columbia. In C. Denholm (ed.), *Canadian trends in school-based child care*. Victoria: Fotoprint

–. 1983. Beyond the three r's: Child care in educational settings. In C. Denholm, R. Ferguson, and A. Pence (eds.), *The scope of professional child care in British Columbia*. Victoria: University of Victoria

–. 1986. Child care workers in Canadian schools: What do they do? *Journal of Child Care* 2:27–34

–. 1988. Hiring school-based professionals. *Child and Youth Care Administrator* 1:17–20

–. 1989. Child and youth care in school settings: Maximizing support and minimizing friction. *Journal of Child and Youth Care Work* 5:53–61

–. 1991. Challenges and questions facing the development of child and youth care work in Canadian educational settings. *Journal of Child and Youth Care* 6:1–10

Denholm, C., Ferguson, R., and Pence, A. (eds.). 1983. *The scope of professional child care in British Columbia*. Victoria: University of Victoria

Denholm, C., Chrest, S., and Pylypa, R. 1991. Profiles of selected school-based programs in Victoria and Vancouver, British Columbia. *Journal of Child and Youth Care* 6:83–99

Diekmeier, J. 1991. Instructional methods in the classroom: Strategies and approaches for teachers and child and youth care workers. *Journal of Child and Youth Care* 6:23–36

Dinkmeyer, D. and McKay, G. 1976. *Systematic training for effective parenting*. Minnesota: American Guidance Service

–. 1983. *Systematic training for effective parenting of teenagers*. Minnesota: American Guidance Service

DuRand, J. and Newfeldt, A.H. 1975. *Comprehensive vocational service systems*. Toronto: National Institute on Mental Retardation

Egan, G. 1985. *Change agent skills in helping and human service settings*. California: Brooks/Cole

Ferguson, R., Martin, R., and Wilson, K. 1989. Distance education: The tip of the iceberg. *Journal of Child and Youth Care* 4:55–69

GAIN Act. 1978. Sec. 2, subsecs. 1 and 2. British Columbia, Family and Children's Resources, Ministry of Human Resources

Goocher, B.E. 1975. Behavioral applications of an educateur model in child care. *Child Care Quarterly* 4:84–92

Gordon, T. 1975. *Parent effectiveness training.* New York: Signet

Haberlin, L. 1976. Child care workers in elementary schools: A developmental model. Unpublished manuscript

Hall, E.M. and Dennis, A.A. (eds.). 1968. *The report of the provincial committee on aims and objectives of education in the schools in Ontario: Living and learning.* Ministry of Education

Holt, J. 1974. *How children fail.* New York: Dell

Houndle, C. and Ricks, F. 1981. Child care workers in school settings. In C. Denholm (ed.), *Canadian trends in school-based child care.* Victoria: Fotoprint

Hubbard, B. and Phillips, S. 1981. Child care workers and school counsellors within the traditional school: A process model. In C. Denholm (ed.), *Canadian trends in school-based child care.* Victoria: Fotoprint

Hughes, K. and Lougheed, V. 1991. Effective partnerships between teacher and child and youth care worker: Experiences at Storefront School, British Columbia. *Journal of Child and Youth Care* 6:75–81

Jarrett, A. 1991. Accountability and the school-based child and youth care worker. *Journal of Child and Youth Care* 6:57–61

Jarrett, A.S. and Klassen, T. 1986. *Planning for positive behavior in the classroom.* Toronto: Dellcrest Resource Centre

Kameen, M. 1979. Guest editorial. *Elementary School Guidance and Counselling* 13:150–1

Kanfer F.H. and Goldstein, A.P. 1984. *Helping people change.* New York: Pergamon

Klassen, T. 1981. School-based child service in Ontario: A provincial overview. In C. Denholm (ed.), *Canadian trends in school-based child care.* Victoria: Fotoprint

Klein. A.F. 1975. *The professional child care worker: A guide to skills, knowledge, techniques and attitudes.* New York: Association Press

Krueger, M. 1980. *Intervention techniques for child care workers.* Wisconsin: J. Tall

Laycock, S.R. and Findlay, J.A. 1971. *Educational needs of emotionally disturbed children in the schools of British Columbia.* Educational Research Institute of British Columbia, Report No. 5, Vancouver

Lazure, D. and Roberts, C.A. (Co-Chairmen). 1970. *One million children.* Commission of Emotional and Learning Disabilities in Children, Ottawa

McMorran, S. 1981. Student perceptions of school counsellors and child care workers in school settings. In C. Denholm (ed.), *Canadian trends in school-based child care.* Victoria: Fotoprint.

Marlett, N.J. and Hughson, E.A. 1979. *Rehabilitation programs manual.* Calgary: The Vocational and Rehabilitation Research Institute

Mayer, M.F. 1958. *A guide for child care workers.* New York: Child Welfare League of America

Meisels, L. 1975. The disturbing child and social competence in the classroom: Implications for child care workers. *Child Care Quarterly* 4:231–40

Menolascino, F. (ed.). *Psychiatric approaches to mental retardation.* New York: Basic Books

Neil, R. 1981. Child care counsellors in public elementary schools: A model for the team approach. In C. Denholm (ed.), *Canadian trends in school-based child care.* Victoria: Fotoprint

Neill, A.S. 1960. *Summerhill*. New York: Hart

Nordstrom, G. and Denholm, C.J. 1986. Student contact, counseling and support: The Shoreline Community School approach. *The British Columbia School Counselor* 7:31–7

Parsons, R.O. and Meyers, J. 1984. *Developing consultation skills*. New York: Jossey-Bass

Porter, F. and Coleman, R. 1978. *The pilot parent program: A design for developing a program for parents of handicapped children*. Omaha, NE: Greater Omaha Association for Retarded Citizens

Robinson, L. 1991. Administrative choices and the implementation of a school-based youth and family counselor program in British Columbia. *Journal of Child and Youth Care* 6:71–4

Standifer, F.R. 1964. Pilot parent program: Parents helping parents. *Mental Retardation* 2:304–7

Strain, P.S. and Kerr, M.M. 1981. *Mainstreaming of children in schools: Research and programmatic issues*. New York: Academic Press

Trieschman, A.E. 1976. The Walker school: An education-based model. *Child Care Quarterly* 5:123–35

Trieschman, A.E., Whittaker, J.K., and Brendtro, L.K. 1969. *The other twenty-three hours. Child care work in a therapeutic milieu*. Chicago: Aldine

Whittaker, J.K. (1979). *Caring for troubled children: Residential treatment in a community context*. San Francisco: Jossey-Bass

Wolfensberger, W. 1972. *Normalization*. New York: National Institute on Mental Retardation

–. 1980. The definition of normalization: Update, problems, disagreements, and misunderstandings. In R.J. Flynn and K.E. Nitsch (eds.), *Normalization, social integration, and community services*. Baltimore: University Park

–. 1983. *Normalization-based guidance, education and supports for families of handicapped people*. National Institute on Mental Retardation, Toronto

Wolfensberger, W. and Menolascino, F.J. 1970. A theoretical framework for the management of parents of the mentally retarded. In F. Menolascino (ed.), *Psychiatric approaches to mental retardation*. New York: Basic Books

Wolfensberger, W. and Thomas, S. 1980. *Program analysis of service systems' implementation of normalization goals*. New York: Training Institute for Human Service Planning, Leadership and Change Agency

5
Child-Life Programs: Fostering Coping and Development of Children and Families in Health Settings

Carolyn Larsen, Roy Ferguson, and Leigh Parish

Introduction

Child-life programs have been emerging throughout Canada primarily during the past twenty-five years. The first prototype was introduced in 1936 at Montreal Children's Hospital. Then one of a handful in North America, this program later served as the backdrop for what appears to have been the first book to describe this field of work (Dimock 1959). Designed to reduce anxiety and foster sound development, child-life programs are based primarily in inpatient and outpatient settings of acute-care pediatric hospitals and general hospitals with pediatric services. According to the Canadian Council on Health Facilities Accreditation (1991), child-life services should include provision for orientation to the hospital environment, normal and therapeutic play activities, parent and sibling education, patient and family emotional support, and preparation for medical procedures.

The inclusion of child-life programs in North American hospitals has been recommended by the Association for the Care of Children's Health (ACCH) (1977), the American Academy of Pediatrics (1986), The Canadian Pediatric Society (1979), the Canadian Institute of Child Health (1979), and special work groups of Canada Health and Welfare (1982; 1985). There are 346 child-life and related programs listed in the 1990 edition of the ACCH *Directory of Child Life Programs in North America*.

This chapter will begin with an overview of the philosophy of health and medical care, the populations served, and the psychological and developmental effects of hospitalization, illness, and medical treatment. The role and functions of child-life programs will then be described and illustrated. The chapter will conclude with a look at some of the central professional issues, including organization, standards, education and training, program research, and professional identity.

Philosophy and Trends in Health and Medical Care

The Western perception of health care is confined largely to that of medical diagnosis and treatment of illness (Jacobs 1979). Within such a medical model, both health promotion and the developmental and psychological needs of children and families have secondary status.

Broadening Concepts of Health and Care

A more holistic and comprehensive view of health has long been promoted by the World Health Organization, which defined health as 'a state of complete physical, mental, and social well-being and not merely the absence of disease and infirmity' (Dunn 1959). The traditional medical model has shifted somewhat towards a more holistic model. More consideration is given to both the interaction between the individual and his or her environment, and to the integral functioning of mind and body, with health care being increasingly regarded as an enterprise where 'humanism and science must be inextricably intertwined' (Turner and Mapa 1979:xi).

This perspective is now widely embraced in medical environments for children, spurred, no doubt, by the large body of literature documenting both the worrisome sequelae to hospitalization and the apparent impact of more supportive environments. It is within this context that child-life programs have begun to flourish and care has become more family-centred.

Two sociological, observational studies of hospitalized children, one in America (Beuf 1979), the other in Great Britain (Jacobs 1979), suggest that a continuing threat to coping, self-esteem, and development is, to a certain extent, inherent to our system of medical care.

Beuf's (1979) main thesis was that the depersonalization and enforced helplessness apparent in childrens' hospitals is akin to that of Goffman's total institution. For instance, she notes that children are made to assume positions associated with lowliness and submission, to engage in forced interaction, and to accept the regimentation of the various routines — including playtimes — in environments which accord first priority to the aims of efficiency and medical training. Jacobs (1979) proposed that the dispassionate scientific diagnosis and treatment, fragmentation of care, and the denial or neglect of the feelings of child patients, parents, and staff alike are attributable to three forces predominant in the health care systems of the Western world. These are identified as (1) the natural sciences medical model, with its focus on pathology as opposed to health, (2) specialization and the large number of functionaries encountered at various points during an illness, and (3) professionalization and the ensuing assumption of control by others of certain major life events.

Populations Served

Number and Nature of Child and Youth Hospital Patients
According to the Canadian Institute of Child Health (Avard and Hanvey 1989), the number of hospital admissions in 1983 was approximately equivalent to 30 per cent of all infants, 10 per cent of preschoolers and adolescents, and 5 per cent of school-aged children. This was noted to represent a decrease of about 30 per cent for all ages, except infants, since 1970 and to include a disproportionately greater number of economically disadvantaged and Native children.

Although admissions have decreased, those who are now admitted to hospital are sicker, on average, than those who were admitted formerly (Kenny 1990). For many children with severe anomalies or chronic and life-threatening diseases, the hospital becomes a major part of their lives due to frequent or lengthy stays and regular outpatient treatment. The population includes, for example, those receiving highly technical care, children who have been abused or neglected and are, possibly, awaiting placement outside the family, newborns who must spend the first several months of their lives in an intensive care environment, children and youth who have become disfigured or who have incurred major loss of functioning, and suicidal adolescents.

Time Spent Receiving Health Care
Whereas the primary reason for hospitalization is medical diagnosis and treatment, in most cases a very small percentage of time is actually taken up by medical activities. Two unpublished studies carried out at Montreal Children's Hospital by G. Kolyvas in 1978 and D. Scanlan in 1980 documented how, and with whom, patients on two separate acute treatment units providing specialized pediatric care spent their daytime, weekday hours. They found that the average amount of time that a child spent in medical care was 6.2 per cent and 7.8 per cent for a medical and an orthopedic surgical unit, respectively. Medical care was defined as: all contacts with physicians, including time off the unit for

surgery, all medical aspects of nursing care, all diagnostic procedures, physical therapies, and the like. The average time, per patient, spent in child-life care was 30 per cent on the medical ward and 13.2 per cent on the orthopedic ward. Patients in the former group were mostly ambulatory preschool and school-age children with chronic or life-threatening illnesses. Those on the orthopedic unit ranged in age from preschool to adolescence and were mostly immobilized in wheelchairs, stretchers, or beds with traction gear.

Effects of Illness, Hospitalization, and Medical Care on Children

Interest in the relationships of illness, hospitalization, and medical care to children's behaviours and development has received increasing attention since reports began to appear in the late 1930s (Prugh, Straub, Sands, Kirshbaum, and Lenihan 1953). Ability to maintain or form trusting relationships, among other problems, was assessed to be jeopardized by the separation of young children from their mothers, even for quite brief periods (e.g., Bowlby, Robertson, and Rosenbluth 1952; Edelston 1943). This was seen to be compounded by arrested physical and cognitive development in the case of lengthy institutionalization of infants and toddlers (e.g., Spitz 1945). Various pathological outcomes were also viewed as deriving from restricted mobility and from surgery (e.g., Bergmann 1944; Levy 1945). In these times, contacts between parent and child were severely restricted, children were frequently uninformed (and even misled) about impending events, and few other measures were taken to safeguard their mental health.

Conditions of care have since been vastly ameliorated, and more current research has identified some of the conditions under which this improvement occurs. There is general agreement that ongoing efforts are required to assist children and their families in their efforts to cope with difficult experiences and to overcome obstacles to sound development. The Association for the Care of Children's Health (1977) outlined the overall situation as follows:

> Threats posed to the emotional security and development of many children and their families by serious illness, disability, disfigurement, treatment, interrupted human relations and nonsupportive environments have been clearly demonstrated by worldwide research studies. The outcomes can range from temporary but frequently overwhelming anxiety and emotional suffering to long-standing or permanent developmental handicaps. (p. 1)

Prevalence of Distress and Developmental Impact
Thompson (1985), covering the 20-year period up to 1984, reviewed 143 studies pertaining to the immediate responses of children to their medical or dental care and 66 studies which explore the emotional sequelae following the experience. Literature previous to 1965 had been reviewed by Vernon, Foley, Sipowicz, and Schulman (1965). Both reviews cite considerable evidence of behavioural and physiological indices of distress in children and youth during medical care and hospitalization and in the days and weeks following. Thompson (1985) also notes tentative findings of changes in aspects of cognitive functioning. Longer term effects have been studied less frequently, and it is their study that is favoured in this review.

Brief Hospitalization for Minor Surgery
In one of the most thorough early studies of children hospitalized briefly for tonsillectomy and adenoidectomy, Jessner, Blom, and Waldfogel (1952) found that most of the 143 children, 23 months to 14 years of age, exhibited at least some behavioural disturbance both during and when assessed a week to 10 days after hospitalization. Months or, in some cases, years following hospitalization, severe or persistent new behavioural disturbances were displayed by 20 per cent of the children. The behaviours included over- or under-eating, nightmares or difficulty sleeping, voice changes or refusal to talk, tics and mannerisms, fears of hospitals, white coats, bodily harm, or death, and regression, with increased dependency, wetting, or soiling. Improved adjustment was noted in about 5 per cent of cases.

In another study examining the effects of hospitalization, Sides (1977) identified 63 per cent of his subjects (aged 1 month to 15 years) as having negative psychological sequelae in relation to their hospitalization.

More recently, two younger tonsillectomy populations in Great Britain were each studied prior to, during, and six months after hospitalization. Dearden (1970) found that 27 per cent of the sample of 4-year-olds had increased pre- to post-hospital upset. Brown (1979) found that 21 per cent of his sample of 3- to 5-year-olds experienced increased general, separation, and sleep anxiety, respectively, and 15 per cent were more aggressive. At the one month post-hospital assessment, twice as many children had presented these symptoms. Nine per cent had poorer general health, and none had increased apathy or eating disturbances.

Hospitalization for Acute and Chronic Illnesses
Both the in-hospital and post-hospital responses appear to have been more severe in the 100 children, aged 2 to 12 years, studied by Prugh et al. (1953) than in those experiencing minor, planned surgery. In the latter case, the children had more serious chronic and newly diagnosed conditions, about 70 per cent of the admissions were unplanned, and the average length of stay was about one week. The findings of this experimental study suggested that children's reactions could be modified, given certain supportive interventions, which included potential parental visiting daily as opposed to weekly, psychological preparation and support for medical procedures, and a program of normal and therapeutic play. Difficulties in adapting to the hospital experience were reported for 92 per cent of those in the control group, compared to 68 per cent of those in the experimental group, despite pre-hospital adjustment favouring the control group. After three months at home again, 58 per cent of the control and 44 per cent of the experimental group, respectively, manifested at least moderate disturbance. Severity of reaction was said to be greater in the control group, and 5 per cent of those in the experimental group displayed improved behaviour.

Factors Associated with Distress in Hospitalized Children
Thompson (1985) has categorized factors relating to distress or developmental differences in hospitalized children, and they are briefly outlined below.

Age
The focus, though not incidence or severity, of anxiety was determined to shift with age among the tonsillectomy patients studied by Jessner et al. (1952). Almost 80 per cent of those under 5 years and almost 40 per cent of 5- to 9-year-olds reacted strongly to hospital and separation. About 30 per cent of the latter expressed apprehension about the operation. Fear of anaesthesia predominated for some 30 per cent of 7- to 9-year-olds and for almost 60 per cent of 10- to 13-year-olds. Needles were the main source of anxiety for about 20 per cent of the 5- and 6-year-olds.

In the sample of Prugh et al. (1953), described above, severe in-hospital reactions were greatest among the 2- and 3-year-olds at 50 per cent versus 37 per cent in the control and experimental groups, respectively, 30 per cent versus 7 per cent among 4- and 5-year-olds, and

27 per cent versus 0 per cent among the school-age children. Three months after discharge, at least moderate disturbance was reported in about two-thirds of the 2- and 3-year-olds and over one-third of the 4-and 5-year-olds regardless of group, compared to 60 per cent and 35 per cent of those from 6 to 12 years in the control and experimental groups. Their experimental interventions seemed to have had greatest impact on the school-age children.

More recently, Simons, Bradshaw, and Silva (1980) estimated that among their young subjects, those from 13 to 36 months experienced the highest incidence of post-hospital behavioural deterioration, at 25 per cent, whereas those from 36 to 60 months had the highest rate of improved behaviour, at 22 per cent. No behavioural differences from pre-hospital to 1-month post-hospital were detected in parents' reports of their school age children in the studies of McClowry and McCloud (1990) and Rae, Worchel, Upchurch, Sanner, and Daniel (1989).

Thompson (1985) concluded that most research suggests that children between 1 and 3 to 4 years are most vulnerable to psychological distress following a hospital experience. However, some of the research on both maternal-infant bonding and infant stimulation with low-birthweight newborns (Thompson 1985) suggests that, whereas there may be no discernible distress response, there can be significant differences in developmental progress among infants from birth to one year of age whether or not they are exposed to appropriate interaction and stimulation opportunities.

Child-Parent Interaction and Family-centred Care
Separation of the child from his or her principal care-givers and family is another major determinant of distress. Hospitalization may bring the first separation of young children from their parents.

Hospital policies and environments are now more receptive to, if not encouraging of, parental presence and participation. In their survey of the 286 North American teaching hospitals, Roberts, Maieron, and Collier (1988) found that, of those responding (95 per cent of the children's hospitals and 64 per cent of the pediatric units in general hospitals), unrestricted visiting hours were reported by 98 per cent and the possibility of parent 'rooming in' by 94 per cent. This is a considerable improvement over the 19.4 per cent claiming unrestricted visiting hours in 36 of 57 Quebec general hospitals to respond to a similar survey by the Canadian Institute of Child Health in 1977 (Larsen 1979) or the 44 per cent indicating that parents were allowed to stay overnight in 55 of the 74 Ontario hospitals responding to a survey by Alcock (1977).

Cardoso (1991) and Popper (1990) offer parent perspectives on a recent experience and recommendations for parent participation in hospital planning, respectively. Intrapersonal factors associated with outcomes include knowledge and understanding about medical experiences as well as prior emotional adjustment.

Unfamiliar or Threatening Events and Preparation
In the hospital and other medical settings, the child is confronted with many unfamiliar and potentially threatening events and experiences, such as the physical environment, strangers, painful or invasive procedures, constant sensory stimulation, ambiguous or altered role expectations, and limited access to developmentally appropriate environments and experiences. These events and experiences are threatening to children, both physically and psychologically, and affect their ability to process information (Gaynard, Wolfer, Goldberger, Thompson, Redburn, and Laidley 1990).

Being informed about anticipated medical events through involvement in preparation programs is now widely accepted as important for the child's psychological well-being. Preparing the child for medical encounters is believed to foster trust in the treatment personnel and to enable the mobilization of the child's coping resources. There is considerable evidence to suggest that effective preparation approaches contribute to less pre-surgical, pre-anaesthetic, post-surgical, and post-hospital anxiety, respectively, as well as quicker and less traumatic physical recovery (Thompson 1985). However, the opportunity for adequate preparation is not always systematically assured, nor are those methods which have shown the most promise necessarily the ones utilized (Azarnoff and Woody 1981; Peterson and Ridley-Johnson 1980).

Personality and Prior Emotional Adjustment
There is considerable evidence suggesting that pre-hospital emotional adjustment is an important predictor of post-hospital behavioural response (Jessner et al. 1952; Prugh et al. 1953; Sides 1977; Stacey, Dearden, Rill, and Robinson 1970). A large proportion of infants, children, and youth admitted to hospital or attending clinics or emergency departments are concurrently experiencing major social and familial upheaval. An example is a seriously burned young child whose parents

have just separated due to marital difficulties. Stacey et al. (1970) observed that children who make poor relationships with others and are socially inhibited, uncommunicative, and aggressive are the ones most likely to be disturbed by hospitalization. Thus, in addition to the fact that hospital, medical, and illness experiences render children psychologically vulnerable, it seems that a large percentage arrive for care already predisposed to such trauma.

Medical Care Experience, Past and Present
Neither previous hospitalization nor the type of medical procedures was related to severity of distress in the studies by Prugh et al. (1953), although the quality of past experiences (Dahlquist, Gill, Armstrong, DeLawyer, Green and Wuori 1986), longer hospitalization, and various planned interventions have been found to make a difference (Thompson 1985). It has been noted that the number of previous hospitalizations (and their durations) experienced by the child is considered to be a predictive factor with respect to the likelihood of hospitalization creating psychological distress (Douglas 1975; Quinton and Rutter 1976; Sides 1977).

The child-life program, through which children often express themselves more freely and function more normally than was the case before its introduction, is a valuable resource both in the prevention and early detection of problems affecting social, psychological, and cognitive functioning or development (Wilson 1979). Interventions can be geared to offset and help overcome some of these problems by child-life as well as other services to which referrals might be made.

Basic Child-Life Interventions
Basic child-life service, wherein a child-life specialist is attached to a specific unit, includes those services directed to all patients on the unit and their families as well as more individually oriented interventions for infants, children, and youth according to need.

A Warm Social Climate
The emphasis on creating and maintaining a social climate in which children can feel psychologically safe and have some control particularly typifies the child-life mandate. Children are encouraged to play freely, ideally in the company of other children, much as they might at home, and to engage in activities that reduce tension, foster individual expression, and contribute to learning and developmental progress.

A core ingredient of such an environment, and the children's motivation to participate, is the presence of, or interaction with, a capable and trusted adult whose actions foster a sense of security.

Play and Other Therapeutic Activities

Play continues to be a basic component of child-life programs because of the rich opportunity it provides for addressing a wide spectrum of needs within a relaxed atmosphere. The power of appropriate play experiences to resolve or bring to light emotional conflict and to promote mastery and self-esteem in the hospitalized child has been described by many (e.g., Brooks 1970; Dimock 1959; Erickson 1958; Goldberger 1990; Lindquist 1977; Plank 1971).

Phillips (1985, 1988) discusses the need to rectify the limited extent to which experimental research has explored the various claims made about the therapeutic outcomes of play. Significant differences in affect or anxiety levels have been documented in children when provided with play opportunities both individually, with a child-life specialist in an intensive care setting (Cataldo, Bessman, Parker, Pearson, and Rogers 1979; Pearson, Cataldo, Tureman, Bessman, and Rogers 1980), and within a supervised play program in an outpatient setting (Ispa, Barrett, and Kim 1988; Williams and Powell 1980). Rae et al. (1989) found that hospitalized 5- to 10-year-olds exposed to two 30-minute sessions of non-directive play therapy, including reflection and interpretation of feelings, reported markedly lower levels of fear than those given diversionary play, verbal support, or no intervention.

Except in units such as isolation or intensive care, where interventions are almost always at the bedside on a one-to-one basis, the play or activity area usually serves as the central working space of the child-life personnel as well as the hub of patients' activities and group life. In this area, over which the child-life service has primary jurisdiction, furnishings, equipment, materials, and activities are selected and adapted with respect to the particular needs and vulnerabilities of the children served.

The 'Safe Haven' Concept

The relief experienced by children who feel that they are in a safe place where they can be themselves is partly assured by the 'safe haven' policy adopted in many programs. That is, neither medical rounds nor procedures are permitted in this space. At the same time, this relaxed and often joyful environment provides an excellent opportunity for physicians, nurses, and other treatment staff to strengthen their rapport with the child.

Planning Individualized Care
Need for special support can not always be foreseen or met on a scheduled basis. Thus, great flexibility is required in the daily plan so as to be able to respond to children when most needed. At the same time, a good system for identifying needs and planning to address them is an important aspect of providing a maximally responsive and responsible service.

As part of the planning for individualized care, patients are prioritized on an ongoing basis by the child-life specialist according to their apparent level of need for assistance in mitigating the potentially negative psychological and developmental impact of the experience. A formal patient classification system may be employed to assist in determining each patient's level of need. Classification systems are based on such indicators as chronicity, prognosis, mobility, isolation, level of anxiety, and developmental or social risk factors. This tool for patient-care planning also serves as a measure of accountability to administrative and funding bodies.

The Child Life Department at Halifax's Izaac Walton Killam Hospital for Children pioneered the development of a classification system in which indicators of need were derived from three categories — emotional, mobility, and medical. The sum of the coded indicators for each child was then associated with one of four possible levels of required intervention. They found that 75 per cent of their patients were in the moderate to maximum category (Skinner 1987). Developing this process further, they now utilize an integrated child-life assessment-intervention plan, by which the particular issues that made patients a priority are identified and matched with specified interventions.

Types of Individual Interventions
Some examples of planned interventions are therapeutic or medical play, self-expressive activity, cognitive and psychological preparation for medical events, emotional support, adaptation of equipment, developmental assessment and programming, and discussion with a parent or prospective foster parent.

Diagnostic and Therapeutic Play
Experiences such as hospital or medical play (e.g., McCue 1988), specialized puppetry (Letts, Stevens, Coleman, and Kettner 1983), and expressive play (Parish 1986) help the child-life specialist determine a child's expectations, perceptions, misperceptions, and attitudes regarding medical procedures, illness, and/or hospitalization.

Preparation for Medical Procedures
Preparation for any stress-provoking events is a shared responsibility of physicians, nurses, and others involved in the care of the child. Because children function at so many different levels of cognitive processing and lack the background knowledge which would make the information more comprehensible, a strictly verbal approach is not usually sufficient. This is especially true for the young child. The child-life specialist may be responsible for providing the preparation for medical procedures alone or in conjunction with members of allied disciplines. Visualization of events and environments along with an opportunity to manipulate objects to be encountered and to engage in some form of rehearsal of the events or of the behaviours deemed helpful are frequently employed approaches (e.g., Cassell 1965; Demarest, Hooke, and Erickson 1984; Ferguson 1979; Ferguson and Robertson 1979; Gaynard, Wolfer, Goldberger, Thompson, Redburn, and Laidley 1990; Schwartz, Albino, and Tedesco 1983). Pre-admission programs for groups of children having planned admissions might also be offered by child-life or nursing personnel, sometimes jointly (e.g., Alcock 1977; Ferguson and Robertson 1979).

Stress-reducing Techniques
Specific stress-reducing techniques, such as physical relaxation, guided imagery, or cognitive restructuring, may be used to help selected children and youth cope more effectively with pain and anxiety-provoking procedures (Alcock, Berthiaume, and Clarke 1984).

Family-centred Care
Child-life personnel have a long history of involvement in family-oriented care. For instance, at Johns Hopkins Hospital in Baltimore, Maryland, the child-life program was responsible for coordinating one of the earliest 'mother live-in programs.' Similarly, child-life departments might be responsible for the hospital's family resource library, such as at Children's Hospital of Eastern Ontario and Alberta Chil-

dren's Hospital, or a drop-in centre for siblings, such as that at L'Hôpital Ste. Justine in Montreal.

Parents often feel ill at ease in the hospital environment in addition to being worried about their child and other responsibilities at home, on the job, or with extended family members. Some are less able to represent their own needs because of age, language or cultural differences, limited mental resources, or emotional fragility. They frequently share their concerns with child-life personnel, who can then serve as their liaison to other members of the team or assist in meeting some of their needs directly. Also, parents may feel more comfortable taking a much needed break if the child-life staff member can spend time with their child. The presence or involvement of parents and siblings in the play area can enhance the children's sense of security, while enabling child-life staff members to become better acquainted with, and extend support to, family members.

Program Design and Staff Assignment
The most common approach to the allocation of services is the long-term assignment of a child-life specialist to a particular inpatient or outpatient service. Those who work regularly with children with chronic diseases in the clinic likely continue their supportive role when the child is hospitalized. This pattern of attachment to a specific diagnostic grouping, in which the child-life specialist moves between outpatient and inpatient settings according to patient need, enabling a continuum of care, has recently been formalized at the Hospital for Sick Children in Toronto. To support a child's transition to another setting or back to home and school, the child-life specialist might occasionally accompany or visit a child and meet with other care-givers.

Some child-life services also have regular centralized group programs, usually more recreational in nature, such as evening and weekend activities, or a kite-making session or a movie night, for patients from various inpatient units. As these programs are available at times when more family members are able to visit, they support the continuation of normal family interactions.

The recommended ratio of child-life personnel to patients has been variously set at 1:5 in Holland (Veeneklaas 1971), 1:10, and 1:15 (ACCH 1979, 1983). According to a 1988 directory (Roberts, Maieron, and Collier), only 21 per cent of hospital child-life programs have a ratio of 1:20 or less. Establishing priorities when the number of child-life personnel are much lower than recommended, and the demands from nursing and medical staff beyond what is possible to meet, is a reality facing most heads of programs. This is a situation in which the afore-mentioned patient classification system could be a useful tool. Clinics and inpatient areas ranking highest for essential services will most likely include those serving children with serious, chronic, and life-threatening conditions (Larsen 1983; Viau-Chagnon and Tallboy 1982). Some services, such as those at Montreal Children's Hospital and the Children's Memorial Hospital in Chicago, have recently adapted to severe personnel cutbacks by establishing a referral system.

Interdisciplinary Communication

Regular, ongoing communication with other members of the health care team concerning patients and their families is a requirement. The child-life specialist's interventions must be based, in part, on up-to-date information about patient and family status, medical precautions, and any anticipated events of importance. Likewise, the work of other team members is aided by insights the child-life staff member might have gained about a child's functioning, concerns, or particular coping styles.

Some of this information exchange takes place on an ongoing, infor-mal basis. In addition, regular daily or weekly meetings with one or more team members are usually scheduled to help ensure that each patient's and family's needs, such as those related to school or continu-ing rehabilitation, are appraised. The most formal communication tool is the patient's medical chart. The child-life specialist's observations, assessments, and plans for meeting the patient's psychosocial needs should be recorded and updated from time to time (Parish and Johnson 1987).

Child-life personnel also work jointly with nurses and others to maintain or modify the environment, physical (Ferguson 1986; Olds 1978) and social, so that these may be developmentally appropriate and foster the comfort, independence, and activity needs of patients and families in general. The social climate can be affected, for instance, by unit policies and procedures related to family activities or by the content of in-service education sessions.

Case Illustrations

To illustrate some aspects of the child-life role in action, two case ex-amples are cited, each of a child hospitalized for lengthy periods. The first is that of a boy whose suffering and drastically altered life circum-stances were the result of an accident.

Paul, seven years old, had been very badly burned. Most of his skin which had not been damaged was used for grafting onto the burned areas of his body. His arms and hands had become contracted from the tense position in which he kept them. Movement was confined to his face, from which angry and frightened eyes looked out, and to his head, which he could turn. All nourishment came through tubes, and for several months he was confined to his tiny isolation room.

Although there was little response to the child-life worker's daily visits during the early weeks, Paul made it clear that he wanted her there. Her early work involved establishing an emotional bond which could help him to cope with the many difficult experiences yet to be faced and would be a motivating force for involvement in activities essential to healthy ongoing development.

An early source of comfort was just having the child-life specialist's hand on his or having his temple gently stroked as she tried to understand his feelings and verbalize them for him. She worked to make his bedside environment visually stimulating and personal, while fostering his identity as a vital member of his family, who were living in another province and able to come for brief visits only. She gradually stimulated his involvement in a variety of play experiences, despite major restrictions, in the hope of restoring a feeling of hope and wholeness as well as a sense of accomplishment, independence, and self-esteem.

Although Paul rejected all initial attempts to accept food by mouth, he was thrilled about doing some cooking in his isolation room. Enthusiastically, he ordered that the wieners which the child-life specialist helped him to fry be cut up and given to many of the nurses, physicians, and others on his unit. He eventually accepted little nibbles of whatever food they prepared in his room. Cooking was to become one of his greatest sources of pleasure. Towards the end of his stay he was escorted to a large oven where he baked his loaf of bread, wearing a chef's hat his aunt had made.

Paul's first days out of his isolation room and in the ward playroom were both exciting and anxiety-provoking. Paul could not relax, fearing pain should anyone accidentally bump into his wheelchair. With some rearrangement of furniture, a protected corner was made. The next hurdle was coping with the stares and questions of the constantly changing group of other children, most of whom were in the hospital for brief elective surgery. The child-life specialist helped Paul learn how to handle this situation, while at the same time allaying the fears of the other children and their parents. Resocialization, following the many months of being restricted to interactions with the various health care professionals, was another important rehabilitative task. The playroom served as an important testing ground for Paul's anticipated re-entry into his family and community life.

The second example deals with a very young child and depicts the role of early intervention. Some practical ramifications are discussed at the end.

During the initial phase of his hospitalization, Louis, a twenty-month-old boy, blind since shortly after birth, remained largely in a fetal position in his crib, severely delayed in his development and withdrawn. His mother, a single working parent, had been overwhelmed and without adequate resources for coping. The child-life specialist, after much reading and consultation with others (such as, for example, a speech therapist), developed a daily handicap-specific stimulation program for the child along with regular encouragement for the mother's efforts and periodic video filming in order to document progress. These films became an invaluable tools for both the staff member and mother in the assessment and modification of their approaches to the child. For the benefit of various members of the staff who were interacting with Louis, the child-life specialist posted at the bedside updated recommended approaches to meeting the boy's needs. Louis made remarkable progress in his development, demonstrating great zest for exploring and manipulating his environment. Similarly, the mother gained increased confidence and commitment in caring for her son to the point where she stimulated the formation of a support group for parents of young, blind children. Teamwork with the social worker resulted in a creative solution, permitting a return to home four days a week and placement in a supportive foster family on the days when the mother worked. Louis was enrolled in a preschool for blind children, first attending while still in the hospital, then continuing once he returned home.

This child was one of approximately twenty infants and toddlers on an acute-treatment medical ward served by one full-time child-life staff member. At any time, about one-third of these patients were identified as experiencing serious social problems. The problems included illnesses associated with particular family lifestyles, failure-to-thrive, and child abuse. This proportion is reminiscent of the findings of

Stocking, Rothney, Grosser, and Goodwin (1972) and represents a segment of those patients and families who would be accorded high priority for individualized child-life intervention (e.g., Evler 1982; Skinner 1987). Additional child-life resources might be available for a few months of the year in the person of a capable, full-time student trainee, who, as another familiar, trusted adult, tuned in to particular infants' unique and subtle behavioural cues, could help address some of these special needs. Ideally, a permanent child-life assistant would be employed full time throughout the year for both this purpose and to provide temporary coverage during vacation periods. Although volunteers can provide invaluable assistance in many aspects of the child-life service's functioning, their assignment to infants and toddlers should only be considered if their attendance is almost as continuous as that of a paid staff member.

Other Child-Life Services
In addition to the above-described basic program, the child-life service, particularly in a children's hospital, might be responsible for certain related services or resources. The most common of these are briefly described here.

Educational Opportunities for the Well Child
Children in the community might have the opportunity to participate in an educational hospital orientation provided either at the hospital or in the community school or nursery. The appeal of such programs lies in their possible preventive effects, particularly for children needing emergency care and who have no time for planned preparation.

School
Children facing long-term or repeated hospitalizations, or frequent day-care treatment, such as kidney dialysis or intensive cancer therapy, require opportunities to continue their school work both for maintaining their academic status and for the additional measure of normalcy the experience provides. Ongoing communication with their home school is an important aspect of this service.

School programs in hospital are occasionally an integral component of the child-life service, as at Izaac Walton Killam Hospital for Children in Halifax, or are provided through a local school board and, possibly, coordinated by the child-life service, as at Children's Hospital of Eastern Ontario and Montreal Children's Hospital. General hospitals usually utilize visiting teachers, who are available through a local school board. In this situation, as exists at Victoria General Hospital, for example, the relationship between the teachers and the child-life specialists is close and complementary.

Patient and Family Libraries

Patient libraries and family resource centres may be among the child-life service's responsibilities. The latter are now in place in most pediatric hospitals. They generally include books, films, and videotapes for parents and children, focusing on a wide variety of issues related to health, illness, and disability. Providing topical information to parents is another means of helping them overcome feelings of helplessness, equipping them to be actively involved in the health care of their children, and, thus, supporting maintenance of their essential parenting role — including informed decision-making with or on their child's behalf. Toy-lending libraries may also be in place, as at Alberta Children's Hospital, providing a source of toys and games for educational, recreational, and therapeutic purposes.

In-House Television Programming

Child-life personnel have become increasingly involved in providing alternate choices to commercial television programs. The in-house channel might feature live programs of interaction with patients as well as good quality educational and entertainment films. A research project at Children's Hospital in Winnipeg documented viewing patterns of patients prior to and following the establishment of their closed-circuit programming (Guttentag, Albritation, and Kettner 1983). Similar programming is now offered at other Canadian settings such as BC Children's Hospital.

Playgrounds

Outdoor play areas allow children to be active in a more non-institutional setting, engage in physical activity, and enjoy the changing seasons and weather (Alcock 1978; Parish and Bean 1987). These play areas require innovative design to maximize access to children who may be on stretchers or in wheelchairs with intravenous infusions running, and who may benefit from challenge provided in a safe environment. The child-life service may hire students from related disciplines to plan and supervise summer playground programs.

Professional Issues

Professional Organization and Standards of Practice

The first North American meeting for some sixty-five child-life and related practitioners was held in Boston in 1965. They were joined the following year by physicians, nurses, social workers, hospital administrators, and others sharing a commitment to fostering the changes needed to make hospitals more hospitable to developing children and families. This led to the establishment in 1967 of what is now called the Association for the Care of Children's Health, a major resource and voice for children with health problems/disabilities and their families. This enlarged group, whose membership now includes parents, meets together yearly for inspiration, mutual support, and planning.

One of the six child-life founders of ACCH was the program director at Montreal Children's Hospital, from which maple was contributed for the making of the president's gavel (which consisted of six different types of wood). Canadians of various disciplines continue to participate actively in this organization of some 4,000 members and in its chartered affiliates across the country. The head office is now situated in Bethesda, Maryland.

Professional Organizations

Issues specific to child-life practice and professional organization were only partially addressed in the multidisciplinary ACCH conferences. Thus, from 1972, various annual pre-conference meetings were held, culminating in the formation of the Child Life Council in 1982. This body, whose membership surpassed 1,000 in 1991, is concerned with the establishment of standards of practice and the continuing education and support of its members. The council has, for instance, enunciated a professional code of ethics, philosophical base, child-life specialist competencies, and standards of clinical practice — these latter comprising the Official Documents distributed since 1990. It has also developed a self-assessment tool for program review and sponsors an annual networking and educational conference as well as an active job bank service. On request by hospitals, the council conducts program reviews and provides consultation. Initially under the umbrella of the multidisciplinary ACCH, the council and its sister organization, the Child Life Certifying Commission, became independent in 1993, although continuing to share head office space and certain resources.

The Canadian Association of Child Life Directors was formally established in 1987 and meets annually (as they had done informally for several years) to address issues affecting the quality of child-life services in Canada. Members of this body have endorsed the Official Documents of, and participate actively in, the Child Life Council.

Accreditation of the Medical Facility
To qualify as a medical teaching facility, the facility's accreditation must be renewed every three years. In 1991 the Canadian Council on Health Facilities Accreditation, in response to initiatives by the Canadian Association of Child Life Directors, published standards and related indicators for child-life services in acute care settings. Evaluation of the facility's child-life service, now a component of the accreditation process, is based on relative compliance with defined standards, including indicators such as the stated purpose, goals, objectives, policies and procedures, the service's human and physical resources, staff orientation, development and continuing education, patient care arrangements, and quality assurance procedures.

Professional Certification
The Child Life Certifying Commission, formed in 1986, grants professional or provisional certification to practitioners meeting minimum standards of education, practice, and professional involvement. This credential offers some assurance to the employing institution and child-life service of the individual's ability to provide an acceptable level of care. Canadian applications are evaluated by a regionally-representative committee composed of Canadian child-life program directors, and there are now some 600 certified child-life specialists.

Education and Training
Among the required child-life specialist competencies referred to above, the Child Life Council has emphasized the ability to apply theories of growth and development, family systems, multiculturalism, and styles of learning at different developmental levels as well as knowledge and skills specific to children's needs in medical environments. To qualify for child-life specialist certification, candidates must have completed both adequate course work in these topics at the bachelor degree level and supervised practice in a medical setting. Child-life assistants should have related training at the college diploma level. A master's degree is recommended for program directors.

Several bachelor degree programs in the United States now offer a major in child-life, and a few offer master's degrees. In Canada, educational opportunities that are specific to child-life are limited. The University of Victoria's School of Child and Youth Care includes a child-life preparation stream within its undergraduate program. In Hamilton, a one-year postgraduate diploma program in Child Life Studies is offered by McMaster University's Faculty of Health Sciences. Child-life programs in pediatric and general hospitals usually provide fieldwork opportunities in conjunction with suitable local university and college programs. A child-life internship program is existent at Izaac Walton Killam Hospital for Children in Halifax, while BC Children's Hospital and the School of Child and Youth Care at UVic are in the process of developing one in western Canada.

The field has some practitioners whose original training includes education psychology, recreation, nursing, occupational therapy, and social work (Mather and Glasrud 1981; McCue, Wagner, Hansen, and Rigler 1978), suggesting a certain degree of theoretical and practical overlap with these professional fields.

The question of how specialized the training should be (Larsen 1980, 1986; Mather and Glasrud 1981) remains open, given the limits it may impose on breadth or depth of basic knowledge and skills, not to mention employment potential outside of health care settings.

Program Research

In the past few years reports have appeared on the only two experimental studies to examine the impact of an established, comprehensive child-life program. One took place in an emergency department, with samples of 372 subjects (Alcock, Feldman, Goodman, McGrath, and Park 1985a) and 625 subjects (Alcock, Goodman, Feldman, McGrath, Park, and Cappelli 1985b), the other with 228 children hospitalized at least three days (Wolfer, Gaynard, Goldberger, and Nicholson-Laidley 1987a; Wolfer, Gaynard, Goldberger, Laidley and Thompson 1987b). Hall (1977) had earlier conducted a sociological study of two hospital play programs in Great Britain during the introductory phase, making observations of 189 children. These three studies are briefly considered here.

In the Emergency Department

Alcock et al. (1985a, 1985b) examined selected effects of a time-limited child-life intervention with children, four years and older, awaiting sutures for an injury just incurred. Interventions included access to painting, games, crafts, and reading materials as well as preparation for the suturing, with particular emphasis on teaching stress-reducing techniques. There were some statistically significant differences in favour of the group exposed to child-life interventions, such as less self-reported anxiety among the oldest children (from eleven to fourteen years) and increased play and other activities both by children and by parents with their children. Otherwise, anxiety levels on the various measures were not appreciably different for younger children in the three groups.

During Hospitalization: Two Studies
Two very different kinds of programs, program research, and outcomes, respectively, should be mentioned here. Hall (1977) conducted a six-month sociological study of the introduction of a play-leader on each of two pediatric wards of general hospitals in Wales and England, respectively. Allowing local authorities to select and direct the work of these new staff members, as they might under ordinary circumstances, Hall's aim was to study 'what difficulties might lie in the way of the implementation of play programs' (p. 61). The former teachers who were selected each failed to develop therapeutic dimensions such as, for example, getting involved in discussions with the child about his or her illness, and they worked in relative professional isolation. Hall found no conclusive evidence of significant upset in the children, but he did identify some of the organizational and role difficulties needing to be addressed if such programs were to bring about the intended occupational, educational, and therapeutic benefits.

In somewhat opposite circumstances, Wolfer, Gaynard, Goldberger, and Nicholson-Laidley (1987a) and Wolfer, Gaynard, Goldberger, Laidley, and Thompson (1987b) studied the impact of a model comprehensive child-life program on children's stress and coping levels. This program was instituted on one floor of a children's hospital highly motivated to establish a child-life program. Up to this time, the two-floor hospital had employed a single recreational worker (1987a). Recognized leaders in the field from Canada and the United States were consulted about the theoretical framework and projected program. Three child-life specialists — two American, one Canadian — were selected on the basis of their experience and established competence. They and one coordinator had six months (before data collection for the experimental group began) to translate the stress and coping paradigm into a program integrated with nursing and other services. Each was responsible for one twelve-bed unit and worked with patients on an individual basis. Two child-life assistants were trained and given responsibility for the morning and afternoon playroom sessions, which served all patients on the floor. A volunteer generally assisted at each session.

The child-life specialists met the child on admission, developed and maintained care plans, carried out therapeutic play, planned and implemented preparation for all medical procedures, determined with the child which coping mechanisms would be used, made a daily stress vulnerability assessment, maintained a supportive relationship (often doing 'the little things,' like changing the snack), and planned appropriate play experiences in the group playroom.

Despite statistically significant poorer pre-hospital adjustment and other disadvantages, according to the scores on measures such as observable distress, cooperation and pulse rates during medical procedures, understanding of the reason for hospitalization and knowledge of medical procedures, and several physiological indicators of recovery from surgery and anaesthesia, the experimental group demonstrated significantly less stress and greater coping ability than did the control group. Moreover, the gap between the group scores for procedural distress and coping increased markedly from the first to the third procedure. The authors suggested that the effects could be cumulative with increased exposure to the systematic, ongoing supportive and preparatory activities. In the preliminary report (1987a), this group difference was reported to be greatest among the youngest children, aged three to five years.

Brief Reflections on the Three Program Evaluations
If there is a tendency for the effects of child-life interventions to be cumulative, it might be more difficult to demonstrate their effectiveness immediately following their application, such as in an emergency setting. That is, in the long run effects might emerge as differences. In fact, there is some support for this possibility in the preparation research literature, with the finding of greater physiological arousal immediately after viewing a peer-model film at the time of admission, yet significantly lower arousal than in the control groups both the evening prior to the operation and at the post-hospital checkup (Melamed and Siegel 1975, 1980). It is also possible that the child already experiencing physical trauma and pain is less receptive to preparation interventions, or that preparation immediately preceding the medical proce-

dure leaves insufficient time to assimilate and muster coping strategies. Faust and Melamed (1984) found that while their slide-tape peer-model intervention was effective with those having surgery the next day, for many having surgery the same day it was less effective than a control film about a boy going fishing. Further, ongoing preparatory interventions have been demonstrated to be more effective than preparation in a single session (Visintainer and Wolfer 1975) with younger as well as with older children.

The extent to which the findings of Hall (1977) and of Wolfer et al. (1987b) would apply to other programs is unknown. Given that they each represent a program near the opposite ends of a spectrum in terms of sound theoretical framework, planning, receptiveness of setting, staff expertise, staff to patient ratio, clarity of role, and professional support, it seems plausible that the effects of existing child-life programs might fall somewhere between.

Role and Professional Identity

Gaynard, Hausslein, and DeMarsh (1989) explored the child-life specialist role, using an ethnographic observational approach, tracking five staff members for several full days each in four different hospitals. Based on precise time-keeping, they were able to calculate the percentage of time spent in various types of direct care, interactions with various health team members, and administrative tasks. A high degree of consistency from one setting to another was reported. Patient support occupied the greatest amount of direct care time, followed by therapeutic play, then preparation interventions. Less time than expected was spent in activities specific to assessing and promoting development — about the same as in parent or family support and diversional activities. These authors note the potential for trivialization of the role by those not understanding the goal behind engagement in simple supportive tasks. They suggest that restricted role perceptions are probably enhanced by the relatively limited amount of time spent by the child-life specialist in interdisciplinary communication and education, particularly charting.

Rubin (1992) discusses the sociocultural factors fostering marginalization of child-life within the health care system and suggests preventive approaches. Thompson and Stanford (1981) address possible resistance to the child-life role on the part of various other health professionals in their comprehensive introductory text book for child-life students. During the current economic recession, considerable reductions to the number of staff have been experienced in some hospitals — a move predicted as ill-conceived (Brazelton and Thompson 1988).

Interdisciplinary Consultation and Education
Given their greater exposure to the child's or family member's point of view coupled with their particular knowledge about children, child-life specialists can make a unique contribution to various hospital planning bodies. Child-life personnel frequently participate in the orientation and in-service education of other health care professionals and hospital workers. In a few cases formal teaching appointments to medical schools (McMaster University and University of Manitoba) have been made.

Conclusion
The developmental and psychological needs of children and youth are now more carefully considered in the design and delivery of pediatric care. Child-life programs have played a significant part in this change. A tremendous amount of progress has been made during the past few years in establishing sound professional standards, and the structures needed for fostering adherence to these standards by both individual practitioners and medical settings alike. These moves can be expected to strengthen the ability of both parties to sustain children and families throughout their medical care experience, enhancing their capacity to cope and to achieve optimal growth and development.

References
Alcock, D. 1977. Hey, what about the kids? *Canadian Nurse* 73:38–41
–. 1978. Developing an outdoor playground. *Dimensions in Health Services: Journal of the Canadian Hospital Association* 55:32–7
Alcock, D., Berthiaume, S., and Clarke, A. 1984. Child life intervention in the emergency department. *Children's Health Care* 12:130–6
Alcock, D., Feldman, W., Goodman, J., McGrath, P., and Park, J. 1985a. Evaluation of child life intervention in emergency department suturing. *Pediatric Emergency Care* 1:111–15
Alcock, D., Goodman, J., Feldman, W., McGrath, P., Park, M., and Cappelli, M. 1985b. Environment and waiting behaviors in emergency waiting areas. *Children's Health Care* 13:174–80
American Academy of Pediatrics. 1986. *Hospital care of children and youth.* Elk Grove Village, IL: Author
Association for the Care of Children's Health (ACCH.) 1977. *Statements of policy for the care of children and families in health care settings.* Washington, DC: Author
–. 1979. *Child life study section position paper.* Washington, DC: Author

–. 1983. *Child life position paper*. Washington, DC: Author
–. 1984, 1990. *Directory of child life programs in North America*. Washington, DC: Author
Avard, D., and Hanvey, L. 1989. *The Health of Canada's children: A CICH profile*. Canadian Institute of Child Health, Ottawa
Azarnoff, P., and Woody, P.D. 1981. Preparation of children for hospitalization in acute care hospitals in the United States. *Pediatrics* 68:361–8
Bergmann, T. 1944. Observations of children's reactions to motor restraint. *Nervous Child* 4:318–28
Beuf, A.H. 1979. *Biting off the bracelet: A study of children in hospitals*. Philadelphia: University of Pennsylvania Press
Bolig, R. and Gnezda, M.T. 1984. A cognitive-affective approach to child-life programming for young children. *Children's Health Care* 12:122–9
Bowlby, J., Robertson, J., and Rosenbluth, D. 1952. A two-year-old goes to hospital. *Psychoanalytic Study of the Child* 7:82–94
Brazelton, T.B. and Thompson, R.H. 1988. Child life. *Pediatrics* 81:725–6
Brooks, M. 1970. Why play in hospital? *Nursing Clinics of North America* 5:431–41
Brown, B. 1979. Beyond separation: Some new evidence on the impact of brief hospitalisation on young children. In D. Hall and M. Stacey (eds.), *Beyond separation: Further studies of children in hospital*. London: Routledge and Kegan Paul
Canada. Department of Health and Welfare. 1982. *Child and adolescent services in general hospitals*. Ottawa: Health Services Directorate
–. 1985. *Child and youth long term services*. Ottawa: Health Services Directorate
Canadian Council on Health Facilities Accreditation. 1991. Standards for child life services. In *Accreditation standards for acute care facilities*. Ottawa: Author
Canadian Pediatric Society. 1979. Resolution on the child in hospital. *Dimensions in Health Services: Journal of the Canadian Hospital Association* 8:52–67
Cardoso, P. 1991. A parent's perspective: Family-centered care. *Children's Health Care* 20:258–60
Cassell, S. 1965. Effect of brief puppet therapy upon the emotional responses of children undergoing cardiac catheterization. *Journal of Consulting Psychology* 29:1–8
Cataldo, M.F., Bessman, C.A., Parker, L H., Pearson, J.E.R., and Rogers, M.C. 1979. Behavioral assessment for pediatric intensive care units. *Journal of Applied Behavior Analysis* 12:83–97
Child Life Council. n.d. *Official documents*. Bethesda, MD
Dahlquist, L.M., Gill, K.M., Armstrong, D., DeLawyer, D.D., Green, P., and Wuori, D. 1986. Preparing children for medical examinations: The importance of previous medical experience. *Health Psychology* 5:249–59
Dearden, R. 1970. The psychiatric aspects of the case study sample. In M. Stacey (ed.), *Hospitals, children and their families: The report of a pilot study*. London: Routledge and Kegan Paul
Demarest, D.S., Hooke, J.G., and Erickson, M.T. 1984. Preoperative intervention for the reduction of anxiety in pediatric surgery patients. *Children's Health Care* 12:179–83

Dimock, H. 1959. *The child in hospital: A study of his emotional and social well-being.* Toronto: Macmillan

Douglas, J. 1975. Early hospital admissions and later disturbances of behavior and learning. *Developmental Medicine and Child Neurology* 17:456–80

Dunn, H.L. 1959. High level wellness for man and society. *American Journal of Public Health* 49:786–92

Edelston, H. 1943. Separation anxiety in young children: A study of hospital cases. *Genetic Psychology Monographs* 28:3–95

Erickson, F. 1958. Play interviews for four-year-old hospitalized children. *Monographs for the Society of Research in Child Development* 23(3)

Evler, G.L. 1982. Nonmedical management of the failure-to-thrive child in a pediatric inpatient setting. In P. Accardo (ed.), *Failure to thrive in infancy and early childhood.* Baltimore: University Park Press

Faust, J. and Melamed B. 1984. Influence of arousal, previous experience, and age on surgery preparation of same day of surgery and in-hospital pediatric patients. *Journal of Consulting and Clinical Psychology* 52:359–65

Ferguson, B.F. 1979. Preparing young children for hospitalization: A comparison of two methods. *Pediatrics* 64:656–64

Ferguson, B.F. and Robertson, J. 1979. Making hospital preparation child-centered (with a little help from Emily). *Journal of the Association for the Care of Children in Hospitals* 8:27–31

Ferguson, R.V. 1986. Hospital environments for children. *Paedovita* 1:61–9

Gaynard, L., Hausslein, E., and DeMarsh, J.P. 1989. Child life specialists: Report of an observational study. *Children's Health Care* 18:75–81

Gaynard, L., Wolfer, J., Goldberger, J., Thompson, R., Redburn, L., and Laidley, L. 1990. *Psychosocial care of children in hospitals: A clinical practice manual.* Bethesda, MD: Association for the Care of Children's Health

Goldberger, J. 1990. Issue-specific play with infants and toddlers in hospitals: Rationale and intervention. *Children's Health Care* 16:134–41

Guttentag, D.N.W., Albritation, W.L., and Kettner, R.B. 1983. Daytime television programming. *Pediatrics* 71 (4):620–5

Hall, D.J. 1977. *Social relations and innovation: Changing the state of play in hospitals.* London: Routledge

Hall, D. and Cleary, J. 1988. The development of play for children in hospitals: British and European perspectives. *Children's Health Care* 16:223–30

Ispa, J., Barrett, B., and Kim, Y. 1988. Effects of supervised play in a hospital waiting room. *Children's Health Care* 16:195–200

Jacobs, R. 1979. The meaning of hospital: Denial of emotions. In D. Hall and M. Stacey (eds.), *Beyond separation: Further studies of children in hospital.* London: Routledge and Kegan Paul

Jessner, L., Blom, G.E., and Waldfogel, S. 1952. Emotional implications of tonsillectomy and adenoidectomy on children. *Psychoanalytic Study of the Child* 7:126–69

Kenny, N. 1990. *Shaping the future of children's health care.* Keynote address at the annual conference of the Association for the Care of Children's Health, Washington, DC

Larsen, C. 1979. L'enfant hospitalisé. *L'infirmière canadienne* 21:24–7

–. 1980. The child life professions: Today and tomorrow. In *Child life: An overview*. Washington, DC: Association for the Care of Children's Health

–. 1983. The child life worker's contribution within an oncology setting. In J.E. Schowalter, P.R. Patterson, M. Tallmer, A.H. Kutscher, S.V. Gullo, and D. Peretz (eds.), *The child and death*. New York: Columbia University Press

Letts, M., Stevens, L., Coleman, J., and Kettner, R. 1983. Puppetry and doll play as an adjunct to pediatric orthopedics. *Journal of Pediatric Orthopedics* 3:605–9

Levy, D.M. 1945. Psychic trauma of operations in children and a note on combat neurosis. *American Journal of Diseases in Children* 69:7–25

Lindquist, I. 1977. *Therapy through play*. London: Arlington

McClowry, S.G. and McLeod, S.M. 1990. The psychosocial responses of school-age children to hospitalization. *Children's Health Care* 19:155–61

McCue, K. 1988. Medical play: An expanded perspective. *Children's Health Care* 16:157–61

McCue, K., Wagner, M., Hansen, H., and Rigler, D. 1978. Survey of a developing health care profession: Hospital 'play' programs. *Journal of the Association for the Care of Children in Hospitals* 7:15–22

Mather, P.L. and Glasrud, P.H. 1981. Child life workers: Who are they and what are they doing? *Children's Health Care* 10:11–13

Melamed, B.G. and Siegel, L.J. 1975. Reduction of anxiety in children facing hospitalization and surgery by use of filmed modeling. *Journal of Consulting and Clinical Psychology* 43:511–21

–. 1980. *Behavioral medicine: Practical applications in health care*. New York: Springer

Olds, A.R. 1978. Psychological considerations in humanizing the physical environment of pediatric outpatient and hospital settings. In E. Gellert (ed.), *Psychosocial aspects of pediatric care*. New York: Grune and Stratton

Parish, L. 1986. Communicating with hospitalized children: Words are not enough. *Canadian Nurse* 82:21–4

Parish, L. and Bean, N. 1987. An activity house at the Children's Hospital of Eastern Ontario: Rain or shine, outdoors is fine. *Children's Environment Quarterly* 4 (3):42–3

Parish, L. and Johnson, P. 1987. Charting in the medical records: Guidelines for child life workers. *Children's Health Care* 16:28–33

Pearson, J.E.R., Cataldo, M., Tureman, A., Bessman, C., and Rogers, M.C. 1980. Pediatric intensive care unit patients. *Critical Care Medicine* 8:64–7

Peterson, L. and Ridley-Johnson, R. 1980. Pediatric hospital responses to survey on prehospital preparation for children. *Journal of Pediatric Psychology* 5:1–7

Phillips, R.D. 1985. Whistling in the dark?; A review of play therapy research. *Psychotherapy* 22:752–60

–. 1988. Play therapy in health care settings: Promises never kept? *Children's Health Care* 16:182–7

Plank, E.N. 1971. *Working with children in hospitals* (2nd ed.). Chicago: Year Book Medical Publishers. (1st edition published in 1962, Cleveland: Case Western Reserve University.)

Popper, B. 1990. A parent's perspective: The changing role of parent involvement in the health care system. *Children's Health Care* 19:242–3

Prugh, D.G., Straub, E.M., Sands, H.H., Kirshbaum, R.M., and Lenihan, E.A. 1953. A study of the emotional reactions of children and their families to hospitalization and illness. *American Journal of Orthopsychiatry* 23:70–106

Quinton, D. and Rutter, M. 1976. Early hospital admissions and later disturbances of behavior. *Developmental Medicine and Child Neurology* 18:447–59

Rae, W.A., Worchel, F.F., Upchurch, J., Sanner, J.H., and Daniel, C.A. 1989. The psychosocial impact of play on hospitalized children. *Journal of Pediatric Psychology* 14:617–727

Roberts, M., Maieron, M., and Collier, J. 1988. *Directory of psychosocial policies and programs*. Washington, DC: Association for the Care of Children's Health

Rubin, S. 1992. What's in a name: Child life and the play lady legacy. *Children's Health Care* 21:4–13

Schwartz, B.H., Albino, J.E., and Tedesco, L.A. 1983. Effects of psychological preparation on children hospitalized for dental operations. *Journal of Pediatrics* 103:634–8

Sides, J.P. 1977. Emotional responses of children to physical illness and hospitalization (PhD dissertation, Auburn University). *Dissertation Abstracts International*, 1978, 38: 917–B

Simons, B., Bradshaw, J., and Silva, P.A. 1980. Hospital admissions during the first five years of life: A report from the Dunedin multidisciplinary child development study. *New Zealand Medical Journal* 91:144–7

Singletary, G. 1991. Infant education team. *Child Life Council Bulletin* 9:4

Skinner, L. 1987. Paper presented at the annual conference of the Child Life Council, Halifax, Nova Scotia

Spinetta, J.J. and Maloney, L.J. 1975. Death anxiety in the outpatient leukemia child. *Pediatrics* 56:1,034–7

Spitz, R. 1945. Hospitalism: An inquiry into the genesis of psychiatric conditions in early childhood. In R. Eissler, A. Freud, M. Kris, and A. Solnit (eds.), *The psychoanalytic study of the child*, Vol.1. New York: International Universities Press

Stacey, M., Dearden, R., Rill, R., and Robinson, D. 1970. *Hospitals, children and their families*. London: Routledge

Stocking, M., Rothney, W., Grosser, G., and Goodwin, R. 1972. Psychopathology in the pediatric hospital — implications for community health. *American Journal of Public Health* 62: 551–6

Thompson, R.H. 1985. *Psychosocial research on pediatric hospitalization and health care*. Springfield, IL: Charles C. Thomas

Thompson, R.H. and Stanford, G. 1981. *Child life in hospitals: Theory and practice*. Springfield, IL: Charles C. Thomas

Turner, G.T. and Mapa, J. 1979. *Humanizing hospital care*. Toronto: McGraw-Hill Ryerson

United States Public Health Service, Office of the Surgeon General. 1979. *Healthy people: The Surgeon General's report on health promotion and disease prevention*. Washington, DC: Department of Health, Education, and Welfare

Veeneklaas, G. 1971. Psychosocial guidance in a children's hospital. *Newsletter, American Association for Child Care in Hospitals*. Sept., 2–3

Vernon, D.T.A., Foley, J.M., Sipowizc, R.R., and Schulman, J.L. 1965. *The psycho-*

logical responses of children to hospitalization and illness. Springfield, IL: Charles C. Thomas

Viau-Chagnon, M. and Tallboy, F. 1982. Le rôle de l'éducateur auprès des enfants mourants. *Santé mentale au Québec* 1 (2):74–8

Visintainer, M.A. and Wolfer, J.A. 1975. Psychological preparation for surgical pediatric patients: The effect on children's and parents' stress responses and adjustment. *Pediatrics* 56:187–202

Williams, Y.B. and Powell, M. 1980. Documenting the value of supervised play in a pediatric ambulatory care clinic. *Journal of the Association for the Care of Children's Health* 9:15–20

Wilson, J.M. 1979. Child life. In P.J. Valletutti and F. Christopolos (eds.), *Preventing physical and mental disabilities: Multidisciplinary approaches.* Baltimore: University Park Press

Wolfer, J., Gaynard, L., Goldberger, J., and Nicholson-Laidley, L. 1987a. A final report on the ACCH research project to measure the effects of child life programs on stress, coping, and adjustment in hospitalized children. Paper presented at the annual conference of the Association for the Care of Children's Health, Halifax, Nova Scotia

Wolfer, J., Gaynard, L. Goldberger, J., Laidley, L., and Thompson, R. 1987b. An experimental evaluation of a model child life program. *Children's Health Care* 16:244–54

6
Child Day Care in Canada: A Child and Youth Care Perspective
Alan Pence, Patricia Canning, and Sandra Griffin

Child day care is usually defined as non-familial, full, or part-time care of children while their parents work or study. While this care is offered in a variety of licensed and unlicensed settings which are either home-based or centre-based, this chapter will review the history and the present status of *centre-based child day care in Canada*, its role in relationship to families and the labour force, its changing importance in contemporary society, its service and regulatory structures, and its training requirements at the undergraduate degree level within the context of a child and youth care perspective.[1]

The nomenclature which identifies this area within the broad scope of child and youth care has been in transition for a number of years. At present, the terms 'day care,' 'child day care,' and 'child care' are used interchangeably.

History

The history of organized group day care in Canada goes back over 160 years to the 1820s. Infant schools were the first group day care centres supported from sources other than parental payment alone and were intended, in part, to serve the child caring needs of working parents. The infant schools established in both Canada and in the United States were based on earlier British models; the 'golden age' of the infant school movement in North America was the late 1820s and the early 1830s. The factors contributing to the development of these early day care programs and those effecting their demise have, in large part, continued to exist throughout the long history of day care in Canada. These influencing factors have contributed to day care's unique, multifaceted identity today. Various aspects of that identity will be considered briefly in the following section.

By 1830 infant schools had developed three specific models, each appealing to or developed for a different stratum of society or for a different child population. The three models were: Robert Owen's employment-driven model; The London Infant School Society's social concern model; and the North American development of these two forms in a 'school preparation' model (Pence 1986).

Owen's model, the earliest of the three, was the most closely tied to familial needs arising from increased industrial labour force participation. During the early part of the industrial revolution women were viewed as integral members of the new labour force. Robert Owen, an industrialist in the early 1800s, had purchased a textile mill in New Lanark, Scotland. In his desire to make New Lanark a model industrial town, he established an 'Institution for the Formation of Character.' This institution, or school, contained an infant school for the children of the families working in the New Lanark mill. Children from the 'age at which they could walk' were able to attend the school while their parents worked (Owen 1841). The plan was conceived as both a service to the working families and a positive learning environment for the young children. Owen was quite specific in his directions to the male and female teachers hired to work in the infant school. In strong contrast with schooling practices at that time, the children were not to be beaten or forced to engage in rote activities. Song, dance, and outside exercise were all parts of Owen's curriculum.

Owen's experiment attracted attention both within and outside Britain. It had particular appeal for a group of London philanthropists, who visited New Lanark on several occasions and ultimately hired Owen's own infant school instructor, Mr. Buchanan, to be the founding instructor in a London-based infant school. Other programs in London soon followed. However, the motivation for the creation of the London-based programs was considerably different from that which had motivated Owen's experiments. Well-to-do Londoners were extremely concerned about the large numbers of young children who populated the streets and learned various means — most often illegal — to survive on them. These children were major contributors to London's high crime rates. To many of the good citizens of London, the infant schools represented both a means of getting these children off the streets and, not incidentally, a way of instructing them about issues near to the hearts of the city fathers, such as property rights and the ways of good citizenry. Lord Brougham, one of the philanthropists responsible for bringing Buchanan to London, noted that 'planting a sufficient number of Infant Schools for training and instructing those classes of people will at once solve the problem of prevention' (Roberts 1972:155). These programs of social control and instruction can be considered the 'London model.'

The principal advocate of the London model was Samuel Wilderspin, an individual engaged by the London Infant School Society to travel throughout the British Isles propagating the model and its accompanying rationale. The pedagogical approach utilized by Wilderspin was adapted from the Lancasterian or monitorial model of instruction, whereby older child monitors were appointed to watch over groups of younger children while a central instructor lectured about the focal topic. Wilderspin noted in one of his publications that, by such means, 'it is possible to have two-hundred or even three-hundred children assembled together, the oldest not more than six years of age, and yet not have one of them cry for a whole day' (Albany Infant School Society 1829:7).

Knowledge of the infant schools came to North America in the mid-1820s and was represented there by both the Owenite and the London models. Because the London model was better documented (through accounts in a number of magazines and newspapers), it became the more common model for North American programs. In North America, however, another factor influenced the creation of these programs, as was summarized in the editorial of an 1820s Boston newspaper article: 'at the age of entering primary schools these *poor* children will assuredly be the *richest* scholars. And why should a plan which promises so many advantages, independent of merely relieving the mother from her charge, be confined to children of the indigent?' (May and Vinovskis 1977:79). Given this additional impetus, infant schools rapidly spread the length of the Atlantic seaboard, 'from Halifax to Charleston.'

Many of the rationales and forms of programs that are familiar today were evident in North America as early as the 1830s. Then, as now, programs were developed as a resource for working parents and also as a way to ensure that children received the benefits of 'early instruction.' In addition, similar to the current attempts to correct the effects of a 'deprived' or 'disadvantaged' environment on young children, programs were often designed to 'reform' children from poor home situations.

The flowering of day care under a variety of sponsors and using a variety of approaches was short-lived in North America. By 1840 virtually all infant school programs had ceased to function — the result of fundamental changes in family and economic life in the pre-1850 period.

The early nineteenth century in both Great Britain and in North America witnessed a significant shift in both the location and the economic base of family life. The transition was away from rural settings with largely self-sufficient households towards urban locations of wage-based employment. The onset of industrialization brought with it major expansion of urban centres and fundamental, significant shifts in family structure and responsibilities. Initially, as seen in New Lanark, it appeared that women as well as men would no longer be at home with their children but would be employed in the factories. It was necessary to provide alternative care for the children of these workers. During this period, day care received the support of the public and politicians. However, after an initial movement towards both male and female occupation outside of the home in urban centres, requirements for female labour lessened and a new model of the family emerged. This change in family members' responsibilities lessened the need for day care services and indelibly stamped one particular family model on the North American psyche.

The new family model, termed the Victorian family by some (Strickland 1983), defined specific spheres of influence for men and women. Men (fathers) became the breadwinners while women (mothers) became the keepers of the house. The world of men was that of business and competition, 'the turmoil and bustle of an active, selfish world'; women were the domesticators, as delicate and refined as the 'haven from strife' for which they alone had responsibility (Kraditor 1968:47). Part of the responsibility of mothers within the family circle was as caregivers to their children; insofar as mothers were expected to be their children's primary caregivers, there was no need for such programs outside the home. Thus, the creation and popularization of the Victorian family spelled the end of the infant school movement.

The Victorian family model, with its tightly defined roles and responsibilities for both parents and children, remained the dominant family ideal throughout the remainder of the nineteenth century and past the midway point of the twentieth century. In Canada, the rurally based, domestically centred family was numerically larger than families reflecting the Victorian model for well into the twentieth century, but the latter had enormous power as a model to be emulated. Most of us, our parents, and our grandparents were reared within its symbolic sway, and it is difficult for many to imagine social stability without its enforcing structure.

A change in acceptable male and female roles, albeit a temporary one, occurred during the Second World War. In addition to taking men far away from their homes, the war brought with it a need for women in Canadian industrialized urban centres to work in factories and other 'out-of-home' places that had traditionally been the domain of men. If women had to work, their children would need caregivers. Day care again became a national rather than a personal or familial need. The federal government offered cost-sharing of day care services with the provincial governments. The two most industrialized provinces — Ontario and Quebec — signed agreements. It is clear that this support of day care was for the 'war effort' and not to support working parents, as evidenced by the fact that in order to receive federal funding support, at least 75 per cent of the children in the programs had to have mothers working in 'essential industries' (that is, essential to the war effort). By 1946, the federal government had withdrawn all such funding; this reflected the general belief that now that the war was over families would return to 'normal,' with father employed out of the home and mother at home caring for the children.

The Contemporary North American Family

Although the Victorian family model has existed as fact and as ideal for a century and a half in North America, its zenith was reached in the post-Second World War period of 1945–55. In the flush of excitement accompanying a return to home, normalcy, and stability, families sought and found security in the roles of male breadwinner and female nurturing child rearer. The baby boom of the late 1940s and early 1950s was, in part, an affirmation of this return to the established ideals and roles of the Victorian family model.

This peak lasted for approximately one child-rearing generation; by the mid-1960s the children of that return to 'normalcy' were themselves of child-bearing age, and deep shifts in values and ideals, which would have profound effects on families and children, were becoming evident. There was an increase in marriage and divorce rates, a decline in typical family size and fertility rates, a significant increase in the number of female-headed, single-parent families, and a major increase in the number of married women in the out-of-home, paid labour force.

The marriage rate in Canada (which is calculated as the number of marriages per 1,000 single, widowed, and divorced population) has been strongly affected by broad social and economic events. A review of marriage statistics from 1921 to the present indicate this relationship. During the Great Depression of the 1930s, many marriages were postponed or cancelled and the marriage rate fell to a low of 653 per 1,000 for men and 660 per 1,000 for women. An unprecedented increase in the rate occurred with the onset of the Second World War. The rate soared to 1,228 for men and 1,212 for women by 1942 (includes remarriages). The period of the 1950s and 1960s, described as a 'prosperous and confident period' (Statistics Canada 1991:77), saw the maintenance of a high marriage rate at a relatively young age. The mean age for marriage was 25 years for men and 22.5 years for women. During this period only 5 per cent of Canadians were still single by the age of 50. The number of marriages in Canada peaked in 1972 (Statistics Canada 1990a). Beginning with the early 1970s, the marriage rate began a steady decline, while the average age for marriage began to rise. In 1987 and 1988 the number of marriages increased slightly. In addition, a significant phenomenon of the late 1980s was an increase in the prevalence of common-law unions. In the six-year period between 1984 and 1990, the percentage of Canadians aged 18–64 living in common-law unions rose from 17 to 28 per cent (Statistics Canada 1990b).

Divorce also has become more common in recent years. During the 1920s, the divorce rate per 100,000 was less than 8 per annum. Throughout the 1950s and early 1960s, the divorce rate was fairly stable at 35 to 40 per 100,000 population. Subsequent to the liberalization of the divorce laws in 1968, the rate of divorce soared: 148 in 1972; 235 in 1976; and almost 280 per 100,000 in 1981 (Statistics Canada 1983). By 1989 the divorce rate was 307.8 per 100,000 (Statistics Canada 1991).

While an increasing number of Canadians are getting married and divorced, the average household size has been decreasing. In 1961 the average family consisted of 3.9 people. Since then, the decline in family size has been steady. In 1976 the average family size was 3.5. By 1986 the average family size was 3.1. (Statistics Canada 1991). This decline is mainly attributable to lower fertility rates. The general fertility rate dropped from 116.6 in 1956 to 50.6 in 1986. The number of families having 4 or more children decreased from 16.4 per cent in 1961 to 8.7 per cent in 1981 (Statistics Canada 1981). By 1986, the number of families who had 4 or more children living at home was down to 5.4 per cent (Statistics Canada 1987).

The increase in divorce in recent years has resulted in an increase in single-parent families, the great majority of which are headed by females. While the number of male-headed families has remained fairly constant over the last twenty years, female-headed families have increased by almost 30 per cent. In 1982, Perreault and George suggested that Canada was on a steady course towards more single heads of families and projected that by 1991 an estimated 12 per cent of families would be headed by a single parent, and, of these, 80 per cent would be women. Indeed, by 1986, 12.7 per cent of families were headed by single parents and 82.2 per cent of these families were headed by lone-parent women.

Beginning in the late 1950s and accelerating through the 1960s and 1970s, the entry of an increasing number of women — more specifically, of mothers — into the labour force has been one of the most significant transformations in North American society in this century (see Figure 6.1). Increasingly, women are choosing to participate in out-of-home work in much the same way as men, although women are much more likely than men to hold part-time jobs with fewer benefits and less job security (Statistics Canada 1991). In 1988 women accounted for 44 per cent of the total Canadian labour force compared to 34 per cent in 1970 (Statistics Canada 1991).

The fastest growing segment of women in the labour force has been women with children, and the younger the age of the child the more rapid has been that group's increase in the labour force over the last ten years. A statistical report on women in Canada notes:

Prior to 1981, mothers with children aged 3 to 5 registered lower participation rates than women overall and such was the case until 1986 for mothers of younger children aged less than 3. In 1988, the participation rate for mothers with children under 3 years was 58.3%, slightly higher than the rate for all women (57.4%) and mothers with older preschool children aged 3 to 5 registered a rate of 65.1%. (Statistics Canada 1990a:75)

These trends reflect the economic necessity of two salaries to raise a family as well as changes which have occurred in the roles of women over the past twenty years. With the dramatic increase in the number of families with working mothers, there has been a re-evaluation of the role that child day care plays in Canadian society. Since the 1840s, child day care has been considered by most Canadians as a welfare-related service for that minority of families who do not fit the Victorian family ideal. However, the Victorian or traditional family model, where the father works in the paid labour force and the mother remains at

Figure 6.1

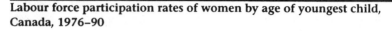

Labour force participation rates of women by age of youngest child, Canada, 1976–90

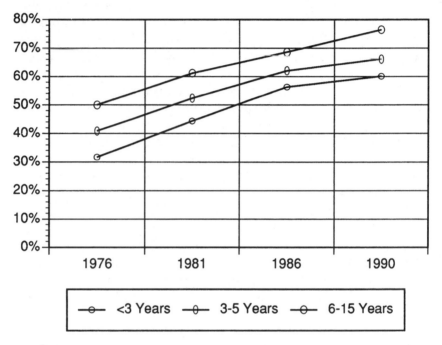

Source:
Statistics Canada, Women in Canada: A Statistical Report (1990). Catalogue 89-503E;
Statistics Canada, 1990 Labour Force Annual Averages. Catalogue 71-220

home as primary caretaker for the children, has now become a *minority* phenomenon, representing less than 33 per cent of families (Figure 6.2). The need for child day care is no longer restricted to the few; it is now a necessary service for the many. As a result of this significant change in Canadian family life, child day care has assumed a level of social and political importance heretofore unknown in Canada.

Beginning with the 1970 report by the Royal Commission on the Status of Women, followed closely by the First National Canadian Conference on Day Care in 1972, the issue of child day care has become an increasingly important policy issue. Commencing with the Second National Day Care Conference in Winnipeg in 1982, issues related to women in the labour force and the consequent need for child care assistance have been well covered in the popular media and were the sub-

Figure 6.2

Proportions of dual-earner, traditional and sole support one-parent families with at least one child younger than 13 years of age, Canada, 1988

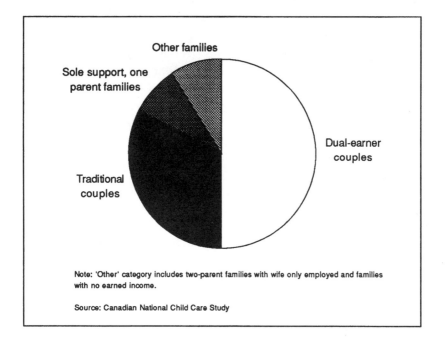

Other families

Sole support, one parent families

Dual-earner couples

Traditional couples

Note: 'Other' category includes two-parent families with wife only employed and families with no earned income.

Source: Canadian National Child Care Study

ject of a number of child care task forces in the 1980s. The Liberal government established a task force on child care within the Status of Women Office in May 1984. At the same time, an interprovincial task force on child care was also created, linking the provincial ministries responsible for the status of women. In November 1985, a special parliamentary committee on child care was formally announced by the Conservative government of Brian Mulroney. During the late 1980s and early 1990s, a number of provinces and, indeed, individual cities and municipalities established task forces to examine the need for, and issues related to, child day care. Reports and studies from these various task forces make a significant contribution to our greater understanding of the complex relationships among families, labour force participation, and child care needs.

Not since the period of the infant schools a century and a half earlier has there been such a high level of interest in and support for child care. As part of an announced National Child Care Strategy, Bill C-144, the Canada Child Care Act, was introduced in Parliament in July 1988. This controversial bill, which advocates protested would do little to improve the availability, affordability, and quality of child care in Canada, was delayed during a Senate review and died on the table when the September 1988 federal election was called. Although the Conservative government included a commitment for national child care legislation in both their 1984 and 1988 election campaigns, in February 1992 Minister of National Health and Welfare Benoit Bouchard announced that the government would not proceed with child care legislation. The minister presented his decision not to proceed with the national child care legislation as a matter of priorities. He announced a child-benefit package that he noted was intended to replace the child day care initiative on the government agenda. The intent of the benefit package, according to the federal government, was to focus on the estimated one million children who were living in poverty in Canada. Bouchard stated, in a media briefing, 'I had a choice to go on child care. I had a choice to go on this side. And I went on this side. The fact of the matter is I don't have the resources to do [both]' (Lavoie 1992:A11). A coalition of national organizations, which included the Canadian Day Care Advocacy Association, The National Action Committee on the Status of Women, the Canadian Labour Congress, the National Anti-Poverty Organization, and the Child Poverty Action group, denounced the initiative. The coalition stated that 'a comprehensive, high quality child care system must be a key part of a strategy to fight child poverty' (Canadian Day Care Advocacy Association 1992:1).

However, even in the absence of national child care legislation, a number of provinces have begun to undertake specific initiatives to increase both the quantity and quality of child care spaces. For example, the minister of community and social services in Ontario has stated that: 'Child care is a basic service, like schools and hospitals [and] publicly funded child care should be available for those who want and need them' (Ontario 1992a:1). The Ontario Child Care Reform consultation paper describes a provincial child care strategy based on the provision of high quality child care services that are affordable, accessible, and soundly managed (Ontario 1992b). In British Columbia, Finance and Corporate Relations Minister Glen Clark announced 17 million dollars for child care as part of the 1992 provincial budget, which included new responsibilities and new dollars for the Ministry for Women's Equality to 'provide for the coordination, analysis and implementation of programs which result in the stabilization of existing child care services; an increased number of child care spaces; and improved quality of services to children' (British Columbia 1992:214). Developments in the territories are underway as well. Based on extensive public consultations, a child care strategy for the Yukon was first announced by the minister of Yukon health and human resources in January 1989. The objectives of the strategy focused on increasing the availability, affordability, and quality of child care services in the Yukon (Yukon 1989).

Accompanying heightened interest in the further development of child care services taking place in a number of provinces and territories is a more generalized awareness of preschool children with special needs. Influenced in large part by recent legislation in the United States, promoting integrated services for young children, the impact of mainstreaming children with specials needs into child day care programs is being felt across the country (Canning and Lyon 1989).

The current debates and discussions go beyond the question of increased services to examine the broader social policy question of how parents can best be supported in their child-rearing activities. Changes in governmental and employer benefit structures, such as extensions of maternity and paternity leave, leave for child sickness days, assured labour force re-entry after extended time taken off for parenting duties, and changes in the tax structure supportive of parent options must all be considered in the debates regarding the future of child care in Canada (Canada 1986).

Although the broader parental benefits and services picture is part of child care discussions of the 1980s and 1990s, the focus for this chapter will remain on the more limited aspect of child day care *services* and, yet more specifically, on child day care centres in Canada. The following section will provide an overview of the Canadian child day care services structure, noting in particular the federal-provincial partnership which characterizes it.

Canadian Child Day Care Service: A Federal-Provincial Partnership
As noted earlier in this chapter, the creation and development of child day care services is intimately linked to family form and roles and to labour force characteristics and expectations. The shifts over the last two to three decades in these two major socioeconomic variables have altered the basis on which arguments for increased child day care services are being made. However, those arguments have yet to fundamentally alter the funding and regulatory systems on which such services have traditionally been based.

It is difficult to generalize about the Canadian child day care system because of its decentralized nature and the diversity of its composition and regulation across the provinces. The act by which Canada was declared a country, the British North America Act (BNA Act), designated which services were to be the responsibility of the Canadian federal government (such as defence and transportation) and those which were to be primarily the responsibility of the provinces (such as welfare and education). Since services to children and families were viewed as 'welfare' issues, these were considered a provincial matter. Child day care services were thus categorized within this welfare structure.

A century later, this welfare orientation was reflected in the Canada Assistance Plan (CAP) passed by Parliament in 1966. This plan provided for assistance to needy Canadians, who required financial assistance or who required social services to prevent, overcome, or alleviate the causes and effects of poverty or child neglect (Canada 1966). Under this act, the federal government agreed to provide matching funds to the provinces for various services, including child day care services to 'needy' Canadian families. Since child day care is no longer considered by many as a 'welfare' service but, rather, as a service required by the majority of Canadian families regardless of income, the appropriateness of CAP as the major vehicle for funding of child care services is increasingly under question. However, with no obvious plans in place to develop a national child care strategy, it is unlikely that alternate funding vehicles will be proposed by the federal government. In addition, in 1990 the federal government put a 'cap on CAP' for the three provinces considered to be 'have,' rather than 'have not,' provinces: British Columbia, Alberta, and Ontario. The consequence of this change is that the three provinces cannot cost share all expenditures related to the services delivered under CAP. It is difficult to project what the consequences of this change may be to the development and delivery of child day care services in these three provinces.

Since the provinces and territories are responsible for regulations governing child day care services, the regulations are distinct and different from province to province. For example, staff to child ratios for children under the age of twelve months varies from a low of 1:3 in six provinces to a high of 1:7 in Nova Scotia. The total number of children allowed in any one child care facility varies from a low of fifty in Prince Edward Island and Newfoundland to no limit in seven other provinces and territories. Grants available to child care services in the provinces and territories span a range from start-up grants to salary enhancement grants, capital funds, renovation grants, relocation grants, and operating grants, to name a few. Some provinces and territories offer a broad range of these grants, while others offer only one or two.

Given this diversity in programs, regulations, and monies available in the provinces for child day care, a major debate in Canada has centred on the question of the quality that such care represents. Traditionally, discussions of quality in child care have centred on the regulations and the power of government to close facilities not meeting those guidelines. Typically, regulations establish a 'minimal' level of acceptable care, below which programs will not be allowed to remain open. Adequate funding to ensure enforcement of even those basic standards is, however, often lacking. The public may then be provided with a false sense of security regarding what the possession of a licence actually indicates and how well enforced those regulations may be.

Even when adequate funding is available for monitoring compliance with regulations, questions are often raised regarding the mechanical nature of regulations: square footage space requirements, number of toilet facilities, staff-child ratios, lighting, heating, and so on. The desirable aspect of such regulations is that they are measurable. However, what can be missed in such 'measurables' are the nature and quality of staff-child and child-child interaction, which, while not unrelated to questions of space and ratios, are at the heart of evaluating developmentally appropriate practice.

Even if it were possible to add this interactional element to the regulatory guidelines, the direct measure of such an element would be extremely challenging to monitor. No doubt the additional time required for monitoring would take away significantly from the already inadequate funds available for direct child care services. One way to create higher quality care for young children is to provide better trained professional caregivers.

Training for Child Day Care Employment

The knowledge we have accumulated in the past half-century highlights the need to consider the group care of young children as professional work. Such work requires specialized knowledge and training. However, the job of child day care workers has not been and is still not being perceived in all quarters as a 'professional' career. This is clearly reflected in the fact that in Canada only limited, if any, formal education or professional training is required for child day care employment. Interestingly, in a recent study on the wages and working conditions of child care staff in centre-based programs in Canada, 68 per cent of child care staff possessed some kind of postsecondary certificate, diploma, or degree compared to 41 per cent for the national employed labour force (Schom-Moffatt 1992). However, the postsecondary education reported in this figure was not confined to early childhood care and education related credentials. The percentage of child care staff with training specific to child care was 58 per cent (this figure includes workers who reported any ECCE-related credential, which would span the range from completion of a forty-hour training program to a degree earned at a college or university.)

While there is no one environment which is right for the needs of all children, we can say with some confidence that there are certain characteristics, both physical and human, that need to be present if we are to have developmentally positive and appropriate environments for children. The quality and organization of physical space, the availability of materials, and the numbers and abilities of adults involved are all related to quality care (Day and Sheehan 1974; Griffin 1986; Doherty 1991). It is the caregiver, however, who is central in the environment, and 'the interaction between caregiver and child is probably the most important indicator of quality' (Doherty 1991:ii).

It is widely reported and accepted that the quality of the staff determines to a high degree the quality of the program (Decker and Decker 1978). According to the U.S. National Day Care Study (Ruopp, Travers, Glantz, and Collen 1979), one important factor which affects the quality of a program is the presence of staff with specialized knowledge of child development, early childhood education, or child day care. In a recent review of the literature on factors related to quality care, Doherty (1991) states that:

> Research clearly indicates that caregivers with some college education and/or post secondary school training in child development or early childhood education exhibit higher rates of positive caregiver behaviours than do caregivers who have only a high school diploma or less. They are also more likely to provide developmentally appropriate activities for the children and children in their care receive higher scores on various measures of child development. (p. ii)

An examination of the existing requirements for the education and training of child day care workers in Canada shows no standard qualification accepted throughout the country. Several provinces do require a certain level of training for particular positions, while others require that a certain percentage of child day care workers in each centre be qualified. For example, in a number of provinces (such as Prince Edward Island and British Columbia) supervisors of centres are required to be graduates of recognized training programs and must possess prior child day care work experience. Others (such as Manitoba, Ontario, and Quebec) require postsecondary training but not experience. In some provinces, all staff must have some training (e.g., Prince Edward Island), while other provinces require that a certain percentage of staff in each centre be qualified (Manitoba, Quebec, and Nova Scotia). Still other provinces have no specific training requirements (e.g., New Brunswick, the Yukon, and the Northwest Territories) but do require good health and suitable personal qualities. This disparity in regulations is reflected in the diversity of child day care training programs available.

The education of child day care personnel is carried out through a variety of educational institutions operating at a number of levels. There are continuing education programs for those already in the workplace; vocational school programs, usually of less than a year's duration; one-, two-, and three-year community college certification and diploma programs; and four-year baccalaureate and postgraduate programs available to those pursuing a career working with the group care of young children. Most often the disciplinary context of these training programs is early childhood care and education, although child studies and child and youth care programs provide alternatives at the four-year degree and graduate degree levels in Canada.

The 'typical' child day care worker may have been through any one or none of these programs. The variability of staff training levels can be seen in Table 6.1, which is based on a 1991 wages and working conditions study (Schom-Moffatt 1992).

The need for a government commitment to establish the professional qualifications for child day care workers and the need for standardization of these qualifications across jurisdictions is great. Ontario's Ministry of Community and Social Services prepared a report which identified areas widely thought to be of importance in ECCE programs and then examined the curricula in various provinces to determine the extent to which there was agreement and consistency across training programs (Goelman 1992). Overall, the review concluded that while there was a significant amount of similarity in the content of ECCE training programs across Canada, there were noted differences in program length. In fact, the length of programs focused

Table 6.1

Early childhood care and education-related credentials, Canada and by province, 1991

	Percentage with credential			
Province	Any ECCE-related credential	ECCE-related certificate	ECCE-related diploma	ECCE-related bachelor's
BC	63	54	15	3
Alta.	28	16	13	3
Sask.	34	21	13	4
Man.	50	32	23	10
Ont.	79	26	50	7
Que.	50	29	24	7
NB	39	28	7	8
NS	64	29	21	19
PEI	46	31	13	4
Nfld.	44	20	15	14
Yukon	21	7	12	5
NWT	52	30	21	0
National	58	27	31	7

Source: Schom-Moffatt (1992)

on training child day care staff at the basic level ranges from forty-hour programs (completion of which is required to work in a centre in Saskatchewan) through to three-year diploma programs (such as the ones offered through community colleges in Quebec) and four-year degree programs offered through a number of training institutions in Canada.

It would be appropriate for there to be a number of different levels of qualification acceptable for different positions within the child day care profession. Many argue that program directors, supervisors, and administrators should be educated to at least a baccalaureate level, while certificate and diploma qualifications may be appropriate for staff with less extensive responsibilities. In fact, it can be suggested that there is a continuum of competency required which is reflective of the range of the simple to the complex demands of the field, and this range can be appropriately reflected in a continuum of articulated certificate, diploma, and degree programs which would train individuals to undertake a broader span of authority and increasingly complex responsibilities within the field. As competent practice and professionalism are intrinsically tied to education and career options, development of an education and career ladder is a significant challenge to the field in the coming years (Pence and Griffin 1991).

As indicated, there is a wide variety of education and training programs for this area within the broad scope of the child and youth care field. The following description will highlight the essential components of four-year degree level education and training programs within the context of a professional child and youth care orientation.

All degree programs preparing people to work with groups of young children in child day care should cover at least four essential curriculum areas: (1) liberal education; (2) human development within the context of family and society; (3) knowledge specific to the child day care profession; and (4) a substantive field placement experience.

Liberal Education
Professional programs must be based on a belief in the value of a liberal education. This is not exclusive to child and youth care but is true for all professions. A general education helps to promote the improvement and the advancement of any profession and indirectly affects the service provided by professionals. Liberal arts courses enhance students' breadth of knowledge, help to develop the ability to think critically and analytically, and enhance problem-solving and communication skills. Regardless of place or level of education, all students of child care should endeavour to enhance their general education.

Human Development within the Context of Family and Society
Specific professional education in child care has been expanding significantly in recent years. Traditionally, programs attempted to educate people to meet the needs of children within the child day care environment without reference to outside factors. The increasing knowledge of human development, and enormous changes in the family and our society, necessitate an ever-expanding professional knowledge base in order to meet the needs of children. The education and training of child day care personnel must address three specific areas. First, child day care workers must be knowledgeable about human development in order to provide a safe, stimulating, and appropriate environment for young children. Second, education and training must encompass an understanding of the family, its changing roles and needs, and the role of the child day care worker in supporting the family. Third, the child day care worker must be prepared as a 'professional' with a broad understanding of both social issues and changes that have direct relevance to the lives of children and the ways in which public policies affecting children evolve and are implemented. Each of these three specific areas will be described in greater depth.

Human Development

The essential component of the professional study of child day care is a sound knowledge of human growth and development, both normal and atypical. Human development courses must address the physical, cognitive, linguistic, social, and emotional aspects of development. Different theories on learning and development need to be examined.

Education and care at all levels have been influenced by different perspectives and a changing knowledge base. The study of human development must include an examination of its social, cultural, and political contexts. Students should remember that knowledge is constantly evolving and not accept it as 'truth.' A critical examination of knowledge is required of any discipline, and knowledge of the issues and questions as yet unanswered is as essential as knowing what has been explained.

Students must be familiar with the norms of development from birth through the early childhood years. The continuous, gradual, and orderly sequence of development as well as the variation in growth and development among individuals needs to be stressed, lest we 'shift from the child and his needs to the adult and his expectation' (Hirsch 1983). Typical and expected behaviour of two-, three-, and four- or five-year-olds is critical knowledge for those working with groups of children. In one study, Canning and Lyon (1984) reported a disproportionately high incidence of suspected behaviourally/emotionally troubled children being identified by child day care teachers as compared to teachers of older children. In this case, such findings may underscore the importance of ensuring that child day care personnel know what constitutes appropriate behaviour for youngsters, lest children be given inappropriate activities or are perceived as having problems because workers lack knowledge of normal development and behaviour.

Knowledge of normal development is also essential to an understanding of atypical development. Child day care centres are places for all children. Increasing numbers of children with suspected or identified handicapping conditions (that is, physical and/or sensory disabilities; developmental disabilities; mental retardation; speech and language problems; emotional disturbance; and/or special needs arising from abusing or neglecting families) are being enrolled in them. To ensure appropriate services and programs, child day care personnel must be able to work with other professionals to identify problems, interpret assessments, and initiate programs for each child and family in need of this special effort.

We cannot state with certainty what the effects of a specific group care experience will be for any individual child or group of children. However, Phillips and Howes note that twenty years of research suggests that children in 'good quality care show no signs of harm' (1986:1). In fact, a more common assertion today is that 'good care is good for children.' Nevertheless, anyone providing such care must examine the research investigating the effects of different kinds of 'out-of-home' care on child development and the potential implications of these findings.

Family
However long a child spends in child day care centres, the family remains the primary socializer (Bronfenbrenner 1974, 1979). According to the U.S. Federal Interagency Day Care Requirements (1980), day care must not only focus on and meet the needs of children enrolled but must also have a social services component that supports family functioning. Support and supervision of child day care in Canada is generally the responsibility of provincial departments or ministries of social services. Administratively, it is perceived as a service to families as well as to children. In fact, in the Ontario review of college training programs for child day care workers noted earlier in this chapter, this important role is acknowledged. Family studies was one of the key areas of curricula strongly endorsed in provincial focus group discussions.

Families exist in many forms. Recent changes in family structure and composition, especially the increase in single-parent families, highlights the need for an increasing sensitivity to children's home backgrounds. The changing nature of families must be recognized and understood by professionals working with children. However, regardless of the form families may take, the function that they play in the child's life and socialization are similar.

Nuclear families often do not function well in isolation, yet many families in today's mobile society lack any kind of extended family or neighbourhood support system; day care may be their only or most important support. It is becoming increasingly difficult for parents to find the support they need. In order to understand the modern family and establish positive and supportive relationships with families, child day care workers must be aware of other all available community services. Courses in the sociology of the family, families in different cultures and societies, the socialization of the child, or parent/child relations should be included in the core curriculum of a degree program.

Society

It is also important that students understand and examine factors in the child's wider social environment. The multicultural nature of Canadian society necessitates an awareness of the ethnic and cultural backgrounds from which children come. To meet the needs of children and their families, child day care workers must not only be able to plan and deliver programs which are culturally relevant and appropriate (Doherty 1991), they must also evidence culturally sensitive and anti-bias behaviour in their everyday interactions with children and families. Women's roles and the sex roles that are considered appropriate are changing, and child day care programs must reflect 'the importance of non-sexist approaches to early childhood practice in regard to developmentally appropriate non-sexist ... activities, gender equity, and role modeling' (Goelman 1992:36).

Technology is changing society and the needs of individuals. Values have changed and continue to do so. Students must develop some understanding of the way in which attitudes towards children and families are translated into the kinds of services provided. In order to be able to work effectively to improve services, they must also know how policies for children and families have evolved and are implemented within the federal and provincial political structure. Courses or components in government administration, social policy, contemporary society, and social issues, including an examination of ethical issues involved in providing group care and the laws and regulations affecting this provision, should be included.

Knowledge Specific to the Child Care Profession
The goal of the applied curriculum is to provide students with the skills required to develop and implement high quality programs for young children. A mentally and physically healthy and stimulating environment for young children does not happen by chance but requires short- and long-term goal setting and planning as well as sound organization and evaluation. Child day care workers must be able to meet each child's social, emotional, and physical needs and be able to manage groups of children effectively.

The child day care setting itself can be viewed as an ecological system in which all the elements influence the child's development. Many areas must be included in the professional preparation of child day care personnel. Courses or components in the following areas should be included in the core curriculum: (1) organizing a healthy and safe environment for young children; (2) meeting children's nutritional needs; (3) group management; (4) planning and implementing activities for young children; (5) curriculum development; (6) observation and assessment techniques; (7) techniques for evaluating children and programs; and (8) program administration.

Students need to develop skills which enable them to involve parents in the children's program. Child day care personnel must be responsible partners with parents and must consider parents' circumstances and desires. This is essential if the program is to benefit the child. At the very least, good communication with parents must be established so that parents feel that day care is an adjunct to, and not a substitute for, their care. Ideally, involvement will go much further. A number of provinces have legislation which requires non-profit child day care centres to have parent representatives on their boards of directors, as parent involvement is seen as a positive contribution to the quality of the programs (Doherty 1991).

Child day care personnel should be knowledgeable enough to offer support to parents. Parent education is the term most often used in this respect, but this education or help must be in response to parents' own perceived needs and not a professional 'how to parent' exercise. Sensitivity to parents' positions and circumstances and an accurate awareness of the child day care provider role is essential.

Students need to develop good oral and written communication skills in practical situations. As well as working and communicating effectively with children and parents, child day care personnel must be able to work effectively as members of the staff as well as with other professionals in the community.

The urgent need for improvement in the status and salaries of those caring for young children and in the funding of programs for children and families necessitates that child day care personnel be encouraged to first see themselves as 'professionals' and work towards being recognized as such. An integral part of a professional's responsibility is lobbying effectively and acting as an advocate for the services and programs in which she/he works. Since child day care is itself part of the emerging profession of child and youth care, professional and advocacy skills should be a priority.

Field Placement
Although few scientific evaluations of training are available, it is generally recognized that an essential component of child day care training

is actual work in centres providing child care. In fact, field placement is seen as a crucial component in the preparation of child day care workers (Goelman 1992). Fieldwork may be given concurrently with classroom training, or it may be provided in blocks of time during which there are no classes. Careful planning, coordination, and supervision are needed to maximize the learning potential of fieldwork.

Care must be taken in choosing the centres in which students are placed. Much of what the student will learn in the centre will be accomplished through modelling the caregiver. The student needs to be in an atmosphere which encourages learning through personal experience and also provides appropriate guidance. Expectations for the students must be consistent with their education and prior experience.

In order to assist the cooperating centres, the educational institution must provide clear goals and expectations for students and supervisors in written as well as oral form. The educational institution supervisor should be familiar with both the academic program and the actual work site. Major responsibility for student supervision should be assumed by those providing the direct service, with clear guidelines for evaluation provided by the institution and the centre in which the student is placed, preferably facilitated by on-site visits from the institution's supervisor.

The institutions seeking cooperating child day care centres must also recognize and acknowledge the extra work required of day care personnel when students join them. Some institutions offer small monetary rewards to centres, while others provide course credits at their institutions. Regardless of the form it takes, appreciation of the value placed on the professional contribution of child day care personnel with regard to educating future professions must be fully recognized.

Summary

Child day care is not a recent phenomenon in Canadian society. Its beginnings go back well over a century and a half. Child care programs, based primarily on the British infant school system, were in existence as early as the 1820s. In fact, during the 1820s and 1830s there was interest and development in the child care field, which, in some respects, was not unlike what we are experiencing today. Similarly, at that time there were also significant changes occurring in family structure and responsibility which often required both mothers and fathers to work outside the home. By the 1840s, however, the Victorian family model, with its specific and differentiated roles for mothers and fathers, was seen as the ideal family form. Women stayed at home and cared for the children while men worked outside the home as the primary wage earners. This situation continued for over a century, with only a minor interruption during the war years when women were required to work outside the home. At that time society responded by establishing day care centres for children. At war's end, however, women quickly returned to the home to care for their children, and day care centres closed abruptly. By the 1960s, society was once again going through changes that greatly affected family and work and which have resulted in an increasing interest in and need for day care provision.

The postwar generation was reaching maturity and beginning families by the mid- to late 1960s and early 1970s. In contrast to the relative social stability of the 1950s, the 1960s brought significant changes in society, which greatly affected the family structure. There was an increase in marriage, remarriage, and divorce rates. Families were becoming smaller and more mobile. There was an increase in the number of single-parent families, headed mostly by females who were required to seek employment outside the home in order to support their children. Married women with young children, particularly those with preschool children, were also joining the work force in unprecedented numbers: a result of both the women's movement and an economic situation which increasingly necessitated two salaries to support a family. These trends are continuing and are expected to do so into the twenty-first century.

Care for children outside the home is a necessity for the majority of families with young children in Canada today. Many families require support in raising their children. Such support was once more readily available through the extended family and community members, but, in our highly urban, mobile society, that function has been increasingly assumed by providers outside of informal kith and kin networks. And most of these children are cared for not in child day care centres but in informal, unregulated arrangements. While it is not possible to suggest, categorically, that such arrangements are of poor quality, research does indicate that there is an increased probability of the care provided in such unregulated arrangements being of poorer quality than that provided in regulated programs (Pence and Goelman 1991; Griffin 1986).

Child day care regulations do not adequately address the issue of quality. Regulations vary from province to province, but in all provinces they deal predominantly with such factors as space, lighting, heating, and staff-child ratios without attention to other variables, which may be more important indicators of the actual quality of the care being provided.

One way to increase the quality of care provided by child day care centres is through the education and training of staff. A recent study reported that just over half of child care staff working in centre-based child care services had some kind of early childhood related credential, and the variability the training programs represented, judging by the credentials, was substantial. There are a number of different levels of qualifications appropriate for different positions within the child day care profession. It is argued that program directors, supervisors, and administrators should be educated to at least a baccalaureate level, while certificate and diploma qualifications may be appropriate for other staff. Certificate, diploma, and degree programs in the field should be sufficiently articulated to ensure that an education and career ladder is well defined for those individuals who choose child day care as a profession.

An ecological approach is basic to any degree program preparing students to work with young children. In fact, the basic principles which define the child and youth care perspective include a focus on children within the context of their families and an understanding of children in their larger environment. As well, a child and youth care perspective includes an understanding of children from a normative developmental viewpoint. And last, but of equal importance, professionalism and professionalization in the field are intrinsically tied to the profession's ability to work as an advocate on behalf of children, families, and child day care workers.

The four main areas considered central to a degree program are: (1) liberal education; (2) human development within the context of family and society ; (3) knowledge specific to the child day care profession; and (4) a substantive field placement which allows students to put theory into practice.

Notes

1 It should be noted that while this chapter focuses primarily on child day care centres, the majority of child day care in Canada is provided by home-based caregivers, most of whom are unlicensed.

References

Albany Infant School Society. 1829. *Proceedings*. Albany, NY: Albany Christian Register

Bower, E.M. 1971. K.I.S.S. and kids: A model for prevention (key integrative social systems). *American Journal of Orthopsychiatry* 42:556–65

British Columbia. Ministry of Finance and Corporate Relations. 1992. *Budget estimates: Fiscal year ending March 31, 1993*. Victoria

Bronfenbrenner, U. 1974. Developmental research, public policy, and the ecology of childhood. *Child Development* 45:1–5

–. 1979. *The ecology of childhood*. Cambridge, MA: Harvard University Press

Canada. 1966. *Canada assistance plan*. Chapter 45. Ottawa: Queen's Printer

–. 1970. *Report of the royal commission on the status of women in Canada*. Ottawa: Information Canada

–. Department of Health and Welfare, National Day Care Information Centre. 1973–83. *Status of day care in Canada*. Ottawa

–. Federal Task Force on the Status of Women. 1986. *Report of the task force on child care*. Ottawa

Canadian Day Care Advocacy Association. 1992. *Bulletin*. Ottawa: Author

Canning, P. and Lyon, M. 1984. Community service needs of pre-school children and their families. Unpublished manuscript. Halifax, NS: Mount Saint Vincent University

–. 1989. Young children with special needs. *Canadian Journal of Education* 14:368–80

Day, D. and Sheehan, R. 1974. Elements of a better school. *Young Children* 30:15–23

Decker, C.A. and Decker, J.R. 1978. *Planning and administering early childhood programmes*. Columbus, OH: Charles B. Mont

Doherty, G. 1991. *Factors related to quality in child care: A review of the literature*. Ministry of Community and Social Services, Toronto

Dowley, E. 1971. Perspectives on early childhood education. In B.A. Anderson, and H.J. Shane (eds.), *As the twig is bent*. Boston, MA: Houghton-Mifflin

Fitzpatrick, E.A. 1911. *Educational views and influence of DeWitt Clinton*. New York, NY: Teachers College Press

Goelman, H. 1992. *Visions of program revision: A report on the early childhood education review project*. Vancouver: Early Childhood Educators of British Columbia

Griffin, S. 1986. Child day care in Canada: Translating research into policy. M.A. thesis, University of Victoria

Hirsch, E. 1983. *Problems of early childhood: An annotated bibliography and guide*. New York, NY: Garland

Kava, T. 1982. *Report on program standards for children in day care and day care staff qualifications*. Ministry of Education, Victoria

Kraditor, A.S. (ed.). 1968. *Up from the pedestal*. New York: Quadrangle Books

Lavoie, J. 1992. Scrapping national child-care scheme puts kids in real danger. *Victoria Times-Colonist*, 27 February

Manitoba. 1983. Manitoba regulation 148. The Community and Day Care Standards Act, Sec. 6. Winnipeg

May, D.L. and Vinovskis, M.A. 1977. A ray of millennial light: Early education and social reform in the infant school movement in Massachusetts 1826–1840. In T. Hareven (ed.), *Family and Kin in Urban Communities*. New York: New Viewpoints

New Brunswick. Department of Social Services. 1984. *Standards for day care facilities.* Fredericton

Nova Scotia. 1978. Day care act and regulations. *Statutes of Nova Scotia.* Halifax: Queen's Printer

Ontario. Ministry of Community and Social Services. 1984. *Standards for day care nurseries.* Toronto

–. 1992a. *The parents' newspaper.* Toronto

–. 1992b. Child care reform in Ontario: Setting the stage. A public consultation paper. Toronto

Owen, R. 1841. Address on opening the institution for the formation of character at New Lanark, delivered on the first day of January, 1916: Being the first public announcement of the discovery of the infant school system. London: Home Colonization Society

Pence, A. 1986. Infant schools in North America, 1825–1840. In S. Kilmer (ed.), *Advances in early education and day care.* Greenwich, CN: JAI

Pence, A. and Goelman, H. 1991. The relationship of regulation, training, and motivation to quality of care in family day care. *Child and Youth Care Forum* 20:83–101

Pence, A. and Griffin, S. 1991. A window of opportunity: Part II. *Interaction* 5:24–9

Perreault, J. and George, M.V. 1982. Growth of households and families in Canada in the 1980s and 1990s. *Canadian Statistical Review* 57:vi–xv

Phillips, D. and Howes, C. 1986. Indicators of quality child care: Review of research. In D. Phillips (ed.), *Quality in Child Care: What Does Research Tell Us.* Washington, DC: National Association for the Education of Young Children

Prince Edward Island. Child Care Facilities Board. 1980. *Guidelines to the regulations for child care facilities act.* Charlottetown

Quebec. 1983. Child day care act. *Gazette officielle de Québec* 115 (44). Quebec City

Roberts, A.F.B. 1972. A new view of the infant school movement. *British Journal of Educational Studies* 20:154–64

Ruopp, R., Travers, J., Glantz, F., and Collen, C. 1979. *Children at the center.* Cambridge, MA: Abt Books

Schom-Moffatt, P. 1992. *Caring for a living: A national study on wages and working conditions in Canadian child care.* Ottawa: The Canadian Child Day Care Federation and The Canadian Day Care Advocacy Association

Statistics Canada. Ministry of Supply and Services. 1979. *Canada's families.* Ottawa: Supply and Services

–. 1981. *Canada's families.* Ottawa: Supply and Services

–. 1983. *Divorce: Law and the family in Canada.* Ottawa: Supply and Services

–. 1987. *The nation: Families: Part 1.* Catalogue 93–106. Ottawa: Supply and Services

–. 1990a. *Women in Canada: A statistical report.* Catalogue 89–503E. Ottawa: Supply and Services

–. 1990b. *Report on the demographic situation in Canada 1990.* Catalogue 91–209E. Ottawa: Supply and Services

–. 1991. *Canada yearbook 1992.* Catalogue 11-402E/1992. Ottawa: Supply and Services

Strickland, C. 1983. Victorian domesticity. Unpublished manuscript. Georgia: Emory University

United States. Department of Health, Education, and Welfare. 1980. *Federal Interagency Day Care Requirement — F.I.D.C.R.* Washington, DC

Yukon. 1980. *Yukon day care regulations.* Order in council. Whitehorse

–. Ministry of Health and Human Resources. 1989. *Working together: A child care strategy for the Yukon.* Whitehorse

7

Infant Development Programs

Dana Brynelsen, Helen Cummings, and Valerie Gonzales

Introduction

This chapter will provide a brief overview of infant development programs in Canada and the major social, political, and legal forces which have contributed to their growth.[1] Infant development programs are one of many forms of health, education, or social services designed to provide early intervention for infants at risk for developmental problems or diagnosed as delayed or disabled. Early intervention refers to those procedures which restructure the environment in order to facilitate the development of an infant or young child. Infant development programs in Canada, as described in this chapter, are primarily home-based and provide services to families with infants from newborns to three years old. It should be noted, however, that some populations of disabled infants, such as the visually impaired or hearing impaired, may be served by more specialized resources.

Like other human services in Canada, infant development programs vary considerably from province to province and from community to community. This wide variation in programs makes it impossible to provide a detailed description of these services. However, this chapter will cover some similar and dissimilar features that relate to program objectives, population serviced, services provided, and parent involvement as well as provide a historical perspective on the development of services for disabled or delayed infants and preschoolers, a description of the skills and knowledge base required by infant development program staff, and an outline of current trends in the field.

Programs for delayed and disabled infants and young children form part of the range of services for persons with disabilities in many parts of Canada. Some of these services have their roots in developments which took place in the nineteenth and early twentieth centuries. These included services for persons with visual and hearing impairment or mental disabilities. However, services for persons with disabilities developed largely after the Second World War and reflect changes in society's perception of people with disabilities. Changing social values and attitudes towards persons with disabilities have led to increasing acceptance of and support for their right to participate as fully as possible in the communities in which they live.

These changes have been accompanied and strengthened by an advanced understanding of handicapping conditions and by the development of effective strategies for ameliorating the impact of a handicap. New concepts about the nature of intelligence and the potential contribution of facilitating environments towards intellectual development have also contributed to development of services; they represent significant departures from concepts held in the past.

Prior to the Second World War, intelligence was widely considered to be 'fixed.' It was thought that a person was destined at birth, by genetic endowment, to be either bright, normal, or slow. With few exceptions, professionals and the public alike did not consider environmental factors to have much influence on the development and growth of a child. This was particularly true of children with mental disabilities. Mental retardation was believed to be inherited, incurable, and irremediable (Blatt 1971). It followed, therefore, that the professional advice given to families of children with severe mental disabilities was largely negative; families were encouraged to abdicate responsibility for these children. Institutionalization was an accepted and common practice. Families who chose to keep a mentally disabled son or daughter at home had little support. Children with severe mental disabilities were not eligible for school. Descriptions of the low level of functioning of institutionalized or isolated persons in the community perpetuated the myth that persons with mental disabilities were 'ineducable' and were 'threats' to society.

The Second World War and the period following brought many changes to North America. One major change was the awakening of North Americans to their prejudices and practices relating to minority groups. Although the Civil Rights Movement had its roots in racial issues, it rapidly expanded to encompass discrimination towards other groups, including persons with disabilities. In the late 1940s and early 1950s, parents of children with disabilities formed local, provincial or state, and national associations for the mentally disabled. A primary goal of such parents' groups was to create educational opportunities for their sons and daughters. In a direct challenge to professional beliefs, these parents believed that their children could learn and would benefit from an education. Families of significant political and social stature, such as the Kennedy family in the United States, joined this movement.

In 1961, President John F. Kennedy formed the President's Committee on Mental Retardation, which had a mandate to prepare a national plan to combat mental retardation. The president's committee stressed the need for service in areas such as early diagnosis, home support, and early education. Services developed were to be comprehensive and community centered and were to provide a continuum of care. Within three years, major changes were made to American federal legislation, and comprehensive planning was underway in every American state (Kott 1971).

Public interest and support for services for children with mental disabilities or those at risk for school failure was accompanied by a rapid growth of research in the field of child development. In 1961, the notion of 'fixed' intelligence was challenged by the publication of Hunt's *Intelligence and Experience*. This was followed by a number of other landmark works which asserted that environmental experiences may alter the developmental course of infants and children (Skeels 1966), and that early years were 'critical' periods for such changes (Bloom 1964). Although subsequent analysis of earlier research (Clarke and Clarke 1976) has resulted in a more temperate view of the importance of some aspects of experience in infancy, the myth that mental retardation is inherited, incurable, and irremediable was shattered. As a result of these findings and in response to public pressure, the American federal government passed legislation in 1968 to fund model preschool programs, such as Headstart, for children with disabilities.

In some ways, Canadian interest and development of services paralleled the American experience. The parental movement in mental retardation spread as quickly in Canada as it did in the United States. Between 1948 and 1970, 320 local chapters of the Canadian Association for the Mentally Handicapped were created by local parent initiatives across Canada (National Institute on Mental Retardation 1981). In 1964, three years after the creation of the President's Committee on Mental Retardation in the United States, Ottawa sponsored the first Canadian federal/provincial conference on mental retardation in Canada.

Judy LaMarsh, minister of national health and welfare, stated that 'the main purpose of the conference was to indicate practical steps that might be taken to coordinate and improve services for mentally retarded persons' (LaMarsh 1965:v). Throughout the proceedings, participants reiterated the need for early education, including home visiting programs, staffed by trained persons, to establish adaptive programs of home care early in the child's life.

Unlike the United States, however, the Canadian federal government has much less jurisdiction over the provinces in matters relating to health, education, and welfare. Therefore, nation-wide reforms were much less evident in Canada. Nonetheless, by the mid-1970s parents and professionals in every Canadian province were discussing, planning, or implementing programs for infants and preschoolers with developmental problems. Canadian interest in this area was not generated solely by American research and social reform. Other major influences were the normalization movement, the reallocation of federal and provincial funds under the Canada Assistance Plan, and the support and influence of public health nurses.

The concept of normalization was first formulated in Denmark in 1959, when it was incorporated into Danish law governing services for persons with mental disabilities (Bank-Mikkelsen 1969). One definition of normalization was: 'making available to the mentally retarded, patterns and conditions of every day life which are as close as possible to the norms and patterns of the mainstream of society' (Wolfensberger 1972:27). This concept spread throughout Europe and Canada and was adopted in principle in the early 1970s by the Canadian Association for the Mentally Retarded. The era of institutionalization of infants and young children was drawing to a close. Families were choosing to keep sons and daughters at home, and they looked to the community for support and education. In many communities, this support was developed by parent associations of the mentally disabled; it involved group programs for preschool children and home visiting services for infants. A new cost-sharing federal/provincial formula under the Canadian Assistance Plan emerged in the early 1970s, and provincial governments had increased monies available to fund community-based programs for infants and preschoolers with disabilities. Public health nurses — strong advocates of service to families with children with developmental problems — were influential in many areas. Thus, parent interest, available government funds, and professional support from public health nurses were factors which contributed to the rapid growth of many services for infants and children with disabilities in the early 1970s. Among these services were infant development programs.

Components of Infant Development Programs

Growth of Services

Infant development programs vary significantly across Canada (Shipe 1985; Kendall, Brynelsen, and Lapierre 1985) for a variety of reasons. In a survey of Canadian early intervention programs conducted in 1985, there were 138 infant programs employing 410 staff. In 1990, an attempt was made to update the survey. Responses were received from half the provinces, and when these statistics were added to the 1985 figures, it indicated that there were at least 189 programs employing 517 staff (Brynelsen 1990). The field continues to expand in each province, and, thus far, no province has cut back this service once it has become established. However, because there is no legal mandate, federally or provincially, for the specific provisions of these services, no standard federal or provincial database exists.

Administration and Program Coordination

In the early years, many local programs developed before expert assistance was available (Sauer 1975). This is still the case in some provinces. Only British Columbia, Newfoundland, Nova Scotia, and Alberta have full-time provincial coordinators available to advise, train, monitor local staff, and encourage standard practices. Saskatchewan has a part-time provincial coordinator, and the Prince Edward Island coordinator is available only for programs serving mentally disabled children (Brynelsen 1990).

Provincial guidelines for the operation of infant development programs were published in British Columbia (Brynelsen 1992) and are now an integral part of the ministry contracts that the provincial government draws up with the sponsoring societies of each infant program. In 1985, Saskatchewan revised the guidelines it had adopted from British Columbia, and, in 1986, Ontario established new guidelines for the operation of its programs (Marfo 1991). Additionally, British Columbia has a provincial steering committee composed of parents and professionals, whose mandate it is to provide direction and support to staff and programs, to advise the government on the operation of the infant program, and to assist in the development of staff training and program evaluation. A similar structure now exists in Alberta and Saskatchewan, although neither province appears to involve parents at the provincial level. A proposal was submitted to the provincial government of New Brunswick in 1990 to set up a similar structure (Brynelsen 1990).

Whereas the majority of provinces transfer provincial funds to regional offices for community-based management of the infant programs, the province of Newfoundland is unique in that it provides the only centralized, publicly-funded program in Canada. Managed by a provincial coordinator and an assistant, approximately twenty-four full-time child management specialists and four early intervention workers (1988 figures) provide home services to families of developmentally delayed children (Marfo 1991). An advantage of a centralized system is the ability to monitor accountability and administer uniform practices across the province, although Marfo also notes that remote regions of the province and specialized populations, such as Native people, may not receive the same level of services as do the more urban centres. A centralized program can, on a practical level, be difficult to manage in provinces with a large geographic area; as an alternative, British Columbia has established a regional adviser, who reports to the provincial coordinator. Four part-time advisers, each an experienced infant consultant, assist the coordinator in program evaluations, assist in the training of new staff in local communities, and provide direction and support for the operation of infant programs in their respective regions (Brynelsen 1990). An advantage of a system that combines provincial and regional coordination is the ability to facilitate individualistic development of local programs that can meet the unique needs of a variety of rural and urban communities.

Program Evaluation
With the rapid expansion of infant development programs and ever-changing models of parent-identified and theoretically-based services, program accountability becomes an essential component of administration and professional responsibility. However, the domain of program evaluation remains, by and large, an undeveloped field. Since the mid-eighties, British Columbia's infant development programs have participated with Dr. David Mitchell in the development and field testing of a program evaluation scale that is intended to have broad-based applicability to early intervention programs on an international level. The fifty-item scale covers fourteen domains, including such diverse

issues as assessment procedures, curricula, transdisciplinary approaches, cultural sensitivity, integration, and administration (Mitchell, Brynelsen, and Holm 1988). British Columbia is, at present, the only province involved in a regular process of evaluating program operation. By the end of 1992, the majority of the forty-four established programs will have completed one evaluation, and some will be beginning a follow-up review.

Training
Programs to train staff adequately prior to employment are not yet available in Canada; only the University of British Columbia and the University of Alberta offer specific courses on early intervention at an undergraduate level (Marfo 1991). The University of British Columbia now has a one-year graduate diploma program in infant development and early intervention. Much more initiative is needed to train personnel at both the undergraduate and graduate level. Saskatchewan, Alberta, and British Columbia hold provincial meetings and/or in-service training sessions for all infant development workers two to three times a year. At this time, only British Columbia and Ontario have established associations concerned with professional ethics and practices.

There is no legal mandate for infant development programs, there are few provincial staff available for support and consultation, and pre-service and in-service opportunities are generally inadequate, yet, surprisingly, there are a number of inter- and intra-provincial similarities between programs. These similarities may be explained in part by the high interest and excitement in this field, which has encouraged informal but frequent information sharing among parents and professionals. The following description will cover broad areas of service provided by most infant development programs in Canada.

Rationale for Infant Development Programs
Infant development programs in Canada are based on one or more of the following assumptions.
(1) Infancy is an important period of life, and delays in development during this period may have long-term, cumulative effects on the patterns of development of any child as well as the patterns of interaction between the child and his or her family.
(2) Intervention for children with developmental problems may be most effective if begun as early in the child's life as possible.
(3) Because the family unit is the most crucial source of learning and

emotional support for the infant, interventions aimed at strengthening the family's functioning influence the infant's development (Sameroff and Fiese 1990).

(4) People, events, and experiences beyond those provided by early intervention programs also function as determinants of child behaviour and development (Bronfenbrenner 1979; Dunst, Trivette, Hamby, and Pollock 1990).

Program Objectives

In the early years of infant development programs, the common feature of most programs was a dominant emphasis on skill teaching as the most efficacious means to facilitate the development of the child. Currently, a considerable evolution is taking place across Canada, acknowledging that sound family functioning is an essential factor in the provision of a supportive and developmentally-appropriate environment for the child (Brynelsen 1990; Marfo 1991). A child-focused approach is being replaced with family-centred intervention that emphasizes sensitivity to, and facilitation of, family coping strategies and resources *as well as* the identification and introduction of developmentally-relevant infant intervention activities (Bailey, Simeonsson, Winton, Huntington, Comfort, Isbell, O'Donnell, and Helm 1986). The challenge to infant workers is to be able to maintain a flexible but relevant balance between acknowledging broader-based family needs and meeting more specifically-focused infant needs (Bailey and Blasco 1990). Central to a family-centred approach is the recognition that the most critical environmental contribution to infant development is the nature and quality of the parent/child interaction.

The commitment of infant programs to these objectives is reflected in provincial guidelines, such as those recently revised for Ontario (1986), which include: (1) assisting parents of at-risk infants to recognize, understand, and adjust to their children's normal developmental needs and their special needs and disabilities; (2) assisting parents of at-risk infants to develop their abilities to plan, problem solve, and advocate for their children's ongoing developmental and special needs; and (3) assisting with at-risk infants in the ongoing development of their family unit.

In Alberta, four of eight statements of philosophy are family-centred, and, similarly, in Saskatchewan, four of the five goals mention the family, with one of them specifically referring to providing 'opportunities for families to develop mutual support networks within their communities' (Saskatchewan 1985). This shift in focus from child to family mirrors the trend in the United States; however, the incorporation of specific infant intervention strategies and activities into a more broadly focused family-centred service remains a major challenge (Marfo 1991).

Population Served

Infant development programs generally serve children from birth to three years or until they are eligible for preschool (Kendall et al. 1985). In some communities, preschool may be available for children aged two or two-and-a-half; while in others, preschool may not be available at all, and, thus, some children remain involved in an infant development program until school age (Kendall et al. 1985). Children identified as either disabled or developmentally delayed in one or more skill areas or as at significant risk of delay constitute the majority of those referred for service.

Infants at risk for delay may be defined in a variety of ways, but they include children who have experienced adverse prenatal, neonatal, postnatal, or socioeconomic factors that are thought to contribute to developmental disabilities. Sameroff and Chandler (1975) provided evidence for the need to consider family variables in the decision-making process regarding long-term outcome. Their research acquired further empirical support from studies such as that by Kochanek, Kabacoff, and Lipsitt (1990), who report that parent traits (e.g., maternal education) are better predictors of adolescent status than is the child's own behavior from birth to three years. Although most infant programs have relatively broad criteria for determining eligibility, political and social factors preclude endorsement of a truly universal access to infant programs (Brynelsen 1990). The consequence is that many children, who, by nature of family or ecological circumstances, are more likely to experience developmental problems are not referred for early intervention services.

Most infant development program populations are cross-categorical and serve children representing a variety of developmental problems. However, the availability of a more specialized resource in a particular community — a home program for deaf children, for example — means that certain groups of children might not be served by an infant development program. Most provinces have special programs for children with visual and hearing impairments; these services include itinerant teachers, home visiting services, and other resources. These are usually available from the time of diagnosis, but they vary considerably. A rural child with visual impairment, for example, may be involved in an infant development program because the worker for the Canadian National Institute for the Blind can visit only infrequently.

Participation in the infant development program is voluntary, although in some programs active parental involvement is required. The family generally remains in the program until the infant 'catches up' to the norm for his or her age (as might be the case for a premature high-risk infant) or becomes eligible for preschool. In some situations the families leave the infant development program if referred to a more specialized resource, such as a treatment center for children with multiple disabilities, or if the parent chooses to discontinue service.

Service Delivery

Structure

In most provinces, provincial governments provide funds to community sponsors which operate and staff the infant development programs (Kendall et al. 1985). Sponsors include hospitals, health units, school boards, and private non-profit societies such as associations for mentally disabled persons, preschool societies, or infant development program societies. One major provincial difference is the degree of professional and parental involvement in directing and monitoring the service.

In some provinces, such as British Columbia and Saskatchewan, the provincial guidelines for the operation of this service specify that local programs be directed by committees composed of parents involved in the infant development program and representatives from a range of professions and agencies. These representatives often include public health nurses, physicians, psychologists, social workers, therapists, and early childhood educators. In other provinces, program administration may be the sole responsibility of an executive director for a sponsoring society, a physician, or a supervisor of a health unit. As noted previously, the province of Newfoundland and Labrador has a centralized, government-run program staffed by child management specialists (interventionists) based in nineteen centres over five regions; overall program responsibility is managed by a provincial coordinator and an assistant coordinator.

Referrals

To encourage early referrals, many infant development programs have an open referral policy, in which a wide range of professionals and parents may participate. The majority of such referrals are from public health nurses, physicians, other community professionals, and parents. Such a policy may be established because most provinces do not have universal surveillance of the child population. Generally, a surveillance system, involving regular developmental assessments of children annually or more frequently, ensures early and appropriate referral to social, educational, or medical services. Without such a system, however, assessments and referrals are not the mandated responsibility of any individual or agency. Parents who have had concerns about their child's development have sometimes waited up to three years for confirmation of a problem and subsequent referral to a program (Robinson and Sheps 1979).

Some parents have described the period between suspicion of a delay or handicap, confirmation, and referral to a program as being the most difficult period to cope with emotionally. The longer this period continues, the more difficult it may be to help parents set realistic goals for their child. This may relate to how the parents perceive themselves in relation to the child. Studies have demonstrated that parents providing 'optimal' home environments believe in their ability to influence their child's development (Tolleson 1978). Parents with prolonged, unsuccessful caretaking experiences may feel unable to influence their child's development; these parents may withdraw more and more from normal parenting practices.

Delays in both diagnosis and assistance may play a significant role in decision-making at the time of diagnosis. Such delays have led parents to seek out-of-home care for their child (Brynelsen 1983). Therefore, early referrals to infant programs are generally encouraged; an open referral policy that accepts referrals from parents and from a wide range of professionals may be of benefit.

Services Provided

Home Visits

Most infant development programs provide home visits to families on a regular basis. In some instances, families are visited for one or two hours weekly or bi-weekly. In some programs, the frequency and duration of visits is determined by the family. Workers who see families on that basis may be concerned that the latter have control over their involvement with the program and not become overly dependent on the staff. However, frequency of visits may also be determined by the number of families on the caseload; in situations where staff have a large service area, families may be seen less frequently than desired by either the staff or the parent.

Assessment and Program Planning

During the course of home visits, information is shared that enables staff and the parent to determine the skills and needs of the infant and family, to develop a program plan, and to evaluate progress. Information may be gathered by one or more of the following methods: interviews with the parent and other involved professionals; observation of the child, home, and family; and informal or formal testing of the child.

Most programs have a standard intake procedure. Information is collected on the child's growth and development, the parents' concerns and priorities for their child, and the results of previous assessments by other professionals. These might include family physicians, pediatricians, physiotherapists, psychologists, speech and language pathologists, child care workers, and social workers involved with the family.

Observation of the child and discussion with family members during home visits provides a valuable source of information about the child's abilities, likes and dislikes, temperament, motivation, home environment, interaction with the parent, and parenting styles. Although there are ongoing opportunities for unstructured observation during the course of visits, a number of assessment tools have been developed to measure some of the above areas. Familiarity with these tools enables staff to become more accurate and objective observers. In some instances, formal administration may be useful and required on a regular basis. Included in measures of this type are the Family Strengths and Resources Assessment, Assessment of Family Needs (Bailey and Simeonsson 1988), and the Parent Behaviour Progression (Bromwich 1983).

Another useful method of deriving information is by testing the child. There are many different tests in use in infant development programs in Canada. Norm-referenced tests compare an individual child's performance to a normative group of other children the same age. Some in common use in Canada include the Bayley Scales of Infant Development (Bayley 1969) and the Gesell Developmental Schedules

(Knobloch, Stevens, and Malone 1980). The Bayley is designed to be administered by trained psychologists and is used more frequently in areas where staff are psychologists or have access to psychological assessments. Criterion-referenced tests compare a child's performance on an item to a sequence of skills. A Canadian example is the Vulpe Assessment Battery (Vulpe 1977). The third type of test is curriculum-referenced. These tests provide teaching activities for each item included on the scale. Most infant development programs have a variety of curriculum-referenced tests available, such as the Hawaii Early Learning Program (Furuno, O'Reilly, Hosaka, Inatsuka, Allman and Zeisloft, 1979) or the Carolina Curriculum for Infants and Toddlers with Special Needs (Johnson-Martin, Jens, Attermeier, and Hacker 1991). A useful description of the assessment and planning process is found in the text *Teaching Infants and Preschoolers with Handicaps* (Bailey and Worlery 1984) and *Interdisciplinary Assessment of Infants* (Gibbs and Teti 1990).

Assessment in an infant development program is a complex and ongoing process (Fewell 1983). Information sources are varied; infants with diagnosed disabilities are often assessed by a range of professionals, and a number of test results must be taken into consideration in planning an education program. The tests used in infant development programs have serious limitations (Zelazo 1982). Many are not standardized, and those that are may often be standardized on a non-disabled population. There is little research available to help staff select the most beneficial tests or to adapt a particular test to accommodate a child's handicap. Assessment data must also be constantly updated to reflect the current status of the child, so that program objectives can be developed for the child and family. Infancy is characterized by rapid change; therefore, the assessment process must be ongoing.

Parent-Professional Roles
Developing a program of activities that is continually responsive to ongoing changes in the infant and family is a challenge. This challenge is more readily met when staff work in partnership with parents, through a collaborative process, to set objectives and determine intervention activities (Bailey 1987; Brynelsen 1984; Mittler and Mittler 1983). If parents have access to assessment data and assistance in interpreting the data, they may be in a better position than staff to make decisions. They know their infant better than staff in terms of what he or she is able and willing to do. They also know what important skills they want

their infant to acquire. By involving parents there is also a greater chance that the infant's program will fit into the family routine and not be seen as an additional burden.

Contemporary research supports a parent-professional partnership, which is family-directed and embodies consideration of the following issues, articulated by Dunst, Trivette, and Deal (1988), who recommend: (1) a *proactive approach*, with interventions focused on strengthening the family; (2) *empowerment*, where interventions empower and enable families, helping them develop skills, knowledge, and competencies that will allow them access and control over resources; and (3) *partnership*, in which families and professionals pool their strengths.

Parents are more likely to remain motivated if the activities they helped design are fun and are seen as part of 'regular' family life. Visits by program staff will not result in significant developmental change in the infant. It is the parents' involvement with their child and the daily interactions and activities they provide that bring change, not only for the infant but also for themselves as parents.

Group Activities

Most infant development programs emphasize home-based services. In terms of providing assistance and support to families of infants and young children, home-based programming offers real benefits. Parents are in their own territory; the infant is in his or her own world. Problems of generalizing information from another setting to the home are lessened. Other family members may be involved more readily. Patterns of behaviour in a child which may not be observed in strange settings may be obvious at home. Assessments in familiar settings may help bring out the best abilities in children, which, in turn, can lead to more effective programming. However, many infant development programs also recognize the importance of providing group-based activities for infants and parents.

Homes can be isolating for parents of young children. There are advantages to some group activities in addition to home visits. These might include parent and tot groups, parent education workshops, or parent support groups. Groups can provide opportunities for parents to observe how other parents interact with their children, showing them alternative models of interaction which may help them with their child. Groups can also provide educational opportunities for infants and parents that are not accessible to them in the home. For young children, meaningful participation with peers can have important benefits for social and communication development (Guralnick 1990; Odom, McConnell, and McEvoy 1992). Therefore, an increasing number of infant development programs are offering parents a range of options and settings for involvement beyond the home program. Parents may then select from these options those that best meet their needs.

Liaison with Other Professionals
Staff in infant development programs generally work closely with other community professionals in providing services to families, in sharing skills and resources, and in keeping the community up-to-date on the program. Many children in infant development programs have been assessed by and are receiving services from other community professionals. Involvement in an infant development program may also lead to increased or new contact with community professionals. It is important that involved professionals are informed that a family has been referred, are kept up to date on the progress of the infant, and are encouraged to work closely with the program staff in planning. Consulting professionals, such as physiotherapists or speech and language pathologists, may visit a child's home with staff to assess the child or to provide specialized input into the program. In other situations, infant development staff may accompany the parent and child to a clinic or hospital for specialized consultation. In some programs, infant development staff may act, if so requested by the family, as case coordinators to facilitate information sharing between the involved professionals and the family.

Resource Materials
Most infant development programs have a resource library of books, toys, and equipment. Parents can borrow children's books, books on normal development in infancy, and books relating to specific disabilities. Books written by parents who have a child with a handicap are also valuable resources for both parents and staff (Pivato 1984; Schaefer 1983). More specialized books also form part of the library and are used by staff or parents to learn more about the impact a handicap may have on development.

The staff use toys to illustrate their value in encouraging the development of a particular skill or increasing exploration and manipulation in play. Equipment and aids to mobility may also be available through an infant development library.

Referral to Preschool
In many communities, preschools are available for children at age two
or three. Infant development staff are involved in assisting parents to
select an appropriate preschool for their child. Many communities
have a range of preschool options available. These might include regular preschools, special needs preschools, and integrated preschools. The
degree of parent involvement in preschools varies considerably, as do
hours of operation and program goals. Provincial funds to support the
education of children with delays or disabilities in preschools after
they leave infant development programs are available in most provinces, but they are not available for preschool children on the comprehensive scale that they are available for school age children (Kendall et
al. 1985). In small communities or rural areas preschools may be few or
non-existent.

Selecting an appropriate preschool may take several months; it can
involve visits to preschools with the parents, assisting them in the transition, and following up with the preschool teacher and parent. In
some communities (e.g., in British Columbia), a new professional position has been created, that of preschool liaison consultant; this individual works with the family, child, and preschool staff, addressing
issues such as transition, evaluation, program planning, and problem
solving. Parents may find it difficult to leave an infant development
program, and the staff can do much to alleviate parental anxiety and
make the transition productive.

Infant Development Program Staff
The following describes the knowledge base, skills, attitudes, and personal characteristics which staff need to work effectively with infants,
their families, and other community professionals. Ferguson and Bry-
nelson (1991) provide a more detailed description of training in this
field.

Knowledge Base

Normal Growth and Development
It is essential for staff to understand the normal patterns of neuromotor, conceptual, play, and social development in infants and young
children in order to plan with parents developmentally-appropriate
programs for the child. Normal family development and family sys-

tems theory should also be covered and include patterns of family growth and change, parent/child interactions, and social systems as they relate to the family (Dunst et al. 1990).

Learning Theories

The current focus of infant development programs is to support and facilitate the growth of both parents and their children. It follows that staff must understand the principles of adult as well as child learning (Anastasiow 1985). The theoretical bases for the (1) relationship between experience and behaviour; (2) principles of learning, concept-formation, motivation, and problem-solving strategies; and, (3) processes of cognitive, adaptive, and perceptual development should also be part of the infant worker's conceptual foundation.

Impact of a Delay or Handicap on Child and Family

Knowledge of various significant handicapping conditions, current treatment, and therapeutic approaches is important. It is also important to understand the effects of stress on the family following the diagnosis of an infant with a handicap and to be aware of the coping strategies which can be supported (Bailey and Simeonsson 1988). Cultural and value-related differences between families must also be understood so that families can be assisted to build on their strengths (Featherstone 1981; Chud and Fahlman 1985; Lynch and Hanson 1992).

Assessment, Program Planning, and Evaluation

The focus in this area should be on functional assessments and programming which recognizes the expressed needs of the family and the child (Bricker and Cripe 1992).

Roles of Other Professionals and Community Resources

The role of the infant development staff is that of 'generalist,' gathering information from a variety of sources and translating it into daily practical use for the family. Therefore, it is important to understand the specific skills and roles of other professionals involved in services to children and families and their potential contributions. An understanding of the function of various community resources available to children and families is essential to helping the family use these services effectively.

Skills

Application of this knowledge requires the development of specific skills. Communication skills include the ability to listen, provide useful feedback, and recognize and respond to changing family interactions. Mastery of these communication skills requires the ability to summarize goals and activities in an understandable form, be it verbal or written. Teaching in the home requires skills in reassessing involvement with the family. The worker must also have skill and flexibility in carrying out assessments with the parent and planning relevant activities to encourage development (Leviton, Mueller, and Kauffman 1992). This involves using information and recommendations from the parent and from other professionals involved with the child and family in ways which ensure that each feels that his or her contribution is respected and valued (Mitchell 1983).

Attitudes and Personal Characteristics

The attitudes and personal characteristics of staff are those required by other professionals working in the human service field. These include the ability to accept and respect the individuality of each family, to value each person no matter how severe his or her handicapping condition, and to believe that people have the ability to change and adapt when opportunities are provided. Flexibility, humour, and the ability to manage time are necessary, given the independent nature of the work. It is also a decided asset if staff are parents themselves and have firsthand knowledge of the challenges of parenting.

Professional Preparation

Staff currently employed in infant development programs have backgrounds in a variety of fields related to early intervention. These include special education, early childhood education, nursing, psychology, therapy (occupational, physio, and speech), social work, family studies, and child care. These areas may involve two to eight or more years of postsecondary education. Past experience in working with young children and families is generally requisite to employment.

Professional Literature

At present, newsletters of a regional or provincial nature share information about new activities in the field, current staff training opportunities, new resource books, and other available materials. Two provinces,

British Columbia and Ontario, have registered societies representing professionals employed as staff in infant development programs. No Canadian journals directed specifically to infant development programs exist. American journals of interest to staff include *Journal of Early Intervention, Infants and Young Children, Topics in Early Childhood Special Education,* and *Infant Mental Health Journal.* Given the multidisciplinary nature of the field, staff must keep up with new developments published in other professional journals, including medicine, nursing, therapy, education, and psychology.

Current Trends and Challenges

The concluding section focuses on current trends and challenges facing infant development programs in Canada today. While some issues have been present since the inception of early intervention services, others have emerged and grown as the field has evolved. Each issue carries with it its own sense of urgency, given available resources. Three major topic areas are briefly addressed: (1) meeting the needs of families in today's social climate; (2) the role of the educational community in professional preparation and research; and (3) program coordination at a provincial and national level.

Family Needs and Social Trends

Infant development staff have typically functioned as generalists, in a transdisciplinary role, gathering information from a variety of sources and translating it into practical use for the family. Increasingly, the family, child, and interventionist interact in a dynamic partnership, sharing skills and collaborating on short- and long-term objectives. Additionally, infant development workers assist families in identifying and advocating for their own and their child's needs as they begin to participate within the larger community structure. As noted earlier in this chapter, parents have played the major role in the acquisition and development of rehabilitation, recreation, education, and family support services for children with special needs. Collaboration with caring, informed professionals can serve to further advance this advocacy process.

The challenge remains, however, to not overlook the original consumer of early intervention — the infant with special needs. Within the context of a family-centred service, it is critical to remain aware of the conceptual, neuromotor, and emotional needs of the infant. However, rather than relying solely on a 'skill teaching' model, parents and interventionists can work in partnership to create broader-based intervention activities that are developmentally relevant and adapted to the child's personality and family lifestyle. In this way, sound family functioning is not sacrificed in an effort to have the child 'pass all the skills on a checklist' or reinforce the illusion that it is possible to 'fix' the disabled infant.

Another, and very significant, family-based challenge concerns adapting early intervention services to meet the needs of families in a rapidly changing society (Brynelsen 1990). The era of the majority of Canadian households being represented by a two-parent family with mother at home full-time is past. At present well over 50 per cent of Canadian women with children under three years of age are employed, over 13 per cent of all families are single-parent families, and the number of blended families continues to increase. The composition of many communities is also rapidly changing; new social-economic groups are emerging to join the ranks of other groups who have not been well-served by infant programs in the past. Infant programs have, traditionally, served middle-class families competently, but aboriginal families and families coping with severe financial and social stresses have not universally benefitted from early intervention services. Added to this are new family groups which include recent immigrants, families where addiction is a problem, and families where one or both parents have mental limitations. Despite the existence of divergent regional communities across Canada, these national trends indicate the presence of major social changes that must be acknowledged and incorporated into program planning (Brynelsen 1990).

Educational Preparation and Research Needs
The second major challenge to early intervention in Canada is the need to increase the availability of educational opportunities for infant development workers and the need to develop a stronger foundation of Canadian-based research. The need for more broadly-available educational options has been an issue since the inception of early intervention services in North America. Professional organizations and universities in the United States responded relatively rapidly to this deficiency in pre-service training, whereas Canadian universities, as noted earlier, have made only small gains over the last two decades (Marfo 1991). Reviewing the responsibilities of an infant interventionist, as outlined in this chapter, highlights the necessity of developing at least a four-year university level program for adequately training per-

sonnel to function competently as interventionists in this rapidly expanding profession. Additionally, more initiative is needed to provide ongoing in-service education and increased options for advanced or more specialized training as well as encouraging clinically-trained interventionists and interested academics to pursue postgraduate degrees.

Although there is a growing body of research relevant to early intervention, there are a number of problems associated with the translation of this research to practice in infant development programs. First, existing research comes from a multitude of disciplines, from pediatric neurology to adult education. Locating relevant research and translating it into practical application is often difficult for individual practitioners. Few staff employed in infant development programs have the training and resources to easily access and interpret such research. Second, much of the existing data derived from evaluation of early intervention efforts are subject to serious methodological and design flaws. The field is new and the problems associated with the evaluation of programs for infants and their families are many (Bricker 1984; Marfo 1991; Marfo and Kysela 1985). These problems include small sample sizes, population differences, inadequate tools to measure change, and insufficient funds for research. The field is also characterized by conflicting theories of human development and learning, which lead to controversies about which aspects of child and family development are most relevant.

There is a great need for new partnerships to be formed among government, university, and field interventionists in order to carry out methodologically sound research and to develop evaluation tools and curricula that are sensitive and responsive to Canadian society (Brynelsen 1990). Such cooperation could lead the way in providing both for increased funding for much needed Canadian research in this area and in ensuring that the results of such research are made fully accessible to practitioners in the field.

Provincial and National Coordination

The final issue addresses the need to continue the process of developing stronger provincial and national linkages across Canada for all those involved in early intervention services. At an administrative level, this includes establishing a provincial coordinating mechanism in every province in Canada. Progress has been made in this regard;

however, until *all* provinces have such a structure, it will be difficult to establish a consistent level of policy and procedures among programs, to monitor standards in service delivery, and/or to monitor equality of access in the distribution of resources within and across the provinces. When such structures are in place, the ensuing communication and coordination can have a ripple effect in the creation of a unified, political voice for infant development and for moving early intervention up on the agenda of the federal government (Marfo 1991). Additionally, regular communication among provincial coordinators would facilitate the development of a provincial and national database as well as the establishment of a national clearing house on early childhood and family services (Brynelsen 1990; Marfo 1991).

Summary

The intent of this chapter has been to provide a brief review of infant development programs in Canada. Since the inception of the first program in the early 1970s, there has been a rapid expansion of this service in various parts of the country. However, this growth has not been accompanied by the development of regional or provincial resources sufficient to meet staff training needs, to provide expert consultation on program direction, or to adequately address the changing social needs of families who have infants with developmental and disabling conditions. Implicit in each of the current issues reviewed in the preceding section is the need for infant programs to become more visible: first within the communities where they operate, so that more parents have an awareness of this avenue of support; second, in academic communities, so that the development of new training programs and research can be expedited; and, finally, in our socio-political environments, so that the base of funding support for infant development programs can be enhanced.

It is now time to link families, professionals, academics, and government officials in a collaborative, interactive partnership. This may help ensure that adequate and relevant educational, health, and intervention services are universally available to all families who have young children with developmental needs.

Notes

1 Infant development programs are also called infant stimulation programs or early intervention programs, but throughout this chapter they will be referred to as infant development programs.

References

Alberta. Social Services and Community Health. 1980. *Early intervention program for families with developmentally delayed children*. Alberta

Anastasiow, N.J. 1985. Parent training as adult development. In S. Harel and N.J. Anastasiow (eds.), *The at-risk infant: Psycho/socio/medical aspects*. Baltimore: Paul H. Brookes

Bailey, D.B. 1987. Collaborative goal-setting with families: Resolving differences in values and priorities for services. *Topics in Early Childhood Special Education* 7:59–71

Bailey, D.B. and Blasco, P.M. 1990. Parents' perspectives on a written survey of family needs. *Journal of Early Intervention* 14:196–203

Bailey, D.B. and Simeonsson, R.J. 1988. *Family assessment in early intervention*. Columbus, OH: Merrill Publishing

Bailey, D.B., Simeonsson, R.J., Winton, P.J., Huntington, G.S., Comfort, M., Isbell, P., O'Donnell, K.J., and Helm, J.M. 1986. Family-focused intervention: A functional model for planning, implementing, and evaluating individualized family services in early intervention. *Journal of the Division of Early Childhood* 10:156–71

Bailey, D.B. and Wolery, M. 1984. *Teaching infants and preschoolers with handicaps*. Columbus, OH: Charles E. Merrill

Bank-Mikkelsen, N.E. 1969. A metropolitan area in Denmark: Copenhagen. In R. Kugel and W. Wolfensberger (eds.), *Changing patterns in residential services for the mentally retarded*. Washington, DC: President's Committee on Mental Retardation

Bayley, N. 1969. *Bayley scales of infant development*. New York: Psychological Corporation

Blatt, B. 1971. Some persistently recurring assumptions concerning education of the mentally retarded. In J.J. Rothstein (ed.), *Mental retardation: Readings and resources*. San Francisco: Holt, Rinehart & Winston

Bloom, B.S. 1964. *Stability and change in human characteristics*. New York: Wiley

Bricker, D. 1984. An analysis of early intervention programs: Attendant issues and future directions. In B. Blatt and R. Morris (eds.), *Perspectives in special education*. New York: Scott and Foresman

Bricker, D. and Cripe, J.J. 1992. *An activity-based approach to early intervention*. Baltimore: Paul H. Brookes

Bromwich, R. 1977. Stimulation in the first year of life? A perspective on infant development. *Young Children* 32:71–82

–. 1981. *Working with parents of infants: An interactional approach*. Baltimore: University Park Press

–. 1983. *Manual for the parent behavior progression (PBP)*. California State University, Department of Educational Psychology

Bronfenbrenner, U. 1979. *The ecology of human development*. Cambridge, MA: Harvard University Press

Brynelsen, D. 1983. Problems experienced by line staff in management of children with multiple handicaps. In G. Schwartz (ed.), *Advances in research and services for children with special needs*. Vancouver: University of British Columbia Press

–. (ed.). 1984. *Working together*. Vancouver: National Institute on Mental Retardation and British Columbians for Mentally Handicapped People

–. 1990. Historical perspective on infant development programs in Canada. In *Proceedings of the Atlantic conference on early intervention: Current issues and future directions*. Department of Child Study, Mount Saint Vincent University, Halifax, Nova Scotia

–. 1992. *British Columbia infant development program policy and procedures manual*. Vancouver: Infant Development Program of British Columbia

Chud, G. and Fahlman, R. 1985. *Early childhood education for a multicultural society*. Vancouver: Western Education Development Group, Faculty of Education, University of British Columbia

Clarke, A.M. and Clarke, A.D.B. 1976. *Early experience: Myth and evidence*. New York: Macmillan

Dunst, C.J. 1982. Theoretical bases and pragmatic considerations in infant curriculum construction. In J. Anderson (ed.), *Curricula for high-risk and handicapped infants*. Chapel Hill, NC: Technical Assistance Development System

–. 1983. A systems-level, family-focused approach to assessment and intervention with profoundly handicapped children. Paper presented at Handicapped Children's Early Education Program Conference, Washington, DC

Dunst, C.J., Trivette, C.M., and Deal, A.G. 1988. *Enabling and empowering families*. Cambridge, MA: Brookline Books

Dunst, C.J., Trivette, C.M., Hamby, D., and Pollock, B. 1990. Family systems correlates of the behavior of young children with handicaps. *Journal of Early Intervention* 14:204–18

Featherstone, H. 1981. *A difference in the family. Living with a disabled child*. Middlesex, England: Penguin Books

Ferguson, R.V. and Brynelsen, D. 1991. Education and training of early intervention and programme personnel. In D. Mitchell and R.I. Brown (eds.), *Early intervention studies for young children with special needs*. London: Chapman and Hall

Fewell, R.R. 1983. Assessing handicapped infants. In S.G. Garwood and R.R. Fewell (eds.), *Educating handicapped infants*. Rockville, MD: Aspen Systems Corporation

Furuno, S., O'Reilly, K.A., Hosaka, C.M., Inatsuka, T.T., Allman, T.L., and Zeisloft, B. 1979. *Hawaii early learning profile*. Palo Alto, CA: VORT

Gibbs, E.D., and Teti, D.M. 1990. *Interdisciplinary assessment of infants: A guide for early intervention professionals*. Baltimore: Paul H. Brooks

Guralnick, M.J. 1990. Major accomplishments and future directions in early childhood mainstreaming. *Topics in Early Childhood Special Education* 10:2

Heifitz, L.J. 1980. From consumer to middleman: Emerging roles for parents in the network of services for retarded children. In R.R. Abidin (ed.), *Parent education and intervention handbook*. Springfield, IL: Charles C. Thomas

Hunt, J. 1961. *Intelligence and experience*. New York: Ronal

Johnson-Martin, N.M., Jens, K.G., Attermeier, S.M., and Hacker, B.J. 1991. *The Carolina curriculum for infants and toddlers with special needs*. Baltimore: Paul H. Brookes

Kendall, D., Brynelsen, D., and Lapierre, J. 1985. Survey of infant development programs in Canada. Unpublished report, Faculty of Education, University of British Columbia

Knobloch, H., Stevens, F. and Malone, A.F. 1980. *Manual of development diagnosis*. Hagerstown, MD: Harper & Row

Kochanek, T.T., Kabacoff, R.I, and Lipsitt, L.P. 1990. Early identification of developmentally disabled and at-risk preschool children. Exceptional Children 56:528–38

Kott, M.G. 1971. The history of mental retardation. In J.H. Rothstein (ed.,) *Mental retardation: Readings and resources*. San Francisco: Holt, Rinehart & Winston

LaMarsh, J. 1965. *Mental retardation in Canada*. Opening remarks at federal/provincial conference. Ottawa: Queen's Printer

Leviton, A., Mueller, M., and Kauffman, C. 1992. The family-centered consultation model: Practical applications for professionals. *Infants and Young Children* 4:1–8

Lynch, E.W. and Hanson, M.J. (eds.). 1992. *Developing cross-cultural competence, a guide for working with young children and their families*. Baltimore: Paul H. Brookes

Marfo, K. 1991. The evolution and current status of early intervention in Canada. In K. Marfo, (ed.), *Early intervention in transition: Current perspectives on programs for handicapped children*. New York: Praeger

Marfo, K. and Kysela, G. 1985. Early intervention with mentally handicapped children: A critical appraisal of applied research. *Journal of Pediatric Psychology* 10:305–24

Mitchell, D.R. 1983. International trends in special education. *Canadian Journal of Mental Retardation* 33:6–13

Mitchell, D., Brynelsen, D., and Holm, M. 1988. Evaluating the process of early intervention programmes. In H. Smith (ed.), *Evaluating services: Psychology and disability*. Dublin: Psychological Society of Ireland

Mittler, P. and Mittler, H. 1983. Partnership with parents: An overview. In P. Mittler and H. McConachie (eds.), *Parents, professionals and mentally handicapped people*. London: Croom Helm

National Institute on Mental Retardation. 1981. Historical perspectives on mental retardation. *Orientation manual on mental retardation*. Toronto

Odom, S.L., McConnell, S.R., and McEvoy, M.A. 1992. *Social competence of young children with disabilities*. Baltimore: Paul H. Brookes

Ontario. 1986. *Consultation paper on proposed guidelines for infant development services*. Toronto: Community Services Division, Ministry of Community and Social Services

Pivato, E. (ed.). 1984. *Different hopes, different dreams*. Edmonton: Academic Printing and Publishing

Robinson, G. and Sheps, S. 1979. *Children with developmental handicaps: Is there a gap between suspicion and referral?* Vancouver: University of British Columbia, Department of Pediatrics

Sameroff, A.J. and Chandler, M. 1975. Reproductive risk and the continuum of caretaking causality. In F.D. Horowitz et al. (eds.), *Review of child development research*. Vol. 4. Chicago: University of Chicago Press

Sameroff, A.J. and Fiese, B.H. 1990. Transactional regulation and early intervention. In S.J. Meisels and J.P. Shonkoff (eds.), *Handbook of early childhood intervention*. Cambridge: Cambridge University Press

Saskatchewan ECIP Provincial Council. 1985. *Saskatchewan's early childhood-home based intervention program: Standards and guidelines.* Saskatoon: Saskatchewan Association for the Mentally Retarded

Sauer, D. 1975. Infant home care programme. *Deficience Mentale/Mental Retardation: Canadian Association for the Mentally Retarded* 25:26–9

Schaefer, N. 1983. *Does she know she's there?* Toronto: Fitzhenry and Whiteside

Shipe, D. 1985. Early intervention. In N. Marlette and B. Gall (eds.), *Dialogue on disability.* Calgary: University of Calgary Press

Skeels, H.M. 1966. Adult status of children with contrasting early life experiences. *Monographs of the Society for Research in Child Development* 31:61–9

Tolleson, L. 1978. Parents' beliefs, attitudes and values and their relationship to home environment provided for developmentally delayed infants involved in a home-based intervention programme. M.A. thesis, University of British Columbia

Vulpe, S.G. 1977. *Vulpe assessment battery.* Toronto: National Institute on Mental Retardation

Wilson, R. 1984. Dads only. *Infant Development Programme of British Columbia: Provincial Newsjournal* 2:7

Wolfensberger, W. 1972. *The principle of normalization in human services.* Toronto: National Institute on Mental Retardation

Zelazo, P.R. 1982. Alternative assessment procedures for handicapped infants and toddlers: Theoretical and practical issues. In D.D. Bricker (ed.), *Intervention with at-risk and handicapped infants.* Baltimore: University Park Press

8
Child and Youth Care Work in the Community
Peter Gabor and Valerie Kuehne

Development of Community Programs

Historically, a key development leading to increased involvement of child and youth care workers in the community was the realization that the post-discharge environment is perhaps the key determinant of successful adaptation after institutional placement (Allerhand, Weber, and Haug 1966; Taylor and Alpert 1973). Outcome research suggests that regardless of success during residential placement, what happens after placement will determine whether gains will be maintained or existing problems overcome. In the light of these findings, institutional programs began to develop aftercare components designed to make the post-discharge environment more supportive to the youngster. Child and youth care workers were frequently involved in aftercare programs, continuing their involvement with children individually and in groups and offering their services to parents, especially in the area of child management. The involvement of child and youth care workers in aftercare services was a logical expansion of their role, as it built on the relationships formed with young people in residential care and took advantage of workers' expertise in child management.

A related development has seen the helping professions increasingly favour ecological rather than child-centred approaches. Recognition of the potential hazards of institutional care (Shyne 1973) and the related prominence of the normalization movement (Wolfensberger 1972) have also been factors in this trend. As a consequence, services have been moved closer to the child's natural environment (Whittaker 1977), thereby increasing the opportunity for influencing key systems such as the family, school, and peer group.

These professional trends have also influenced legislative and policy developments. In 1978, the Family Support Worker Program was established in British Columbia, primarily as a means of reducing the need for specialized forms of services (British Columbia 1978). Subsequently, in Ontario a consultation paper issued by the government prior to the drafting of the current Children's Act (Ontario 1982) declared that one of the principles of the new act would be that 'services to children should support, enhance, and supplement the family, whenever possible, rather than compete with the family by providing alternative care and supervision.' The Child Welfare Act (Alberta 1984) in Alberta also states that community measures should be tried first: 'If it is not inconsistent with the protection of a child who may be in need of protective services, the child's family should be referred to community resources for services that would support and preserve the family and prevent the need for any other intervention under this Act' (SA-4). Provisions such as these have had a major impact on child and youth care, legitimizing and encouraging family-oriented and community-based programming.

In the child and youth care field, this move towards the community has resulted in two types of program changes. First, institutional programs, which have traditionally tended to be relatively isolated, have increasingly given way to group home programs. In Ontario, for example, the number of children in institutional placement declined by over 27 per cent between 1970 and 1980 (Ontario 1983). Second, and perhaps more profound, a new class of programs — community-based child and youth care programs — have developed to take their place beside the more familiar group care programs, in some cases as adjuncts and in others as alternatives to the latter. For example, the move to group homes has meant that children were more likely to attend schools in the community rather than remain in in-house school programs. This change has prompted the creation of school liaison programs, which help children adjust to the community and, in turn, assist the community to improve services for children with special needs. Similarly, life skills and community activity programs have been developed to help children function more effectively in the community while continuing to live at home; these programs also increase the resources the community can offer youngsters who might otherwise need group care placements. Family support programs, too, have become prominent, with their goals of helping families as a means of strengthening their ability to maintain children in the home.

In the late 1960s, more and more adolescents left their homes, and most sizeable cities in Canada have seen the establishment of a permanent core of youth living on their own with marginal resources. Many of these young people have left behind abusive or otherwise unsatisfactory home situations; they are often unprepared to make constructive use of their independence. Consequently, they are not only vulnerable to such dangers as prostitution, drug and substance abuse, and sexually transmitted diseases, but they also tend to miss out on their education and on developing age-appropriate work, social, and life skills. A high proportion of these young people are in need of social services, and a range of community programs offering both emergency and long-term services has developed in response to this need. These programs include runaway and street worker programs, life skills training programs, and outreach. The people who staff such programs are not always clearly aligned or identified with any recognizable professional group, but many staff members have been designated as child and youth care workers.

Another trend which has had a strong impact on the delivery of child and youth care services has been an increasing focus on the prevention of problems, a distinct shift from the earlier preoccupation with cure and treatment. Associated with this trend are the efforts aimed at encouraging appropriate development and enhancing well-being and competence, an outlook Maier (1988) has described as 'developmental child care.'

Institutional and other group care approaches concern themselves primarily with reducing the seriousness and impact of already identified problems, referred to in the public health field as a tertiary prevention approach. More preventive approaches involve interventions in the environmental systems in which people live. Such interventions may involve identifying problems early in order to minimize consequences, or they may focus on working with high-risk groups to prevent the occurrence of problems in the first place. In public health these approaches would be considered secondary and primary prevention, respectively. These efforts normally take place in the community and aim to help people make more effective use of their social environment. Community child and youth care programs can in many instances be viewed as operating on the secondary and primary prevention levels. Contract workers and runaway services are examples of secondary prevention programs, while street worker and AIDS information programs serve primary prevention purposes.

Finally, child and youth care work has been affected, no less than other social services, by the increased cost consciousness which has accompanied the recent troubled economic times. More and more, funders scrutinize the costs of services and seek less expensive alternatives. Group care programs tend to be relatively costly because of the need to staff around the clock. Funders, hoping to realize savings, have, therefore, increasingly favoured community child and youth care models. While community programs are usually less expensive than are group care programs, it is important to recognize that not all community programs can be viewed as alternatives to group care. In fact, community projects come in many different forms and vary greatly in costs, ranging from relatively inexpensive recreation programs to highly sophisticated ventures providing intensive services. It may be legitimate to compare some of the latter programs to group care, but a comparison of costs will likely reveal that the community alternative, while less expensive, is still a relatively costly operation. Thus, while economics have favoured the development of community child and youth care, the arguments and comparisons have often been simplistic, comparing the costs of different programs providing different services. Funders have often opted for less expensive alternatives without due regard for needs. As a result, in many jurisdictions, the continuum of child welfare resources has gaps in the area of more intensive, treatment-oriented programs and a proliferation of less expensive programs.

The Range and Variety of Community Child and Youth Care

The growth of community child and youth care has seen the development of numerous innovative programs across Canada. For example, recognizing that for most young people the best possible placement available remains their own home, programs supporting children and families are now commonly available. Other programs aim to relate primarily to the young person, helping with school, social functioning, peer relations, and work.

Family Support Work

Family support work is based on the premise that, in many situations, providing timely help and support to families can be the most effective means of providing help to children and young people. Timely support to the family may preclude the necessity of more extensive and intensive services in the future.

Family support services, which have proliferated over the last several years, can be organized in a variety of different ways. In many instances, however, the role of the family support worker is undertaken by child and youth care practitioners. The objectives usually identified for these programs are enumerated by Gabor and Collins (1985–6): (1) help families manage their daily living situation; (2) help parents acquire child management skills; (3) support parents and children in coping with each other; (4) help families communicate more effectively; and (5) assist families in using community services.

Child and youth care workers providing family support are typically involved with the family for four to six hours per week. This is possible because case loads are usually limited to six or eight. The approach is informal and the focus is on day-to-day issues and difficulties. While family support workers often work directly with children and young people, in some instances the focus of the work is on the parents or other adult caregivers. For example, in one program, child and youth care workers teach conflict resolution skills to adult family members under the assumption that constructive conflict resolution processes within the family will enhance family functioning in general and the well-being of children and young people within the family in particular (Ing and Gabor 1988).

Supporting the Child or Youth in School
Young people experiencing problems at school often develop difficulties in other areas of their lives as well. Because schools are often unable or unwilling to work with young people who have special needs, child and youth care approaches have been developed to help children succeed at school. These programs often utilize teams of child and youth care workers and teachers. Other programs, often referred to as life skills programs, supplement the efforts of schools and caregivers by teaching the practical skills required in daily life.

There is a variety of other child and youth care opportunities in schools. For example, child and youth care workers may act as liaisons between home and school, working in elementary schools and helping families resolve school-related problems. Where adolescents are not attending school regularly, child and youth care workers attempt to help them become constructively involved with school. In still other types of programs, child and youth care workers may be assigned to work on an individual basis with children who have special needs, thereby allowing them to remain in regular classroom settings. Such workers can assist many children, including hearing and visually impaired students and behaviourally disruptive youngsters.

Street Programs
Some of the most innovative community child and youth care work takes place in street programs. Because these projects tend to work with young people before problems have arisen or have been recognized by formal helping systems, these operations have the clearest preventive orientation.

Street programs often attempt to engage young people through the use of outreach techniques and constructive alternatives. Such programs often reach into the schools and provide life skills and job search training, sex education, counselling, and activity centres for all adolescents. In other cases, street-based programs can be targeted on high-risk youth and offer counselling, information, and skill training.

Street programs are often the only means of engaging young people who are alienated from traditional community structures and are, therefore, shut off from mainstream help and support systems. As social pressures and youth unemployment continue to increase, it can be expected that the numbers of young people who become isolated and estranged will grow, increasing the need for street programs.

Community Aspects of Group Care
During the past few years, community dimensions have been added to many residential programs. Child and youth care workers are now commonly involved in family work while the child is in residential care and are often responsible for arranging and supervising visits and offering advice and support to parents.

Many residential programs have also developed aftercare programs aimed at helping children and families with the transition from residential placement. Child and youth care workers are often the key aftercare personnel, offering help, support, and information.

Finally, some community programs resemble residential care. Many of these are clearly the result of the evolution of group care. Day treatment for children with behavioural and emotional problems is one example of this evolution. While extensive community contact is provided and young people continue to reside in the community, a residential care-like environment is still a major component of such programs.

Implications for Child and Youth Care Practice

Definition of Community Child and Youth Care

The move of child and youth care into the community has altered the nature of the profession; workers are now involved in a wide range of tasks, many of which are radically different than those responsibilities traditionally associated with child and youth care work. In turn, additional knowledge and skills, as well as different attitudes and a broader perspective, are now required of workers.

Community child and youth care modifies and expands the role developed in group care. The distinctive feature of residential child and youth care is constant contact with the client within his or her own living environment. The aim of the work is to integrate the 'child's total experience in residence — his specialized treatment requirements with his normative requirements for social, educational, work, and recreational experiences' (Barnes 1980). The work has a dual purpose: (1) the provision of basic care and (2) the mediation of difficulties or problems experienced by the child or those around her/him. Both care and mediation are provided through skilful management of the living situation, using the events and interactions of the child's life to further emotional, social, and instrumental competence (Trieschman, Whittaker, and Brendtro 1969).

Community child and youth care work has similar purposes. The provision of basic care is not, by definition, the mandate of community child and youth care; the enhancement of development is a more explicit focus of the work. Because the child continues to live in the community, child and youth care work increasingly involves contact with the child's family, friends, substitute caregivers, teachers, and others. As the child continues to be involved with the community, child and youth care interventions must be undertaken with due regard to the influence and impact of key people and systems in the child's life. Indeed, at times, these people and systems become the focus of child and youth care work. In brief, child and youth care workers have had to add to their initial core knowledge and skills; they have had to develop an ability to work with adults and adopt a new perspective, shifting from what was previously a child-centred orientation to one that recognizes the importance of the social environment to the development of the child (Garbarino 1982). Moreover, work in the community may inadvertently or deliberately lead to the worker's involvement in local politics. Thus, community child and youth care workers need to develop an understanding of, and sensitivity to, political processes as well as the skills to effectively participate at the political level.

VanderVen (1981) has analyzed the nature of child and youth care work utilizing Bronfenbrenner's hierarchical levels in the ecological system. This analysis helps to elaborate the differences between community and residential child and youth care work and clarifies the contexts within which community child and youth care is practised. Level 1 of the environment is the microsystem, that is, the immediate environment containing the child. Work at this level is directly with children. Level 2 of the environment is the mesosystem, which is a system of direct settings within which the child is involved. Practice at this level involves working through those people responsible for the various settings: facilitating, encouraging, enabling, and coordinating. Work at this level involves indirect contact with children. In applying this schema to the case of child and youth care, it appears that much of this work, both residential and in the community, is performed at Level 1, but some aspects of the work fit the criteria for Level 2.

Consider, for example, the case of the child and youth care worker in group care who works directly with the children, that is, at Level 1 of the environment. At the same time, this worker may have the opportunity to work with the child's parents and teachers or to advocate on behalf of the child within the residential program itself. These are all examples of work which takes place at Level 2. The community child and youth care worker may also be involved in work at both levels. Leading a recreational program, teaching job search skills, and managing an emergency program for runaways could be considered examples of work at Level 1, while supporting a child within the family, at work, or in school may involve considerable work with parents, foster parents, employers, teachers, and other adults, and could be considered examples of work at Level 2. The respective proportions of work at the two levels vary, depending on the design of particular programs and the job descriptions of workers. Nevertheless, in considering the nature of residential and community work, it appears that, on the whole, much of residential work involves direct work with children and can, therefore, be characterized as being performed at Level 1, while community child and youth care seems to involve more frequent contact with key people in the child's life and, thus, operates at Level 2 as well as Level 1.

VanderVen indicates that work at Level 1 requires identification with children, while work at Level 2 must combine identification with both children and their parents. In considering the respective demands of residential and community child and youth care, it seems that this analysis is applicable. Residential workers, who work primarily with children, tend to have a strong identification with their charges, at times to the extent that they seem almost anti-adult (VanderVen 1979). To be effective, community workers must be able to identify with adults as well. VanderVen indicates that such a shift in orientation occurs quite naturally as people grow from late adolescence to adulthood. This suggests that community child and youth care work is suited more to the older, experienced child and youth care practitioner than to the younger worker just beginning a career in the field.

As child and youth care workers move into the community, their practice may at times resemble that of other professionals based in the community. There are a number of similarities between community child and youth care and the practice of other professions, but for child and youth care, struggling with obtaining professional recognition and acceptance, it is vital to demonstrate that its community-based practice is not a duplication of the work of existing professions. Community child and youth care needs to be clear about its underlying philosophy, focus, and approaches in order to be able to show convincingly that it can make a unique contribution to existing services.

While many aspects of child and youth care work are shared with other professions, child and youth care is unique because of the particular combination of values and approaches which characterize it. The context of practice is, of course, the child's everyday living environment. Child and youth care workers involve themselves for several hours at a time in the events and activities of their client's day. The practice is holistic: oriented towards growth, development, and the enhancement of human functioning. The underlying philosophy is essentially humanistic: there is a belief in the potential of people to live effectively, given the right kind of experiences, supports, and opportunities. Child and youth care practice is action-oriented, practical, and informal, three characteristics which provide opportunities for child and youth care workers to relate to their clients — often young people who are not receptive to more formal, clinically oriented professionals. It should be emphasized, however, that although child and youth care is less formal than other professions, child and youth care workers often make use of powerful and sophisticated interventions. The practice is eclectic, drawing on skills from other disciplines and blending these with the approaches developed in child and youth care. Finally, child and youth care practice tends to be interdisciplinary, and child and youth care workers are often responsible for coordinating and interpreting the efforts of other professionals.

Barnes' (1980) description of the European educateur describes well the distinctive aspects of community — and residential — child and youth care:

> Thus, the educateur, a specialist in working with youth as a 'constant contact practitioner' or generalist, engages with his clients in the thick of whatever they are doing. He can relate purposefully during a wide range of life space incidents or program events, and it is his expertise to structure the nature and operation of these events so that they are therapeutic and growth-inducing for the youngsters involved. The skill of the educateur is in relating directly to children and youth and helping them over the total range of their experience. Through making conscious use of the available milieux, individual and peer relationships, his own personality, and appropriate outside resources, the educateur transforms the whole experience of everyday life, whether in community or residential programs, into an educational and rehabilitative program.

Comparison of Community and Residential Child and Youth Care
Much of the same knowledge and many similar skills are required for the effective practice of both residential and community child and youth care. Workers in both settings must relate effectively to children and need skills in counselling, advocacy, teaching, group leadership, crisis intervention, activity programming, and behavioural management. In residential practice, these skills are used within the context of the group living situation; interventions are usually directed towards the children. In community child and youth care, many of the same skills are required but in different contexts: within families, groups, and organizations. Consequently, child and youth care workers are often called upon to work with adults as well as children. Thus, the community worker must be able to relate to adults, families, and organizations.

A study examining the job functions of child and youth care workers in British Columbia provides useful data for comparing community and residential child and youth care (Anglin 1983). This study describes the job functions of child and youth care workers in various settings and concludes that family support work, a form of community child and youth care, has the highest job complexity, according to the definition used. Residential child and youth care is of a lower level of complexity. While the author of this study points out that specific workers in less complex settings may be performing highly complex work, the results can, nevertheless, be viewed as one measure of the level of complexity in various child and youth care settings. It is also shown that there are many job functions common to all forms of child and youth care. This study suggests that the essential nature of the work is similar in both group care and community care, but some community work is more varied and complex.

Professional Identity
Because community child and youth care is relatively new, neither the field nor the discipline is as yet clearly defined. Community child and youth care is practised in settings as varied as youth recreational programs, drop-in centres, schools, and homes, with the result that child and youth care workers are at times confused with recreational leaders, lay counsellors, teachers' aids, social workers, or others (Ricks and Charlesworth 1982). There is no widely accepted definition of community child and youth care work which could help define the profession or at least indicate what lies within and outside its boundaries. Indeed, there is little consensus about the relationship between community and residential child and youth care or about whether the two are branches of the same profession or different fields altogether.

From time to time, community workers have attempted to form their own associations, as did community youth workers in Alberta in the late 1970s. The attempt failed, but it had the effect of retarding the growth of the Child Care Workers' Association of Alberta for a number of years. In the current troubled economic times, even a unified field of child and youth care is facing an uphill battle in its efforts to gain professional recognition; the task may be impossible if the two branches of child and youth care are contenders for scarce resources. To the degree that community child and youth care tries to go separately, it is distancing itself from roots which can help provide a clear-cut identity and develop its knowledge base and technology. Correspondingly, this distancing can deprive the profession of one of its most vigorous and energetic branches.

The claim to professional recognition is significantly strengthened if child and youth care can define itself to include both community and residential practice. Increasingly, child welfare agencies are developing both residential and community components. A close association of the two branches will make it possible for residential and community child and youth care to draw on each other, thereby enhancing the effectiveness of child and youth care practice generally. Many approaches and techniques perfected in group care — activity program leadership and behavioural management, for example — can be very useful in community work, while community child and youth care can offer a more ecologically oriented perspective as well as concrete approaches to involving families in group care services.

Finally, a united field significantly improves career opportunities in child and youth care. Lack of career opportunities and a lack of variety in the work are two reasons for the high turnover in the profession (Gabor 1975). With the field encompassing both community and residential work, more varied and complex career patterns might be possible. For example, a worker might begin in residential work, move to community work after a few years, then return to group care in a supervisory capacity. The advantages to this type of career progression are twofold: The individual is afforded the opportunity to try a variety of assignments which can, in turn, enhance practice skills as well as prepare the worker for advancement. At the same time, community child and youth care benefits from acquiring a worker with well-developed skills, and group care benefits from acquiring a supervisor who can bring a community perspective to the work.

Education and Career Development
The foregoing discussion leads to a number of considerations about child and youth care education and career development. In the early days of community programs many workers had previous direct practice experience, usually in a residential setting. More recently, more and more people have entered community work without previous group care experience or even extensive direct practice experience.

Educational programs that train people for entry into the field have traditionally emphasized direct work with children. A perusal of the announcements of community college training programs indicates that most of the content is designed to provide direct practice skills. Thus, courses like Observation and Assessment, Therapeutic Activities, and Group Dynamics constitute the largest part of the curricula, preparing people for working with children alone or in groups. Programs, increasingly, also provide at least an exposure to topics which are relevant for community work. Accordingly, courses with titles like 'The

Role of the Child Care Worker in the Family, School, and Community' and 'Family Support and Intervention' are also offered. Such courses attend to the theme of working with adults as well as children in family and in community systems. Although the emphasis on such course content may now be increasing, as recommended by Beker and Maier (1981), it would be appropriate for child and youth care education to give even more emphasis to these themes.

Because much pre-service training is aimed at the direct practice level, it is important to recognize the needs of experienced child and youth care workers who move into community work. Courses leading to advanced diplomas could be offered by existing child and youth care training programs, with scheduling to accommodate part-time study. Similarly, agencies could provide for this need through in-service events and should be prepared to support the efforts of beginning community workers through supervision. At present there are few such supports, with the result that many workers are required to undertake community work without adequate preparation or support.

Current Issues in Community Child and Youth Care
The rapid growth of community child and youth care has resulted in problems as well as opportunities. Some of the concerns relate to the profession itself and some to the way services and organizations are structured in the field. Because community child and youth care is a relatively new field, there is little to guide future developments. In this section, some of the key issues facing the field today will be discussed.

Decentralization of Community-based Services
During the postwar era, provincial governments in Canada assumed an increasing financial responsibility for all social services. As provinces came to fund a large number and variety of programs, they came under increased pressure to ensure comprehensiveness, consistency, and equity in all provincial jurisdictions. Centralized policy-making, decision-making, and program development were viewed as the most reasonable approaches to facilitating the functioning of what had often grown to be very large departments.

However, the 1970s saw increasing discussion and scrutiny of the assumptions underlying the very existence of social services and of the way in which those services were planned, structured, and delivered. The economic constraints of the 1980s and the accompanying deficit budgetary positions of many governments also provided impetus for questioning the structure and delivery of social services. At a time when successive recessions increased the demand for and consumption of social services, many governments were exercising fiscal restraint in attempts to reduce deficit budgeting, with the effect that the funding for social services was barely maintained and, indeed, was often reduced (Kinkaide 1987).

These trends and developments have, in turn, served to focus attention on how social services could be restructured to better reflect current circumstances. One of the more widely discussed models was the decentralization of services. It was argued that the movement from central control to regional or community levels would allow for a service system that would be much less bureaucratic and, therefore, more responsive to local needs. Decentralization also promised to promote more flexibility in decision-making with regard to funding and resource allocation as well as to further citizen participation in service definition and direction (Kammerman and Kahn 1990; Kinkaide 1987; Hurl 1984). Thus, it was hoped, scepticism and doubt about appropriateness and effectiveness of services could be reduced. As well, decentralization would likely result in the development of a system that would be more attuned to a local definition of needs (Lewis 1989), ensuring that only appropriate and needed services were offered. Finally, decentralization would allow the development of a more responsive and functional management structure, which could increase productivity and efficiency in the delivery of services.

A study of decentralization in the Alberta child welfare system in the 1980s, undertaken by Gabor, Nicholson, Charles, and Thomlison (1991), describes several changes which, typically, result in the child welfare system. These changes include the deployment of many specialized services in the regions and the privatization of services.

Deployment of Specialized Services
As conceived in many decentralization plans, Alberta's specialized services, such as treatment resources for children, were moved into the regions. It was planned that each region would have a complete range of resources, thereby eliminating the need to move children great distances from their homes in order to receive services. This objective was largely achieved, as there is now little movement of children between communities and regions. Providing services within regions has a number of advantages. First and foremost, young people can be main-

tained in their community, providing less disruption to natural support systems such as family and friends. Intervention efforts can focus not only on the young person but also on the whole support system, maximizing the likelihood of sustaining long-term changes. Community-based support services can also be accessed and organized to support the case plan goals developed for the individual client. Finally, there is a reduction in service costs because transportation costs for children and their families are reduced.

The decentralization of the delivery system, however, is not without disadvantages. Although there are now more services in the regions than ever before, it did not prove feasible to develop a complete range of services within each region. Cost considerations, a well as the scarcity of specialists, had the effect of leaving gaps in the continuum of services within the regions, particularly with respect to highly specialized services. At the same time, coordination between regions was often not sufficiently effective to ensure that clients had access to specialized services in other regions.

Privatization of Services

A second change in the delivery system during decentralization involved the privatization of services. At the beginning of the Alberta experience, most services had been operated by the government, but, as the decade progressed, an increasing number of services were contracted out to nongovernment operators.

Privatization brought with it a number of advantages. Private operators were capable of responding quickly to emerging community service needs by developing new programs and delivering them in a more flexible manner than was formerly the case. By piloting new program models under private agencies on a limited basis, models could be tested and adjusted to meet needs without a major commitment on the part of the department. Successful programs could then be implemented on a wider basis than was previously possible. Generally the emergence of private service providers helped to revitalize and make more innovative the child welfare system.

Although the benefits of privatization are important, there are also some drawbacks. The method of tendering and contracting for new services has led to a competitive environment between nongovernment service providers, resulting in less willingness to share ideas and information about community-based intervention methods. Moreover, many private operators perceive that when the government purchases services it does so on the basis of cost considerations alone, with little attempt to assess quality criteria. Thus, proposals are drawn up with a view to minimizing costs, often to the detriment of quality considerations (Gabor et al. 1991).

A second drawback associated with privatization concerns salaries in the private sector. Government funding policies have pegged private sector salaries at about 25 per cent lower than those for corresponding government classifications. The result is that there has been a steady drain of skilled professionals from the private sector, resulting in a high turnover rate and difficulty in maintaining an experienced workforce. This is particularly detrimental in child and youth care programs, where many of the problems of young people are related to previous losses of important relationships in their lives.

Overall, throughout much of the decentralization process in Alberta, there has been a shortage of the highly trained, skilled individuals to fill the many newly created specialized positions in the regions. This was particularly true in some of the northern communities, which were perceived by many as less desirable places to live. Consequently, many key regional positions went unfilled for lengthy periods of time, while some were filled, by default, by people who lacked the skills, qualifications, and experience required for the positions. The inability to find well-qualified people to fill key positions greatly impaired the ability of the regions to assume and carry out their new responsibilities of meeting the variety of community-based social service needs. As decentralization and privatization movements progress in other provinces, these problems will continue to challenge social policy developers, social service providers, and front-line child and youth care workers.

Standards for Programs and Practitioners
The proliferation of community-based programs in Canada has undoubtedly been accelerated by economic considerations, by legislative trends (including decentralization and privatization), and by professional developments. However, it can be argued that the quickly growing demand for such programs did not leave a sufficient opportunity for adequate preparation and orderly growth. Under such circumstances, it is hardly surprising that program standards are a key issue needing to be addressed.

A related concern is the matter of standards for community workers. Child and youth care has long been a field where standard credentials have been lacking, leaving agencies with the power to decide who is and who is not a child and youth care worker through their hiring process (Austin 1981). Consequently, many people filling community child and youth care positions have neither child and youth care training nor child and youth care experience. Ironically, at a time when residential care seems to be making headway in upgrading staff qualifications, community care can still be practised by anyone who manages to get a job. And there remains a related concern, even when qualified people are employed in community programs. Because many child and youth care training programs still tend to emphasize work in group care, and because few workers in residential programs have much experience in community work, even trained and experienced child and youth care workers do not usually have preparation appropriate to community work.

The development and implementation of appropriate standards is further complicated by the 'decentralization' and 'privatization' of social services described earlier. Specifically, when services are contracted to private providers (as are many community programs), fees are kept low and benefits are not usually provided. Since there is often no assurance of continued employment beyond the current contract, career opportunities are limited. Thus, experienced workers are not usually attracted to contract work. Moreover, there is constant worker turnover as people leave contract work to take more traditional and stable jobs. The result is that the least experienced or trained people fill many community child and youth care positions. Yet, because of the complexity of the tasks and the need for the ability to work with minimum supervision and supports, community work requires the talents and skills of the most able and experienced child and youth care workers.

The present lack of standards for programs and practitioners leaves the field in a very vulnerable position. This is a situation which must be urgently addressed in order to ensure the quality of the services provided.

Impact on Families

The growing prominence of community child and youth care represents a promising development for families in need of child welfare services. In effect, community child and youth care brings services to families, lessening the chance that children are served in isolation, removed from their family and community. At the same time, community child and youth care workers are in a position to involve family members in the child's treatment. There is considerable evidence now that chances of favourable outcomes in child welfare services are increased if the child and the family can both be involved in the effort to change (Maluccio and Sinanogul 1981).

Community programs appear to be less bureaucratic in their organization and structures than are many child welfare programs as well as being more flexible and responsive in delivering their services. This is of considerable advantage in providing services and designing programs according to the unique needs of individual families. Thus, services can be provided at various times of the week, including weekends; the child or the family or some combination of the two can be the focus of service; and the services can be provided inside or outside the home. Moreover, there is an informality about community child and youth care that is attractive to some families. These qualities make community child and youth care programs more accessible, again increasing the possibility that the family will join in the child's treatment.

As well, community child and youth care services are sufficiently flexible that they can be offered at various points of need. Services can be offered to high-risk individuals and families in the hope that the problems can be prevented. Early service can be provided before a problem has grown too large and complex. Some community services can be designed to take the place of or shorten residential placement. This, in turn, maximizes the chances that the family can be kept united or can be successfully reunited. Finally, services can be offered after placement in order to help the family to accommodate the return of the child and to help support the child's various community involvements.

Overall, community child and youth care work appears to be an ideal medium for delivering family-oriented child welfare programs. It is to be hoped that community programs can maintain their present flexibility and client orientation. To the degree that they are successful in doing this, community child and youth care promises to be influential in increasing the family orientation of child welfare services.

The Need for Research
Although, as the trends and developments described above indicate, community child and youth care is becoming an ever more significant branch of the profession, very little empirical research has been conducted on the topic of community-based programs and practice. It is not surprising, therefore, that as yet there is an almost non-existent lit-

erature in the area of community child and youth care practice, although there are an increasing number of descriptive studies about community programs. In this respect, community child and youth care is not too different from group care, which for many years lacked a research base (Powell 1982) and is just now beginning to acquire adequate literature. From time to time the field of child and youth care is urged to devote more effort to research endeavours (Beker 1979). Community child and youth care needs to take such exhortations seriously if it is to develop a solid professional base.

One part of the research agenda for community child and youth care relates to the issue of adequate educational preparation for child and youth care workers. Pence (1990) suggests that, for too long, the entire field of child and youth care has viewed the worlds of practice and research as separate from one another. Further, he argues that this separation is not only artificial and unnecessary but also dysfunctional. In fact, Pence suggests that

> when one makes this mental and focal shift . . . to the parallel processes inherent in research and in practice, a true accommodation between child and youth care practice and child and youth care research becomes possible. Indeed, at the baccalaureate degree level, a program could not provide professional training in one without impacting on the other. (p. 237)

Pence (1990) goes on to describe six steps of both research and practice that include observing and reporting, interpreting based on theory, planning intervention, implementing a plan, and evaluating and communicating results both orally and in writing. He rightly argues that these six steps are as central to child and youth care practice as they are to research in the field. Child and youth care training programs must make the linkages between these commonly taught processes so that graduates can truly move the field forward. As Pence so aptly concludes:

> With the gift of process — the process of observing, interpreting, planning, implementing, evaluating, and reporting — a professional can . . . learn what will be effective, under what conditions, and for which groups or individuals. And, ultimately, it is that ability, the ability to become a learner-practitioner utilizing systematic feedback and

replicable procedures, which must serve as the foundation for the development of professional child and youth care. (p. 240)

It seems clear that if child and youth care workers are to be well trained for their roles in the community and elsewhere, attention to both research and practice is important. For research knowledge and skills will better equip front-line workers and their supervisors to initiate important, reality-based research and to undertake program evaluations, needs assessments, and the like. Each of these exercises is central to providing higher quality services and care to children, youth, and families in community and other settings.

For example, more studies aimed at describing and analyzing precisely what child and youth care workers do in the community would be helpful in determining the community-specific education required by workers and would help to define community child and youth care and its relationship to other professions. Research is also needed to demonstrate the effectiveness and efficiency of various forms of community-based child and youth care. Presumably, such studies could elaborate on when, for whom, and in what circumstances certain community child and youth care services would be most appropriate.

Answers to such questions are by no means predictable. To date, community child and youth care practice is based on accumulated wisdom, not on empirical evidence. It is not suggested that practice should develop only from empirical evidence, but, rather, that more empirical research is a necessary component of knowledge building. As more research results become available, there may be some surprises which will lead to the re-examination of widely accepted practices.

Beyond empirical research, theory-building studies that often begin with descriptive projects are also invaluable as the field of community-based child and youth care evolves. Front-line workers are usually best positioned to observe and record aspects of their experience that prompt questions. If educated to appreciate the theories inherent in child and youth care practice (e.g., Pence 1990), front-line workers can often see situations that test current models used in training better than can child and youth care educators in their ivory towers. While they generally have few resources with which to take on research projects, agency directors and workers need to be reminded of, and rewarded for, the valuable contribution they make to the field of community child and youth care when they use their skills to document and communicate their experiences through journals and conferences. Encouraging practitioners to link with educators and researchers should become a more common practice. In fact, if child and youth care workers do not initiate such linkages, others will.

Specifically, community child and youth care will attract increased evaluation research activity in the future, because funders will be interested in determining whether increased reliance on community child and youth care is warranted. This type of research provides a starting point, but it tends to be too narrowly focused to provide the information required for the continued development of the profession. If the issues posed above are to be addressed, community child and youth care will need to work harder to generate its own research activities. Realizing that community child and youth care work is often a multidisciplinary enterprise, research should also benefit from the expertise of those professionals involved in community caregiving such as, for example, psychology, social work, education, and nursing. To ensure that this happens and that the research is practical and useful, those who have the greatest stake in the development of the field – child and youth care workers – must take a much greater interest in this area (Krueger 1982).

Summary and Conclusions

Over the past several years, child and youth care work has changed significantly. Fifteen years ago child and youth care was almost always practised in group care situations; today there are numerous community agencies which employ child and youth care workers. The development of child and youth care has been accelerated by a number of trends in the helping professions, most notably ecological concepts and a growing preference for family- and community-based services. As well, increased cost consciousness on the part of government funders has also provided an impetus for the growth of community child and youth care.

The practice of community child and youth care takes place within a wide variety of settings, ranging from street corners to day treatment programs and including schools, homes, and crisis centres. As a result, the definition of the field is unclear and boundaries are ill-defined. As the field struggles to define itself more clearly, it may be tempting to cast a wide net and include all things within the definition of community child and youth care. But the profession would be better served by defining itself in a way congruent with its beginnings. Community child and youth care should build on child and youth care's humanistic philosophical base, its holistic orientation, and on the traditional ability of its practitioners to effectively engage and relate to people. Child and youth care should remain a constant contact practice and should continue to emphasize the goal of helping people transform the events of daily living into growth-promoting experiences.

At the same time, it is important to recognize that community child and youth care is different from group care in two important respects: (1) the context of the practice is the community, and (2) interventions often involve the child's family or others in the community. This suggests that additional skills, knowledge, and research are required for the practice of community child and youth care, and, also, that the work requires a shift from a primarily child-centred orientation to one that can include parents and other adults.

There are several key issues facing the field at this time. Perhaps the most important is that few standards exist either for community programs or for practitioners. Compounding the problem is the fact that, as yet, few educational programs prepare people adequately for community child and youth care work. Consequently, agencies can designate who is a community worker through their hiring process. Too often, under-qualified people are hired, leaving the profession in a very precarious position. In spite of these concerns and issues, the growth of community child and youth care is an exciting development for the field. This field of practice is well situated to play a key part in the ecologically oriented approaches to children's services which are so prominent today.

References
Alberta. 1984. Child welfare act. Statutes of Alberta, Chapter C8.1
Allerhand, M.E., Weber, R.E., and Haug, M. 1966. *Adaptation and adaptability: The Bellefaire followup study*. New York: Child Welfare League of America
Anglin, J.P. 1983. Setting the sights: An assessment of child care job functions and training needs in British Columbia. In C. Denholm, A. Pence, and R. Ferguson (eds.), *The scope of child care in British Columbia*. Victoria: University of Victoria
Austin, D. 1981. Formal educational preparation: The structural pre-requisite to the professional status of the child care worker. *Child Care Quarterly* 10:250–60
Barnes, F.H. 1980. The child care worker: A conceptual approach. Paper prepared for the Conference-Research Sequence in Child Care Education, Pittsburgh, PA
Beker, J. 1979. Editorial: Child care education and trainers. *Child Care Quarterly* 8:161–2

Beker, J. and Maier, H.W. 1981. Emerging issues in child care education: A platform for planning. *Child Care Quarterly* 10:200-9

British Columbia. Ministry of Human Resources. 1978. *The family and children's services policy manual.* Victoria

Gabor, P. 1975. A theoretical exploration of the child care worker position in the treatment institution. M.A. thesis, McGill University, Montreal

Gabor, P. and Collins, D. 1985-6. Family work in child care. *Journal of Child Care* 2:15-27

Gabor, P., Nicholson, H., Charles, G., and Thomlison, R. 1991. The decentralization of child welfare services in Alberta: A case study. Paper presented at the International Conference on the Welfare State in Transition, Budapest, Hungary

Garbarino, J. 1982. *Children and families in the social environment.* New York: Aldine

Hurl, L. 1984. Privatized social service systems: Lessons from Ontario children's services. *Canadian Public Policy* 10:395-405

Ing, C. and Gabor, P. 1988. Teaching conflict resolution skills to families. *Journal of Child Care* 3:69-80

Kammerman, S. and Kahn, A. 1990. Conclusions and recommendations. *Children and Youth Services Review* 12:145-67

Kinkaide, P. 1987. The revitalization of community enterprise: The Alberta case for 'privatizing' social services. In J. Ismael and R. Thomlison (eds.), *Perspectives on social services and issues.* Ottawa, ON: Canadian Council on Social Development

Krueger, M.A. 1982. Child care worker involvement in research. *Journal of Child Care* 1:59-65

Lewis, H. 1989. Ethics and the private non-profit human services organizations. *Administration in Social Work* 13:1-4

Maier, H.W. 1988. *Developmental group care and practice.* New York: Haworth

Maluccio, A. and Sinanogul, P.A. (eds.). 1981. *The challenge of partnership: Working with parents of children in foster care.* New York: Child Welfare League of America

Ontario. Ministry of Community and Social Services. 1982. The children's act: A consultation paper. Toronto

—. 1983. *Three decades of change; The evolution of residential care and community alternatives in children's services.* Toronto

Pence, A. 1990. Worlds apart? Integrating research and practice in professional child and youth care training. *Child and Youth Services* 13:235-41

Powell, D.R. 1982. The role of research in the development of the child care profession. *Child Care Quarterly* 11:4-11

Ricks, F. and Charlesworth, J. 1982. Role and functions of child care workers. *Journal of Child Care* 1:35-43

Shyne, A.W. 1973. Research on child-caring institutions. In D.M. Pappenfort, D.M. Kilpatrick, and R.W. Roberts (eds.), *Child caring: Social policy and the institution.* Chicago: Aldine

Taylor, D.A. and Alpert, S.W. 1973. *Community and support following residential treatment.* New York: Child Welfare League of America

Trieschman, A.E., Whittaker, J.K., and Brendtro, L.K. 1969. *The other twenty-three hours: Child care work in a therapeutic milieu.* Chicago: Aldine

VanderVen K.D. 1979. Developmental characteristics of child care workers and design of training programs. *Child Care Quarterly* 8:100–12

—. 1981. Patterns of career development in group care. In F. Ainsworth and L.C. Fulcher (eds.), *Group care for children.* London: Tavistock

Whittaker, J.K. 1977. Child welfare: Residential treatment. In *Encyclopedia of Social Work.* Washington, DC: National Association of Social Workers

Wolfensberger, W. 1972. *Normalization.* New York: National Institute on Mental Retardation

9
Recreation Services
Gary Young and Kevin Pike

History and Philosophy

As we approach the end of the twentieth century it is interesting to note that, while games and recreation are at least as old as recorded history, the specific history of organized recreation and leisure services in North America is largely a phenomenon of this century. Its formal beginnings can be found in the parks and playgrounds movements of the first third of the century, but it has been the post-Second World War period that has been the most significant in the development of a new parks and recreation and leisure services profession.

Both historically and presently, the parks and recreation movement has embraced the broader objectives of child and youth care services. It is interesting to note how this movement paralleled other services, with its primary focus evolving from, in the early part of the century, a concern for youth at risk tied to the concept of serving lower income communities, to today's commitment to serve all segments of society. In addition, contemporary parks and recreation services have had to deal with a broader range of special needs challenges in order to meet the expectations of society for mainstreaming all children and youth, brought about by the deinstitutionalization movement. As will be pointed out in this chapter, parks, recreation and leisure services have been on a path of convergence with other services, program streams, and professions within the child and youth care sector, almost from the inception of this relatively young profession.

Children, of course, have been 'natural players' from the beginning of time. But as we moved through the twentieth century, play and recreation for children and youth came to be seen, increasingly, as necessary for the development of good citizens. These pastimes were also viewed as a diversion from a growing number of anti-social activities.

Although adult recreation grew in importance, the fifties and sixties were clearly decades which placed emphasis on children. An explosion in the development of ice arenas, swimming pools, and recreation centres was the response to the baby boom generation, and children turned out in ever-burgeoning numbers for organized activities.

Indeed, it was *organized activity* that drew most children. Hockey, figure skating, swimming lessons, competitive swimming — the things the school system did not offer — became more popular and, in fact, became a 'requirement' for every community. As recreation for adults moved from being a secondary and peripheral feature of life to a primary consideration, the expectations of these adults for their children's leisure grew as well. It became essential for each community of any size to provide a pool and an arena. As family size began to decrease and as affluence grew, children were able to actively participate in not just one, but several, of these often expensive activities. In addition, governments saw a mandate to provide recreation for those who could not afford the admission fees. This followed the philosophy that everyone needs and is benefited by positive leisure experiences.

Rick Gruneau of Simon Fraser University notes that the central philosophy for the development of a broad range of public leisure services in the fifties and sixties was based on the principle that these services produced certain benefits. In the last two decades, that philosophy has shifted. Governments are now providing these services simply because people want them, even though there is still the underlying virtue of their being beneficial (Gruneau 1984). As we approach the turn of the century, however, a new view may be taking hold. That view has to do with public recreation — the idea that park and leisure services are, primarily, providers of health, a preventive service that is not only fun but is also a major contributor to the reduction of illness and, thus, a contributor to a reduction in traditional health care costs. The children and youth who grow up in systems where positive leisure experiences are the norm, and who are educated to realize that their health is influenced significantly by the way they spend their leisure time, will become the adults who will create a new order of well-being in our societies.

Evolution of the Profession

As recreation has developed over the past quarter century, the question, 'Are we yet a profession?' has often been posed. For many, especially the younger workers in our field, this becomes an important question as they attempt to establish credibility, competence, and collegial relationships with their former classmates who have joined other established professions, such as education, medicine, and law.

The classic view of a 'profession' includes a clearly delineated definition of the scope of knowledge required for the field. Unfortunately, this requirement is a significant impediment since each member of society holds a personal view of how recreation should be defined. The leaders of the profession have not yet provided a firm, theoretical foundation for the profession.

Recreation conjures up different images for each member of society. Not surprisingly then, the recreation profession has yet to agree on appropriate descriptive definitions of the fundamental words that describe our business, namely, 'leisure,' 'recreation,' 'play,' 'sports,' 'arts,' and 'culture.' Serena Arnold of the University of California suggests that 'as long as recreation is anything done in free time and described by various activities, pursued for pleasure, and as long as leisure is welded to time and is viewed as games for fun, there are no boundaries' (1980:7).

The problem is compounded further when one recognizes that what some consider to be leisure, such as remodelling a home, gardening, or working out at the gym, others consider to be work. The person who does this activity for leisure often reports how much she/he enjoys the opportunity to get away from the humdrum of other life activities. Again, for others, these are not considered leisure activities.

Play

Many child development experts suggest that play is the work of the child. They suggest that play provides an opportunity for children to try on different roles, to experience different sensations, to integrate physical activity with mental comprehension; in short, to use fantasy and fun as the primary tools for exploring the world in which they live. Some suggest that as much as 85 per cent of the total knowledge of a human being is gathered through the play process (Pennington 1988). If this is true, then adults, be they parents, teachers, or other child-related professionals, dramatically undervalue the play activity. Generally speaking, adults see play as something that should be done after education, after chores, and after other 'essential' activities have been completed rather than being seen itself as an essential element in self-development. Robin Moore, author of *Childhood's Domain*, told a Vancouver conference in 1982, 'Adults tend to spend little time ensuring that enriching environments are created where social actions, physical activity, creative thoughts and contemplation can and will occur. In fact, it can be said with some real assurance that we have been moving in the opposite direction.' Education programs are expected to add more and more facts to the curriculum, which is taught within the formal, institutional walls of our various schools. Urban areas are seeing higher and higher population density with a corresponding removal of natural play settings, be they wooded lots, large back yards, or quiet neighbourhood streets.

The Scope of the Field in Relation to Children and Youth

Leisure Time and Recreation
Modern, urban families' leisure patterns have shifted dramatically. The casual informal play opportunities of earlier times appear to be in decline. Children's leisure activities are becoming replicas of adult work, e.g., hectic schedules, numerous planned events, and high levels of energy output. In North Vancouver we have seen child and youth registrations in formal programs and organized sport grow significantly in the last five years, while the school population has remained virtually static.

Numerous writings have properly depicted the probable effects that hundreds of hours of T.V. watching have on children, particularly as this medium describes a world of sexism, violence, stereotypical cultures, and the like. 'One thing is certain: every hour spent passively in front of the T.V. robs children of first hand experiences which are essential to their development,' wrote Jane Knight (1984:5) of Ryerson University.

A recent survey of teenagers by Nancy Hall (1991) indicated that significant numbers find the experience of walking from one point to another in their neighbourhood to be a somewhat fearful experience, one that requires a sense of caution to avoid falling victim to the violence perpetrated by some teen groups. Do those who initiate this violence define these activities as part of their play? Do young people, who are emulating the romanticized action of *The Terminator*, find the joy and fun, traditionally associated with leisure time, in these violent activities?

The recent development of the recreation profession is being shaped by changing conditions of society. Specifically, the challenge of recreation workers serving children and youth is to find ways to counteract the dehumanizing, isolating conditions present in much of today's North American culture. Planned activities require, as a theme, models of positive use of leisure time. Again, the terminology becomes confusing when one attempts to define what is positive across a range of lifestyles and situations.

Historically, play has provided an opportunity for Canadian children to meet in a shared world of play, which has helped to overcome many of the barriers which differentiated and separated their parents. Collective activities, particularly for younger children, often seemed blind to economic standing, colour or ethnic background, and, to some extent, even the sex of the participants. Of course, this is not to suggest that play is the single most important levelling factor in society, and one which will necessarily lead to the creation of a perfectly homogeneous Canadian community. However, the games and play activities of the neighbourhood children encouraged each child to find a position within the 'child culture' of his or her neighbourhood. Each group in this sub-society put some emphasis on a different type of play pattern and, as a result, lifetime friendships were struck, social skills were developed, and life patterns established. Today, recreationists are struggling to create new environments where this type of personal development can be fostered. Structured 'how to' classes are being slowly replaced by drop-in opportunities which are now offered in controlled settings, such as gyms and pools, to replace informal neighbourhood play opportunities which lack the parent-present home as the base.

Another factor which contributed to the development of the recreation profession was Canada's open door to immigrants, particularly from Europe. Many of the common elements in play patterns of the past forty years can be traced to European immigrant groups. When they came to this country, they found a set of recreation activities which, while uniquely Canadian, did have strong European roots. More recently, there has been an influx of a multitude of new ethnic groups, who have brought with them substantially different recreation patterns and games. Children are finding that their play patterns are constrained by the lack of commonality of the games that are passed on to them as part of their heritage.

How difficult it must be for a young teenager to emigrate from Pakistan or Vietnam and integrate quickly with the neighbourhood young people's number-one-ranked activity, sitting around listening to contemporary music and talking with friends (Posterski and Bibby 1987).

While many would argue that music is indeed the universal language and that contemporary pop stars are known around the world, nonetheless, the unique language of Canadian teen groups is a far cry from the predominant characteristics of previous lifestyles for many immigrant children. Yet young people are often those members of immigrant families most receptive to the Canadian culture, and leisure activities can and do form a functional transition forum.

Sports and Recreation

There are many who argue that sport is the essential recreation activity; that in sport, children have an opportunity to develop both their growth and their fine motor movement skills, hand/eye coordination, team work, a sense of cooperation, sportsmanship, a general sense of self worth, and strong relationships with significant adults, other than their own parents. Others argue that this may be true in theory, but that any visit to a minor hockey game will quickly belie all of the good intentions. They point to the outrageous behaviour of some coaches and a sometimes abnormal focus on competition and winning. All these factors lead one to question the concept of positive character development. One can point to the high drop-out rates of teenagers from sport and make a case that the sport delivery system is a failure.

As is the case with our previous discussions, the truth lies somewhere between the two extremes and, again, recreation leaders need to look at the variety of opportunities provided by sport and ensure that these possibilities can lead to positive experiences for the participants. Generally, we have seen dramatic improvements in the delivery of sport in the past ten years as the system has placed more and more emphasis on volunteer training, skill development, and fair play. The recreation profession, in concert with sport administrators, has accepted the challenge for encouraging this development, and future programs will likely see an emphasis on parent education, cross-sport training, and peer counselling.

Cultural Activities and Recreation

Finally, one must ask how music, art, and other cultural activities fit into children's and youth's leisure patterns. How can we develop and cultivate these activities as interests and, hence, develop the creative side of each human being. In *Megatrends 2000*, Naisbitt and Aburdene (1990) note that art is rapidly replacing sport as society's dominant leisure activity. Children have always exhibited creative interests, but only in these last few years of the twentieth century do we see a real encouragement at every level of society to develop these activities. Dance classes, music lessons, and painting classes are becoming more and more a part of children's leisure activities.

As was stated earlier, the concept of recreation or leisure constitutes such a broad and yet such a personal set of experiences that one is challenged to adequately define them. The organizations that deliver programs and services in Canadian society can, however, be more easily categorized. Generally, the service delivery system can be divided into three sectors: the volunteer sector, nongovernmental organizations, and government services.

Service Delivery Systems

Volunteer sector

It should always be remembered, when looking at recreation or leisure services, that the vast majority of recreation opportunities provided to Canadians are organized and conducted by volunteers or by individuals personally collecting nominal fees for providing individual instruction. Most leaders in this particular sector provide their services strictly for benevolent reasons. Often, of course, they are parents drawn into leadership to support their children in Girl Guides and Boy Scouts, 4-H Clubs, community sports organizations, local choirs, and so on. Some are trained, often replicating what they received when they were children themselves, particularly those who provide music instruction. Others begin the activity knowing little about it, but possess the desire to support or enhance the lives of children.

In most communities between 10 and 20 per cent of the population are actively involved in volunteer work in recreation settings. It is a common meeting ground for persons from almost all sectors of society, who collectively pool their efforts to provide recreation opportunities for themselves, their own children, and other members in the community.

As an aside, it is interesting to note that even with the accelerating rate of the breakdown of the traditional family, if there is to be any place in the community where adults who are lone parents or weekend parents meet, it is around these types of recreation activities. It is unfortunate that this common ground is not utilized more as an opportunity to support families in a variety of ways.

As well, these volunteers are increasingly being asked to provide advice to policymakers on matters affecting recreation. They also join with governments and business in partnerships to build new facilities and services. As a consequence, the recreation profession is spending more and more time supporting and facilitating the activities of these various volunteer-based organizations.

Nongovernmental Organizations
There are significant numbers of nongovernmental organizations (NGOs), or societies, which employ several thousand Canadians in the provision of services for children and youth. These NGOs usually provide services to a larger catchment area than the previously noted volunteer organizations, often focusing on larger communities, provinces, or even the nation. Many of these organizations are designed to provide support, encouragement, training, and programs for the aforementioned community-based volunteers. As an example, in the sporting community you would find, at both the national level and the provincial level, a full-time staff responsible for the design of programs, leadership training, sport administration, insurance, championship play, and development programs for elite athletes, all geared to supporting these local, volunteer-staffed, community-based organizations noted in the first category. Normally, these NGO staff groups report to a volunteer board composed of citizens, who have come from the ranks of the local community organizations. Similarly, you would find staff supporting similar organizations in sectors other than sport, such as 4-H Clubs, choral federations, and youth symphonies.

Other NGOs tend to provide more specific programs to particular groups of citizens; for example, the YMCA and the Boys' and Girls' Clubs of Canada provide a number of facilities and professional staff in many urban Canadian neighbourhoods. Boys' and Girls' Clubs recognize that recreation can be a tool towards guidance and, as a result, they see programs as vehicles to assist young persons in their overall development. These types of organizations often gear their services either to specific neighbourhoods or segments of the population, such as those who have special needs or are suffering financial hardship. The professional staffs of these organizations are often expected to provide direct services to children. They are also expected to develop volunteer corps to expand their programs beyond that which they themselves can provide. They, too, usually report through some hierarchy to volunteer boards of directors.

Government Services

In 1974, the ministers of the various provincial governments and the federal government who were responsible for the delivery of sport and recreation services adopted the following resolution:

Whereas recreation includes all of those activities in which an individual chooses to participate in his leisure time and is not confined solely to sports and physical recreation programs, but includes artistic, creative, cultural, social and intellectual activities;

and whereas recreation is a fundamental human need for citizens of all ages and interests and is essential to the psychological, social and physical well-being of man;

and whereas society is rapidly changing and leisure time is increasing;

be it therefore resolved that this Conference recognizes the fact that recreation is a social service in the same way that health and education are considered as social services and that recreation's purpose should be: (a) to assist individual and community development; (b) to improve the quality of life; and (c) to enhance social functioning. Such recognition will indicate the constitutional responsibility of the Provinces and Territories in recreation services. (Posterski and Bibby 1987:23)

This was an important step for recreation. It finally gave clear recognition to the fact that the provincial government had the primary responsibility for delivery of recreation services in the country. This concept was further reinforced at a 1978 conference where the minister of state for fitness and amateur sport stated, 'I do indeed recognize the primacy of the Province in the field of Recreation' (ibid.). The two senior levels of government have agreed 'that Recreation in Canada, in common with other social services, lies within the jurisdiction of the Provinces' (ibid.). In addition, for the first time, the 1974 resolution recognized recreation as a social service on a status equal to health and education. This resolution is unique in that it is the first attempt to clarify both the roles and responsibilities to the profession.

Municipal governments exist as a result of acts adopted by each province and, hence, the form and style of these local governments will vary across the country. However, in every province, the primary responsibility for delivery of recreation services is identified in the various acts that constitute these local governments. As a consequence, the single largest provider of services outside of the voluntary sector is the municipal government. Normally, these services are provided under a department called 'Parks and Recreation,' but one may also find them under 'Leisure Services,' 'Social Services,' or some other departmental name providing facilities, resources, and programs. Individual workers in these municipal services come together, voluntarily, in various provincial recreation associations and, nationally, through the Canadian Parks/Recreation Association, which acts as a clearing house and advocacy group from its headquarters in Ottawa.

Almost all sizable municipal governments have sections, departments, or commissions providing recreational services and, in most cases, they attempt to meet the three purposes stated in the above-noted resolution, namely, community development, improved quality of life, and enhanced social functioning.

The primary reason for decentralizing this responsibility to the local governments rests with the recognition that (a) most volunteer organizations, which should properly be partners in the delivery of services, are community-based, and (b) the direct nature of services provided can best be achieved with constant and ongoing contact with the citizenry. The recognition of municipalities as the principal delivery agent was confirmed in the National Recreation Statement released in 1987. Given that each municipality across this country is unique in its cultural makeup, economic base, and demographics, there are a number of differences in the types of recreation services required to meet local needs.

Most municipal parks and recreation departments operate under some organizational objective for providing quality recreation experiences for the family. In a few cases, this results in the maintenance of a separate children's programming section, but, generally, the professional staff responsible for designing and implementing recreation programs have job descriptions requiring some form of coordinated seniors/adult/youth/children's programming aimed at all residents of the defined communities. Often, the job expectation also notes some anticipation of balance within programming to ensure opportunities for positive leisure experiences in social, emotional, physical, intellectual, and spiritual areas. In the vast majority of cases, the actual programs are led by a part-time, casual, or volunteer staff, who often provide this service out of a commitment to their community. The full-time professional staff, therefore, are generally responsible for identifying program need, designing functional programs, promotion, hiring and supervising appropriate part-time staff, and evaluating the services. Since most recreation agencies have expectations that some portion of the service costs must be recovered from the user, staff are also expected to be skilled in marketing, pricing, and cost control.

The professional staff is often also expected to provide some form of facility management, whether this is overseeing community halls, community centres, swimming pools, ice rinks, arts centres, playing fields, interpretive centres, heritage buildings, outdoor band shells, beach areas, or other outdoor gathering places. These staff usually work in some form of collegial relationship with the staff responsible for providing maintenance and engineering services to these indoor and outdoor recreation facilities. Further, recreation professionals are often also expected to provide support and assistance in one form or another to the locally based community groups that were mentioned earlier.

In the operation of indoor and outdoor recreation facilities, there exists a wide variety of relationships between municipal recreation departments and the volunteer sector. While there is a broad continuum, the following four models might best describe municipal parks and recreation operations.

Municipal Models of Service Delivery

Community Ownership
In this model, municipal governments lease out land and/or facilities to local community groups to manage and operate. These groups sometimes receive an additional subsidy from the municipalities to assist with the operations, but, for the most part, they are responsible for the hiring of staff, the management of the facilities, the development of policies, and the delivery of services. In this type of operation, the staff reports directly to a board of directors and staff members are usually employees of this local organization, rather than the municipality.

Partnerships
In the partnership model, the municipality and a local community association each agrees to provide certain services leading to the overall delivery of programs to the community. Often, the local board of directors takes responsibility for the development of policies and the implementation of programming. The staff that is hired is usually municipal

although the local association has some involvement in the hiring process. These staff members are usually supervised by the municipality, but take many day-to-day instructions from the volunteer community board.

Consultation
In this model, the municipality takes more responsibility for the operation and maintenance of the facilities, staffing, and the development of policies; however, some form of advisory committee is struck to give staff advice on the tailoring of programs to meet the needs of the particular community in which the facility is found.

Municipal Operation
In this situation, the municipality takes full responsibility for providing services, with no organized community group providing advice or participating in decision-making. However, even in these settings, almost every recreation department in the country now tries to involve local volunteer groups and other clients in program development, evaluations, and related facets of the operation. It is important to note that recreation staff must be flexible enough to work in any one of the aforementioned settings and variations thereof.

With respect to children and youth, under normal circumstances, one will find either no citizen involvement or some form of consultative process on the development of children's programming, although one should always expect that, from time to time, child advocates will arise from within the community and speak strongly to a particular point of view. On such occasions, it is necessary to accept the feedback and measure the advice relative to the overall needs of the community before proceeding.

With respect to youth, there is a growing movement across the country for citizens to become more directly involved in youth services, particularly those aimed at what are commonly called the 'at-risk' youth. At-risk youth can best be described as those young people who do not comfortably fit into the traditional programming provided through the schools, community clubs, and recreation departments. Often, the blocks to participation in mainstream programs include a background of negative experiences with similar types of institutions and services. Adult citizen involvement at this level is particularly useful, given that funding of these programs is sometimes difficult to arrange since the provision of services for at-risk youth slides between the mandates of the three levels of government. Fortunately, community groups usually have alternate fundraising possibilities within the community, without which such services often would not exist. As well, citizen participation at this level of programming has a better opportunity to involve the parents of the at-risk youth, who may themselves need support and assistance.

Therapeutic Recreation
Until recently, society has used specialized residential institutions for large sectors of the special needs population. Residential child and youth care workers were typically the front-line staff employed in such settings. Recreation departments, for the most part, had developed only limited services to this population group. However, in the early to mid-1980s a number of governments across the country made a conscious decision to deinstitutionalize many of the services that they had provided to persons with disabilities. In essence, this meant that a larger number of persons with special needs, who previously had been housed or at least serviced by provincially funded institutions, were moved into their local communities, either in their personal residences or in group homes. Suddenly, and properly, they expected services from the local authorities. As noted earlier, the process of deinstitutionalization has been a factor in bringing the work of the recreationist into closer alignment with other child and youth professions.

In the area of therapeutic recreation there is, as well, a continuum of services that varies from one community to another and across organizations. The philosophical base of some recreation organizations prescribes that recreation is the best place to provide opportunities for persons with disabilities to be integrated into the normal lifestyle of the community and, as such, most recreation programs are designed with integration as a possible objective. Often these integrated programs require 'recreation buddies' — volunteers or part-time staff who assist the special needs individual to participate with other members of the community in the various programs until help is no longer required.

Other jurisdictions with different philosophies offer 'segregated programs,' such as wheelchair basketball, in which only persons with disabilities participate. A long and heated debate has raged within the community of care workers as to what model is most effective. It would now seem that many organizations are moving towards recognizing that segregated programs are required by some persons, but that wherever possible, the objective of these programs should be the development of sufficient skills to integrate these people with other recreation participants. The recreation integration programs are then designed to assist, where necessary, with this integration process.

Practitioner Characteristics

Like any profession, the leisure service field has been shaped by the nature of the people who have worked in it and built it over the years. As we have seen, recreational services and the professionals working in it have also been affected by social changes over time. This combination of individuals and broader social forces has shaped the current characteristics of the field. Because it is also a new field, the last forty years have seen a wide variety of people, with a diverse range of skills, assuming staff positions at all levels.

As leisure services merged with one another and paid staff came to replace volunteers, recruiters looked to other disciplines and to the ranks of the volunteers themselves. Initially, it was the field of physical education which supplied the largest number of people. Most of these individuals were working in the school systems and were suitably prepared for a move to the leisure sector. Not surprisingly, in the twenty years following the Second World War, recreation was primarily seen as a physical activity. Staff members were also recruited from more established agencies, such as the YMCA and from the recreational specialist services of the armed forces. Recreation in that era was therefore defined as sport and fitness, with a social component viewed as a fortuitous secondary outcome.

New challenges were predicted in the field, however, and it soon became apparent that future candidates would be needed who were specifically educated for the provision of recreation and leisure services and who were specially trained to operate the growing number of facilities. Dr. John Farina of Sir Wilfrid Laurier University gained national prominence in the early 1980s when, in a national television news story, he predicted 'that man will likely be faced with an ever-increasing block of time which is potentially free.' It therefore followed that 'healthy' activities had to be provided to occupy this time. There was a need for creating and certifying a generation of students, upon whose shoulders this task would fall. At first, recreation education programs were primarily technically oriented, but soon courses in the philosophy of leisure and the history and critical analysis of various leisure practices were offered. In addition, programs branched out into specialized areas, like service to the aged or to people with disabilities. At the same time, research became an important component in post-secondary institutions.

Graduates of these programs, based both at universities and at community colleges, were in great demand. A survey of recreation graduates in British Columbia showed that of those graduating from the UBC program between 1962 and 1980, 84 per cent of the sample were currently in jobs in a recreation or recreation-related field (Gruneau 1984).

Today, there is more competition for the jobs available and there are more graduates available. The growth of programs in recreation education has stopped, however, and there seems to be a disturbing trend towards the elimination of programs at both universities and community colleges as costs rise and cutbacks are made. Recreation programs have been a target. The effect in the field has not yet been felt, but the quality of people looking for work may be affected adversely unless new ways are found to provide appropriately educated leisure practitioners.

None of this is to suggest that there does not exist, at this time, a strong and competent body of people who are providing for the leisure needs of our communities and for our children and youth. As in most of the people-serving fields, especially those encompassing service to children, recreation practitioners tend to be dedicated, committed, and, at times, selfless in their pursuit of improved quality and in the satisfaction of community demand. Virtually all of them have either a college diploma or a university degree. Some have postgraduate degrees. It is significant to note, however, that as many as 50 per cent of today's recreational leaders do not have recreation diplomas or degrees. The field continues to recruit from a broad range of disciplines which provides, in most workplaces, an eclectic range of people, who are at home with many facets of community life. This has been the strength of this field from the beginning and it continues to be to the present. In fact, the related child and youth care professions will likely become a significant source of candidates for employment in the future.

It is also important to note that, in the past two decades, the number of women entering the field has been greater than the number of men. While the senior positions are still primarily occupied by male practitioners, this is changing rapidly. It is not unusual to see a 50:50 mix in most municipal parks and recreation departments. As women begin to assume more senior roles, it might be expected that the nature of the service may change. At this point, the nature of this change would only be speculation.

A final comment on practitioners involves the mix in most leisure service departments of the parks and recreation functions. The nature of the people working in these two disciplines is quite different. While most recreation people are college or university educated, most park practitioners are drawn from the ranks of outdoor park-maintenance staff. The difference in training and background is quite apparent, but it is changing. A group of formally educated park employees is emerging which has increasingly become involved not only with the maintenance of the parks but with the planning and programming functions to meet changing leisure trends. For example, it is not unusual to see a group of children being consulted on the design of a new public playground or the gardener giving lessons on the nature of certain plant species.

Future Trends

So what is the future of the field of parks and recreation and leisure services? Perhaps the most accurate answer would be that the social trends which are driving Western society in general are equally salient for leisure services, but they have their own peculiar meaning for a field which specializes in fun.

A recent workshop of recreation leaders in British Columbia, brought together by the Richmond Parks and Leisure Services Department, identified four major trends which are having a particular impact on the provision of recreation services.

Changing Social Values

In a short period of time, the makeup of communities in Canada has undergone fundamental changes. From a country whose roots were predominantly European, Canada has become a multi-ethnic and multi-cultural society, and many new values have been introduced which challenge the ability of the traditional majority to adapt. We live in a time of independence, both individually and collectively, where neither families nor countries are staying together. Reaching consensus on issues has become a significant challenge as many community debates turn into an adversarial struggle to determine who is right and who will gain the upper hand. These struggles have reached into our youth population, which has joined the political battles over the environment, the economy, ethics, and justice.

As a community-based and community-driven service, parks and recreation is challenged to adapt as well and to provide for all facets of these new communities. It is learning how to deal with non-consensus in the community and how to bring about a collective understanding and acceptance of differences. Planning is becoming a short-term process as the need for flexibility and the toleration of differences becomes paramount.

Changing Roles and Expectations of Government

Local governments are closer to citizens and thus able to be more responsive than other levels of government. For the most part, local governments are more respected by voters at a time when there is widespread cynicism of senior levels of government. Yet while local governments have some of the highest expectations placed upon them, they have the fewest resources with which to respond. Citizens expect more, but also want greater value for their tax dollar. One solution has been to move towards more partnerships with community agencies, the school system, and private agencies. Both effectiveness and efficiency will be critical in the future.

Demographic Changes

In many of the major cities of Canada, populations are growing rapidly. The demands for parks and recreation services matches that growth. Cultural diversity, single-parent families, and an increased incidence of poverty have brought unprecedented pressures on families and children. In addition, our aging population is often more concerned with the welfare and the economic prospects of a huge wave of new retirees than it is with ensuring the newest generations receive maximum opportunity.

A Move to Self-Help

Existing community groups are assuming a broader mandate, and new groups are constantly springing up in response to community conflict, perceived service needs, or current political issues. The environmental movement is active in most community debates. When government does not respond quickly enough to needs or demands, a group will often form solely to lobby for its own priority. When the services provided by government are not seen as adequate, groups will form to provide for themselves. This is seen particularly in recreation as parent groups are taking on the management of a variety of specialty recreation clubs for their children, ranging from gymnastics to ballet, competitive swimming to drama. Parks and recreation departments are gaining expertise in dealing with these groups and have learned the skills of negotiation and conflict resolution.

These trends provide the broad strokes for the parks and recreation field, but there is a wide variety of sub-trends (both negative and positive) which provide special challenges in the area of service to children and youth. The negative trends include:

(1) Society is in a hurry and many parents are unable to provide the amount of time to their children that they and their children would like.

(2) Single-parent families are most susceptible to poverty, and children living without adequate resources present a special challenge to society.

(3) Child neglect appears to be increasing. It is often detected by leaders, supervisors, or coaches in the parks and recreation system.

(4) Even children from functional families are under pressure to perform, whether it be educationally or recreationally.

(5) Many forms of crime are increasing, and its participants are now more likely to be children or youth. A child unable to find self-esteem in a family may turn to street gangs and other anti-social behaviours in order to assert identity.

Fortunately, there are a number of positive trends to report as well. They include the following:

(1) High participation rates continue for children in a wide range of municipally organized leisure programs.

(2) The arts is a growing area of interest in the parks and recreation field, and children are just as involved as adults in everything from drama to community festivals.

(3) The environmental side of the field is attracting a new and idealistic group of youth, which is working with parks practitioners to set examples, on public land, for the general community to follow.

(4) Community youth-oriented sport is active and growing.

(5) Large numbers of committed community volunteers continue year after year to provide voluntary services to a host of recreational and leisure programs.

Conclusion

The parks and recreation and leisure services field is active and changing. Its practitioners are challenged as never before by a growing population, which expects quality and safety, but at the same time wants the latest activity trend. More and more special interest groups are appearing, each with its own unique focus, mandate, and set of expectations, and these groups often require unique, specific responses and support from recreation professionals. Children and youth needs for quality leisure services are increasing dramatically, but these needs can no longer be the only focus of recreation departments, which also must cater to much more active adult and seniors' population groups. As a consequence, the challenges are immense and will continue to increase as society becomes more and more diverse. Partnerships, joint projects, and shared resources among all child- and youth-oriented professions will be essential to meet future challenges.

References

Arnold, S. 1980. Recreation and leisure issues in an era of change. In T.L. Goodale and P.A. Witt (eds.), *Recreation and leisure: Issues in an era of change.* State College, PA: Venture

Farina, J. 1980. In T.L. Goodale and P.A. Witt (eds.). *Recreation and leisure: Issues in an era of change.* State College, PA: Venture

Gruneau, R. 1984. New directions in recreation and leisure services. Unpublished brief. Department of Recreation and Leisure Studies, University of British Columbia

Hall, N. 1991. North Vancouver youth report. Unpublished brief prepared for Youth Speak Conference. North Shore Union Board of Health

Knight, J. 1984. Television: Plague or play partner. *International Playground Association Journal* 8(7):5–6

Moore, R. C. 1986. *Childhood's Domain.* Beckenham, UK: Croom Helm

Naisbitt, J. and Aburdene, P. 1990. *Megatrends 2000.* Englewood Cliffs, NJ: William Morrow

Pennington, G. 1988. You can do it. Unpublished presentation. Canadian Parks and Recreation Conference, Vancouver, BC

Posterski, D. and Bibby, R. 1987. *Canada youth ready for today.* Canada Youth National Recreation Statement, Ottawa: Fitness Canada Foundation

10
Children, Youth, and Disability: A Community Approach to Rehabilitation

Roy Brown

Introduction

It is not possible in a short chapter to give a detailed account of the development and direction of practice in the field of disability. This chapter is aimed at pulling together some of the highlights and approaches in the disability field, with particular reference to children and youth. An attempt is made to look at the relationship between the disability field and the field of child and youth care in general. Indeed, one of the major developments in the past few years is the growing recognition that disability need not be looked at in terms of specific conditions but can be seen as part of a continuum of causation and behavioural variability, which, at one extreme, merges with variations of normal growth. Such a view is not historically consistent with a medical model of disability, but concepts of disability have changed and include a more psycho-social approach, which recognizes that various models are required to understand different disability situations. Such models are important, for they enable people to see conditions or processes from different perspectives. It is not that one is right or wrong, but particular models or specific conceptualizations from different perspectives provide a wider range of approaches within the field of disabilities.

Historical Development

In Canada, as in many other Western countries, the models relating to disabilities were first introduced from Europe. More recently, Canada has been influenced by developments in the United States. It would probably be fair, however, to conclude that today the approaches that are used in Canada have a uniqueness which puts them apart from programs in many other countries. For this reason, Canada is seen as having something to offer which changes philosophy, intervention, and facilities in relation to the field of disability. Very briefly, Canadian approaches to disability began with an institutional model of care which led, particularly in the late sixties and seventies, to the setting up of services through local agencies (some of which were residential but others of which were day programs). These included special schools and sheltered workshops. Gradually, a much more community-based approach developed, involving group homes of small size (e.g., three or four people) and independent living. That is not to say that everywhere in Canada the same approach is employed, but, rather, that trends are developing which highlight particular approaches within a number of cities and, in some cases, rural areas. Presently, the accent is on enabling people to live with their families and in their own homes. As individuals with disabilities age, there is an accent on moving them to community living environments of their choice, which may mean they live singly or in partnership or with the support of a skilled worker. Again, it cannot be said that one approach is always used over the other, but that a trend is developing, which clearly favours community living environments for individuals with disabilities.

Some Canadian provinces still have large numbers of people living in institutions, but, over the years, the numbers have reduced. By far the largest group of individuals who are institutionalized with disabilities is that of the mentally handicapped. Yet, the population that is recognized as mentally handicapped is now, to a marked degree, made up of different individuals from those who were considered to be mentally handicapped twenty years ago. The reasons for this will be discussed later.

Many handicapped children were taught within school programs often based in residential facilities. Thus, the residential school for disabled or handicapped children was very common, but, as a model, this is not very different from facilities for Native groups or for children in need of foster care. The curriculum in such facilities was largely a watered-down version of that of the normal school system, but, over the years, special day schools have been developed for a large number of children. Today, wherever possible, opportunities are being made for children to enter into integrated life within regular school systems. However, what this means, from one school jurisdiction to another, is often highly variable. For some, it means that children attend the same building as do non-handicapped children but rarely mix. For others, it means integration for part of the program, such as physical education.

For yet others, particularly in the early years, it involves sharing classes and teachers with other children of their age groups. However, across Canada, the variation in the degree of integration differs from province to province and school jurisdiction to school jurisdiction. For example, in New Brunswick, there is a very strong focus on integration in the formal sense that children are placed in the same class as non-handicapped children (Csapo and Goguen 1989). In Alberta, integration of this kind appears to be much less, although again it varies from school district to school district. Non-integration may be challenged legally by parents or guardians, and ministers of education are becoming more sensitive to the integration needs of people with handicaps. Today, there are opportunities to challenge rulings on where children are placed, and appeals can be made by parents on behalf of their children, with requests for opportunities to mix with, and be taught alongside, children without disabilities and to have the same access to appropriate curriculum or program plans.

Integration and Society
Among teachers, community workers, and parents, there are often considerable fears about the integration of children with handicaps. There are fears that the integration of handicapped children into regular schools will mean a poorer education for non-handicapped children. To date, there have been relatively few studies on the conditions that promote integration in the fullest sense and no detailed scientific evaluation of the pros and cons of full integration, but there has been a sensitive review of the literature by Porter and Richler (1991). There are many individual records of children with both physical and mental handicaps doing extremely well once they are integrated into the regular school system. In particular, social skills of handicapped children seem to be enhanced when they are in an integrated setting. There is also considerable evidence that children with physical disabilities can do well in much of the curriculum when they are in regular classes. Not surprisingly, many of the negative arguments are based on fears and anxieties or on ill-developed concepts rather than on hard evidence. There are often school personnel, sometimes well-meaning, and others, who are resistive, who have neither studied the issues involved nor utilized parental knowledge, which is often critical in such cases (Mitchell and Singh 1987). There are still many children with a variety of handicaps who are isolated from the normal stream of life. Integration goes further than schooling and must be considered holistically,

including home and local community as well as school. There is evidence that even children with severe disabilities, when provided with these opportunities, often do very well (Porter and Richler 1991; James and Brown 1992).

It must be recognized that our concepts of disability change. For example, fifteen years ago, many people were classified by intelligence or by physical attributes of disability. Today, these criteria may still be used, but very often measures of social and allied domains, such as home living and community skills as well as the extent of a friendship network, self-image, and emotional stability, are seen as predominant measures of performance and adaptability. These additional factors are associated with care and intervention in more normal community environments. For example, children with Prader Willi syndrome, an inherited condition involving abnormal eating behaviour and generally associated with mild or moderate mental handicap, are living longer. Although in the United States the direction is towards institutionalization for persons with this condition, in Canada, home environment, schooling, and integration in the community represent the preferred model of care. Psycho-social, rather than simply medical, models of intervention are providing parents and teachers with resources which can contain, and sometimes modify, abnormal behaviour (James and Brown 1992).

Change and Disability

As times have changed and attitudes broadened, people have not been sent to institutions in the same numbers as in the past. This means that many children, particularly those from deprived environments, now have opportunities to remain within their homes and within regular school systems. The result is that they often do not show the degree or range of handicap that was formerly recognized by professionals working in institutional and other congregate care centres. The fact is that people who have cognitive handicaps, and this can include many that we regard as developmentally handicapped or those who have other problems relating to brain function, often do well when not isolated in congregate care communities that reduce their opportunities to learn. However, opportunity to learn is not the only factor involved in development. Self-image, which has major effects on motivation and one's ability to attempt tasks or to behave appropriately in society, may be critical. Psycho-social models have relevance across disabilities and provide models of practice and understanding which have implications for many fields of intervention.

Another factor relevant to change in the disability field is that many children who would not have survived, even ten years ago, now do so. The involvement of the medical profession in alleviating some of the effects of prematurity, or birth-trauma, means that not only do more children survive but more disabled children survive. Very often, as medicine learns to cope with disease and with physical damage, children perform better in educational and social domains. At times, those who still have cognitive deficits are enabled to live a reasonably long life, which not only affects how we see disabled children but raises issues of an ethical and professional nature concerning society's responsibilities to such children. For example, very premature infants may now survive birth and the neonatal period, and develop sufficiently to attend school. Such children are often more vulnerable, as well as being more often impaired, than are other children. Thus, medical intervention in the early stages of development places responsibilities on other professional groups to provide effective education, home support, and allied interventions, which were previously less in demand. Thus, the progress of one professional system affects diverse areas of the community, raising professional, economic, and ethical issues which often have political implications.

Indeed, for many children the prospects for longevity are increasing because of better management by health professionals and greater reliance on normal family environments. People with Down syndrome often died relatively young due to diseases such as pneumonia, but this can now be treated through the use of drugs like penicillin (Denholm 1991). In other conditions, like Prader Willi, there are management systems, both medical and psychological, which enable diet to be controlled within reasonable limits so that people are healthier and live longer (James and Brown 1992).

Transition periods (e.g., from home to school and from school to work) become extremely important, for they represent periods of change to which children with disabilities appear particularly sensitive. For example, children who are disabled often seem more vulnerable or susceptible to stress and unfamiliarity than do other children, possibly because they do not have the resources or experience to adapt. That is why living in a normal environment is so important for enabling children to learn how to cope with normal stresses. Transition periods are times of great change, and, although some changes may not be common to most children (e.g., death of a parent), other changes, such as going to school, changing school, or going from school to work, *are* common. These situations represent examples of where, at a societal and professional level, we can reduce stress and unfamiliarity (Brown and Hughson 1987). We can prepare people to expect and deal with unfamiliarity by providing support systems during these periods (Halpern 1991). Psychological and social involvement often becomes critical at such times, not just for the individual but for the family. For example, counselling children and parents about transition periods or providing a family with ideas and practical resources can often alleviate situations which would otherwise become crises. Making an in-home rehabilitation practitioner, or, in the employment situation, a peer model, available are some ways of overcoming the problems of difficult periods (Brown, Bayer, and Brown 1992). In fact, such strategies would seem to be cost-effective, since they can prevent breakdowns which can have health, social, and economic consequences throughout the family.

The nature as well as our concept of disability is changing. It is likely that our regular systems of health and education services are coping with more handicapped children — certainly, at least, those with mild disabilities. It is also true that as health authorities improve their knowledge and practice, often in the technical domain (for example, treatment of hearing loss and problems of visual acuity through prosthetic devices), the impact of handicap diminishes through specialized human services.

The above comments underscore two important developments. One is the recognition that disability and handicap are not the same. Disability does not have to remain a handicap. For example, a child with an effective hearing aid is still suffering from a disability but may now hear well. Thus, the handicap is reduced. The second development is our recognition that disability and handicap are not generally the result of linear causation. Complex, multidimensional models are required to understand how different conditions and situations interact with one another to result in a particular 'condition,' which itself changes over the years in both positive and negative directions. Disability is the result of genetics, physical conditions such as pregnancy and birth, changes in the physical circumstances of the environment, and the socio-psychological phenomena which affect each individual and every family. Thus, an ecological approach to intervention involves changes to different aspects of the environment (Bronfenbrenner 1979; Mitchell 1986) and may or may not involve direct intervention with the individual.

Development in Society and Disability

As we pursue knowledge we recognize that disability comes in more forms than we previously realized. It is only in recent years that labels such as 'learning disabilities' have become clearly recognized in the education system. It is only in the last few years that adult students have been provided with university resources in which to deal with learning disabilities. But many parents of young children still find it difficult to obtain services. Learning disabilities are still not clearly defined (Samuels and Brown 1989) but it is probably important to recognize that at earlier stages in the development of our society, the ability to read or write was often irrelevant. It is only in a society that demands certain skills, such as reading or mathematics, that people who cannot develop these skills are likely to be diagnosed as disabled. Thus, a general rule can be applied — the greater the complexity and the more advanced the education and vocational systems of the society, the more likely it is that disabilities will be diagnosed, leading to a higher frequency of disorder.

If one projects such a model into the future, it may be supposed that as the education system and society in general places more technical and professional demands on people, more and more members of our society will be seen as disabled. Pringle, quoted by Segal (1967), suggested as many as 15 to 20 per cent of elementary-aged children may be recognized as needing special assistance for shorter or longer periods because of handicapping conditions. Today, higher figures than that have been put forward for conditions such as learning disabilities alone. Even emotional disturbance is believed to affect 19.5 per cent of boys and 13.5 per cent of girls aged 4 to 11 (Offord 1986). We recognize that many of these difficulties or disabilities arise from environmental causes. Over a person's lifespan, her or his level of disability may change. In many cases improvement occurs, while in others, decrements are noted. What is critical is that, over time, variation between people and within the same person are enormous, making individual predictions about success or failure tenuous (Cobb 1972).

It has been recognized for some time that those experiencing severe deprivation show major increases in intelligence, particularly in their adolescent and young adult years (Clarke and Clarke 1954). The requirement to segregate people, which was once thought appropriate (since protection was seen as necessary for life and individuals were not thought to change), is no longer either relevant or desirable. Institutionalization restricts environmental enrichment and normal experience, and we do not know the extent to which particular children can benefit from intervention. In other words, our prediction models are poor, and it is more important that professionals explore possibilities rather than predict which children will or will not benefit from intervention. To take this one stage further, from a psycho-social or educational point of view, the disability label that is given to a child may not only be undesirable — it may be dangerous. Yet, from a medical standpoint, particular labels, diagnoses, and models enable practitioners to focus on particular symptomology and to provide appropriate treatment. Thus, professionals in different disciplines need to be clear why particular models of description or diagnosis are used. Each one only provides, at best, an understanding of particular aspects of a condition and may be totally inappropriate if used by other disciplines or for other aspects of a condition.

The child and youth care worker, educator, or rehabilitation counsellor may need to know what the problem is from a medical point of view, but their role is to recognize that interventions of a psycho-social nature, using a different model, may help them to enable the individual to overcome handicap if not disability. This very real difference makes it critical that child and youth care workers and others do not use a label or diagnosis employed by one profession to limit their approach to, or jaundice their opinion about, a child. Very often a genetic or physical condition may have certain outcomes, but these outcomes can be ameliorated, depending on the environmental and personal variables outlined above. It is the environmental and personal aspects which are the subject matter of community rehabilitation. In recent years, society has begun to move from a purely institutional, medical, or health model of disability to a multidisciplinary approach, where there is room for social, psychological, and educational models of performance and intervention.

Intervention and Environment

Traditionally, as we have moved away from an institutional model of care, a wide range of specific interventions have been developed to overcome handicapping conditions. Many of these have been behavioural and social; sometimes based around behaviour modification and, later, behavioural management strategies (Martin and Pear 1978) and sometimes concerned with social skills training (Gunzburg 1968; Close and Foss 1988). Basically, the approach has been directed towards specific skills training, whether concerning bus training, budget skills, vocational employment, or inappropriate emotional behaviour within the home. Historically, these developments parallel the changes in our care training models. As institutions have given way to schools, sheltered workshops, and vocational centres, greater emphasis has been placed upon developing a specific training program for the handicapped individual. Each step has had successes and failures, resulting in subsequent developments involving more refined techniques, which apply to an ever-increasing range of skills. Today, education, home-living and social skills, vocational preparation, and leisure time training are seen as part of the holistic picture of intervention. As early as the 1950s Gunzburg (1960), in the United Kingdom, was advocating a social skills model of rehabilitation, with social assessment techniques (progress assessment charts) for all ages of individuals. Development in the 1970s of the Adaptive Functioning Index (Marlett 1976) for the assessment of adolescents and adults with developmental handicaps as well as those living in deprived environments, including institutions, illustrated a more advanced way of measuring social skills. Gradually, however, we have recognized that, although each of these techniques has helped some people, they have been limited and have not solved the problems of many others.

Despite a more holistic approach to disability, we live in a world which is directed towards adult vocational success, thus, most of the rehabilitation models, in practice, are directed towards educating and integrating people into a working society as fast as possible. For example, consider the situation in which an eighteen-year-old in an unskilled or semi-skilled work environment has a physical accident involving brain injury. He is provided with rehabilitation. Yet some of the issues he faces are not related to the physical disability but to the attitudes and behaviours evinced towards him by his friends, family members, and colleagues. They, in fact, form part of the complexity of his condition. Adjustment, counselling, and intervention need to relate to a wide range of situations and behaviours and must reflect the context and disposition of the whole individual. This may include vocational rehabilitation, but issues relating to leisure, home living, and social and community performance must not be ignored.

As we tried new approaches, other problems arose. First of all, we found that individuals do not transfer their skills very well from one environment to another (Ward 1989). To deal with such issues, strategies like Feuerstein's Instrumental Enrichment Technique (1979) have been developed. Such methods generally concentrate on the development and learning of problem solving strategies, which can be applied to a wide range of situations. Although many specific tasks may be employed in the intervention, the aim is to develop an approach which deals with problems or issues in general. Thus, instead of learning a specific skill, the individual is provided with a strategy for dealing with a large number of situations. But such approaches often lack hard evidence in terms of their applicability, though Feuerstein's assessment and intervention techniques have been used with children and adolescents under a wide variety of conditions. Thus, if we can improve problem solving behaviour, this will have more impact than simply enabling the individual to learn specific skills. There has also been some recognition that the issues might be resolved by looking at the environment in which the individual lives, and, thus, the concept of an ecological perspective has come to the fore (Bronfenbrenner 1979; Mitchell 1986). Some (Brown 1992) have argued that it would be possible to predict an outcome from knowledge of environmental conditions rather than from the performance of an individual at any one point in time. Certainly, modification of the environment as well as direct rehabilitation of the individual is recognized as critical.

Normalization

On the environmental side, the studies of normalization have had a major impact. Wolfensberger (1972) and many others have recognized that the environments of most disabled people are artificial, and that the demands made of them are even greater than those made on people without disabilities. Institutions, vocational agencies, special schools, and classes promote problems which non-handicapped children may not have to face. For example, in order to get to a special school or class, children may be bused long distances. Children who are bused to school tend to be more aggressive once they get there than are children who cycle or walk. People with disabilities often face additional challenges. Those with physical disabilities, such as cerebral palsy, may become more fatigued by travel. Those with epilepsy may suffer from greater fatigue and flicker-fusion problems, which can arise during travel and which may make them more susceptible to epileptic seizures. Yet, if a special school is seen as necessary, busing to school becomes very common. This is only one example of many situations which make the environment of a disabled child much more complex than it is for other people — thus Wolfensberger's plea to normalize the environment, including the approaches to rehabilitation. Even basic routines need to be examined; for example, children in care facilities get up at unusual times compared to most children living in a 'normal' family. They also eat under different regimes, and their choices are limited to a greater degree than is the case in most 'normal' environments. Wolfensberger (1983) goes on to suggest that social valorization is a major aspect of normalization. That is, what people do, once disabled, needs to be seen as valued if the person is to be seen as valued. This has led, particularly in Canada, to the development of concepts of quality of life, which encompass other approaches towards the field of disabilities.

Quality of Life
In brief, the term 'quality of life' may be defined as follows: 'The discrepancy between a person's achieved and unmet needs and desires. This refers to the subjective, or perceived, and objective assessment of an individual's domains. This definition assumes a discrepancy model. The greater the discrepancy the poorer the quality of life.' It includes 'the extent to which an individual increasingly controls aspects of life regardless of original baseline' (Brown, Bayer, and MacFarlane 1989:57–8).

Viewed through such a model, many children with disabilities are not able to fulfil their own choices. Indeed, surprisingly little is known about their inner and personal feelings, because, quite frequently, they are not asked, and, frequently, they are not able or allowed to express their ideas. Professionals have concentrated their efforts on the development of objective assessments, including norm-referenced and criterion-referenced procedures which are based on observable behaviour. However, there may be important subjective measures that could be even more critical. Like all children, those with disabilities have worries and anxieties. Very often, the family, teacher, child and youth care worker, or rehabilitation counsellor protect such children from the normal impacts of society on the grounds that they are disabled and, in so doing, also prevent the child from (1) having the experience of learning and (2) discussing and resolving issues which are important. Because of these concerns modern strategies are beginning to involve the development of choice and goal setting; these being in the hands of the person with the disability.

Quality of life measures include what is subjective and can help us to understand more about the internal choices and wishes of people with disabilities. It is not argued that one type of assessment replaces another, but, rather, that it is extremely important to provide a major role for quality of life assessment, which enables a child to promote and project his or her ideas into the intervention process.

Quality of life studies indicate that people with disabilities do not often see themselves improving within traditional models of rehabilitation. Individual self-image is often poor and the locus of control external. The aim of rehabilitation in the field of disability should be to ensure that the child's locus of control is gradually internalized Choice should be in the hands of the child or adult who is disabled, which means that the child and youth care worker or rehabilitation practitioner becomes much more of a processor with a wide range of skills than a director or controller of choice and, therefore, of behaviour (Brown 1992). Because the professional recognizes that learning is more effective when it is directed towards choice, he or she enables the child to utilize preferences. There is dignity in recognizing such choices. The procedures involved may have to move from highly structured or external processes to unstructured or internal processes (Brown and Hughson 1987). Further, because of problems caused by lack of transfer from residential or special school and class environments to the community, it is recommended that as much education and social and emotional experience (and, therefore, intervention) as possible should take place in the child's natural environment, that is, the home and local community. This raises new challenges. In such a model it is recognized that disability is not just a particular feature of a particular child but a process which involves the total family. Thus, one has to recognize that the attitudes of parents, which may include aggressive or protective approaches, have to be modified to become more enabling of the child.

Choice and Structure

Although choice by the consumer is something that is increasingly recognized as important, very often it is seen within the context of allowing people to do what they want. However, the seeking of knowledge about consumer choice, the provision of counselling around that choice, and the development of intervention procedures represent important phases of community rehabilitation practice. As suggested by Brown and Hughson (1987), it would appear that most of our systems, including the behaviour of individuals with disabilities, move from highly structured to unstructured processes. Thus, as learning and behaviour develop there is a gradual removal of external controls (i.e., structure). In their place are internalized mechanisms controlled by the individual. At a very simple level, this is represented by parents directing behaviour or providing environmental controls at an early stage and, later, tolerating more choice and self-expression. However, within the field of disability, developmental stages may be out of step with chronological development. Further, individuals may be more developed in one aspect of behaviour than in another. Our knowledge of disability in the psycho-social domain underscores the variability of behaviour both between and within individuals. This is one of the reasons why the traditional labelling system may have limited relevance to treatments or interventions concerning behaviour. This, of course, has been recognized in a number of ways, not the least of which is in the development of the individual program plan, which provides opportunities for professionals to develop a specialized program for particular individuals in order to help them meet their specific goals and needs.

Although largely looked at from an educational perspective, the concept and the practice of individual programming applies equally to community rehabilitation. Such plans can provide the degree of structure that is necessary for intervention. Structure refers to the degree of formal development of a program in terms of its content, sequencing, administration, and time of application. At one level, it is very precise and controlled, although, as individuals develop skills, it is important to ensure that flexibility and variability are taken into account. Children need to perform behaviour with minimal external cues. As indicated elsewhere, the dangers of providing a wide range of highly detailed and specific tasks must be avoided. Although we need to teach through specific tasks, opportunities for problem solving, understanding, and gaining personal knowledge are important for ensuring that an individual is not only able to function effectively on her/his own but is also able to transfer appropriate behaviour to new situations (Ward 1989). It is for this reason, amongst others, that community rehabilitation provides opportunities for learning not normally seen in the congregate care facility. Within such educational requirements it is important to recognize the role that different modalities (tactile, visual, auditory) play at particular stages of development or learning. When the behaviour of children regresses, for example, when they cannot deal with a particular task, there is often a move to more basic patterns of responding, involving tactile and visual rather than auditory behaviour. Further, responses may become more concrete than abstract within any particular modality.

Although there is not time to go into these processes in depth, the above suggests the range of professional skills that are required by the child and youth care worker and the rehabilitation counsellor when working with disabled children and youth. Further, the description draws attention to some of the confrontations which may occur between people who hold particular societal values and the needs of rehabilitation practice. For example, a number of school boards in Canada have stressed that it is important that teachers should not touch children, yet, within any community rehabilitation model where stress and unfamiliarity cause disturbance and regressed behaviour, it may be critically important to use effective communication, which involves touch, in order to ensure that the child is supported and comforted and can grow to deal effectively with the difficulties he or she is experiencing. Obviously, such issues have professional and ethical implications. They also illustrate why professionals must be experienced in how they provide intervention and why they need to recognize the value system under which they operate.

Education of Professionals

Changing Approaches: Individualization, Empowerment, and Brokerage

Obviously, such changes in direction have fundamental implications for how professionals are educated as well as for the types of ethical standards that they develop in terms of practice. Implicit within the model described is that many of the processes of rehabilitation become individualized. Of course, many services would argue that this is too expensive. The evidence to date suggests that not only is such intervention effective, but it has also minimized the bureaucratic and non-intervention aspects of traditional rehabilitation (e.g., costs of a building), enabling much more of a one-to-one relationship between the individual and the professional worker at much less cost. Also, because programs are matched to the individual, it is likely that improvement can take place very rapidly. This, in itself, is cost-effective, but other aspects of efficiency have, at least in one study, been shown to be no more expensive than is the least expensive traditional agency program (Bayer, Brown, and Brown 1988).

The issues that are raised here are those of empowerment; that is, individuals are enabled to assert their authority and their choices within an environment which is natural to them. This does not mean that 'anything goes,' because structured counselling can and does affect choice in the long-term. The point is that an individual's initial choice is accepted, and, therefore, dignity and personal control are preserved.

As people with disabilities become empowered, they challenge systems, and this is not always popular. It makes them more difficult to 'manage,' particularly if the professional (and this is particularly true in large-scale residential programs and in families where protection is seen as the major goal) finds him or herself challenged by the disabled person, who wishes to carry out more and more activities of choice. But the challenge may also represent normal growth on the part of the child.

Another related and developing aspect of the professional's job is that of brokerage. Brokerage provides for an independent party to assist individuals (families or consumer, child or adolescent) to choose the personnel and programs that they believe best suit their needs. This has been strongly advocated and practised by Fewster and Curtis (1989) and Brown, Bayer, and Brown (1992). In Canada, we have arrived at a position wherein quality of life within a context of choice, empowerment, and brokerage can be seen as an interrelated system which provides highly personalized programs within natural environments. This system contains support networks which enable the relevant others in a child's community to enter the rehabilitation process in order to change the environment as well as the individual. The mediation of such a system requires highly skilled personnel and exceptional professional education. The professional education of personnel in the field of rehabilitation is taking place beyond the school education system and involves rehabilitation counsellors, rehabilitation practitioners, and allied professionals. This area is of direct interest and relevance to child and youth care professionals.

The Professional Education Process

The system of education for rehabilitation practitioners or counsellors is very similar to the umbrella described for the child and youth care worker, that is, one-year certificates and two-year diplomas (occasionally three-year) within community colleges, a bachelor's degree in rehabilitation, such as the one at the University of Calgary, and opportunities for a post-first-degree professional diploma, such as that provided through rehabilitation counselling at York University. The system continues to master's and doctoral programs, which concentrate on the educational, psychological, and social aspects of rehabilitation. As such, this means that there is a ladder of professional education. This is a far cry from the past, where unskilled personnel and volunteers formed the front-line resources for disabled persons. This, of course, does not mean that there is not a role for volunteers, but it does argue for the widespread development of professional workers to apply the skills that have been developed over the past twenty or so years. Unfortunately, practice and research are separated by an ever-increasing time warp. Some of the research work quoted here is still not applied in most service systems.

The argument is that intervention, particularly community intervention within individualized family circumstances, is a highly skilled operation. Individuals who carry out such intervention require a knowledge of child development, management processes, specific knowledge of learning and motivation, knowledge of physical and mental disabilities, well developed counselling skills, and a wide range of experience in the application of skills within the child's normal environment through a variety of practica and internships. As indicated, the model is similar to that in child and youth care except that it concentrates on the field of disability. However, with the increasing knowledge that social environments are associated with handicapping conditions, both of these professions have much to learn from each other and, indeed, are much more closely allied than has been formally recognized.

Ethical Practice and Legal Issues

The professional working in the area of rehabilitation is confronted with a number of ethical issues, which, although common to many practitioners, have certain aspects which require particular attention in the context of working with young disabled people. Many child and youth care and rehabilitation practitioners do not belong to a professional association, either at a provincial or a federal level. Although such associations as the Canadian Association of Rehabilitation Personnel exist, they are frequently not recognized by governments or service systems either as representing the professional needs of their members or as a channel to deal with challenges from the community concerning rehabilitation practice. Traditionally, government departments have paid for services, often through government congregate care systems or through charitable societies organized to run services. Frequently, the latter organizations have been developed by parents to meet the needs of their children. However, the system is changing, partly because of the developments within the field of rehabilitation. These developments have resulted in a move from volunteerism to professionals educated to provide specific services to people with disabilities, not just in formal settings, like schools and agencies, but in informal settings such as individuals' private homes or the normal social milieu of town and country living. This means that much of the rehabilitation process is individualized and that practitioners, instead of working under the eyes of experienced and trained personnel within a facility, are often working on their own, providing personal and complex programs to the child and his or her family. Thus, rehabilitation has moved towards community involvement, necessitating the development of individualized programming within personal community environments. For these reasons, practitioners need to have a high level of skill, because they represent the knowledge-base for provision of on-the-spot intervention. In turn, they are more vulnerable, because they are working in other people's environments rather than in formal facilities. Such developments are likely to increase in the coming years and will probably be paralleled by the move towards privatization of programs. This means that instead of governments directly running services they will be contracted to private profit-making groups who may or may not be directed by client/consumer needs and workers. In other words, there is likely to be a competitive market driven by direct economic issues.

Complicating the matter still further are the developments resulting from human rights legislation and a range of other federal and provincial legislation relating to children and young adults. Regulations may differ from province to province, but, generally, there are some basic issues or rights which have a bearing on the practice of practitioners working with people with disabilities. Not only are there rights concerning normal opportunities for education but expectations about opportunities for family functioning. Legislation governing guardianship and, often separately, trusteeship may involve responsibilities to which the professional must respond. That is, there may be individuals who are appointed on behalf of a child or a young adult to represent their specific needs in addition to, or instead of, parents. This means that the network of consultation has to be broader, and if, as indicated above, rehabilitation moves into the area of personal choice, it needs to be recognized that skills in counselling parents, guardians, and professionals with particular responsibilities relating to children with disabilities must to be put forward in an affirmative manner in order to ensure that an individual's choices are recognized. Indeed, the author believes that this will represent one of the major challenges to effective rehabilitation in the future, since little is understood about the nature of choice and the accompanying processes of structure, which enable effective and individualized service to be delivered.

Issues relating to confidentiality of information are critically important from a professional perspective, and if, as suggested in this chapter, emotional and other aspects of behaviour concerning self-image are involved, then confidentiality not only between the professional and the family of the child needs to be respected, but the worker must recognize the importance of confidentiality between the child and her- or himself. This, of course, is associated with issues such as child abuse. It is recognized that child abuse amongst those with disabilities is much higher than it is in the general population (Sobsey and Varnhagen 1989), and it is incumbent upon the professional worker to officially report the occurrence of suspected child abuse. How this is done, and how involvement with a family can be maintained by the rehabilitation worker, requires experience and a high level of education. Thus, the need for education in counselling. The foregoing, of course, argues not only for comprehensive education regarding professional and ethical matters in college and university training of professionals but makes it clear that, without such education, practitioners are likely to provide less than ideal service and are likely to put their clients and themselves in vulnerable situations.

The need for the formal development of professional associations with requirements for certification are readily apparent. It should be the professional organizations that monitor, along with lay or public input, the standards by which professional members practice. It is also important that a relevant professional body look into alleged professional malpractice in the community rehabilitation field. Of course, these are practical ways in which individual and group practice can be governed. However, beyond this lie concepts critical to the development of effective rehabilitation practice in any community. These relate to the values and philosophies developed on a group and individual basis by the professionals concerned.

Students should examine their own personal value systems and should be aware of how these may conflict with societal or sub-group values, particularly as we live in a multicultural society where individuals and families may express themselves very differently from one another. It is not, for example, the role of the professional to impose a personal value or belief system concerning child rearing on particular individuals or families. (Hughson and Brown 1992). It is suggested that a mature professional is someone who, to a very large degree, can enable the consumer/client to examine and develop values within her or his own family. It is, of course, likely that, within a multicultural society, a wide range of values and views will be held.

Obviously, new and developing professionals will tend to evolve views which are different from those of traditional service systems or service workers. For example, the child and youth care and the rehabilitation practitioner are likely to have views about the importance of consumer choice in relation to programs or interventions. Our society is one in which children, as a general rule, have relatively little choice or control in the systems which provide them with services. The more a child is disabled, the more likely it is that the social structures will control or direct services (in the best interest of the child) while, at the same time, ignoring the child's concepts and patterns of choice. This, of course, often leads to a reduced motivational system for the child, with further damage to self-image.

Future Developments
This chapter has raised a number of issues which are only now being explored within our community. Child and youth care practice and rehabilitation are only now recognizing the critical importance of community involvement. Indeed, it seems likely that much of what has been talked about in these pages could be referred to as community rehabilitation. It is a natural development from congregate and small group care to the use of natural environments and circumstances for rehabilitation. This means that professional workers will need to work much more closely with family members and will require greater skills in counselling, as they professionally represent the consumer and client in developing effective intervention procedures within the home and local community. There is a move from group to individual prac-

tice. In the long-term, it is likely that there will need to be improved links between the education system, as practised within schools, and education and intervention services, which are provided in the home and community. At present, there is a large gap in this area — a gap into which the professionals described in this chapter are likely to move and provide services. In this context, it will be necessary to sort out competing philosophies (e.g., care and intervention) and recognize the need to examine ethical practice in relation to disabilities outside the service agency. Within the health care system it is appropriate that costs have an impact, in terms of research and practice, on types of development. Developments in medicine are likely to greatly influence the types of children with whom the professional community is apt to work. This, in time, affects the qualifications, experience, and practice demanded of child care and rehabilitation practitioners and the nature of the development of formal professional associations representing them.

Traditionally, governments have looked to non-professionals to support disabled people in the community. They have argued for volunteers or the employment of low-paid and relatively unskilled staff. This, of course, represents a short-sighted policy, for it does not provide a flexible environment within which opportunities for development and rehabilitation can take place. Indeed, the policy at present still leans to 'left-over' concepts from custodial and congregate care days, when we believed that it was impossible to rehabilitate children with disabilities. Our changing views, both from a social and biological perspective, argue for a much more enlightened and proactive policy in this regard. The future, then, can be seen both pessimistically and optimistically. On the pessimistic side, it seems likely that fewer dollars will be available, at least in the short-term, for the development of community rehabilitation practice, leading to further privatization, competitive situations, and, if there is little professional regulation, a return to institutional and custodial practices. On the optimistic side, there are the chances for highly developed individualized intervention practices and choices within the community, with skilled personnel who can work with disabled individuals and their families.

If this latter path is chosen, it is likely that we will find more and more persons in need who can benefit from such services. It seems fairly apparent that as we change our approaches to family and child care and support, and as these practices become more diverse, more varied and different types of support are required. It may also be argued that society is moving from a traditional view of family to a multiple concept of child upbringing, where professional intervention replaces, to some degree, the volunteers that have normally surrounded young children. This has fundamental implications for the philosophies and values held by professional practitioners. Although there will obviously be changes in the development of prosthetic devices, medical research, and intervention, it is probably in the community area that the greatest attention will have to be given to the nature of practice and intervention. Thus, the value systems developed must be examined so that field workers are highly knowledgeable not only of the practice of their profession but in their insight into their own beliefs concerning interventions for children with disabilities.

We are likely to see many more disabled children, and more severely disabled children, supported within the community. The need for respite care, and the importance of having highly experienced, front-line professional workers becomes critical. As a result of changes in philosophy and practice we, are likely to see major challenges to current management systems. Traditionally, in a hierarchical model, we have promoted front-line personnel to more and more senior positions, until they have taken over senior management functions. This has often meant that while members of senior management have been very experienced and knowledgeable about the congregate care systems they have worked for, they are less knowledgeable about practice and values regarding disability in the community at large. The types of knowledge referred to in this chapter suggest that if an individual is to work in the community at a front-line level, she/he will be experienced and skilled and, therefore, highly paid. But such persons also need to practice in management. Thus, some form of rotation system between front-line practice and management is necessary. Further, college and university personnel must ensure that they preserve their own individual practice at the front-line level, so that they provide effective modelling along with sound theory and philosophy.

It is perhaps these developmental aspects, more than any others, which are missing from the current system. The future needs to bring into being not only new community services but must also ensure that college and university teachers are contracted into community services on a shared basis, with a recognition that their knowledge must be tested and utilized in practice for the benefit of the individuals with disabilities and for students receiving education in colleges and universities.

Summary

This chapter describes the development of rehabilitation from psychosocial and educational perspectives. It argues that the system is truly developmental, with each stage necessarily predicated on its predecessor. It is strongly suggested that we have now arrived at a point where more holistic and professional services are required. It is also argued that both child and youth care and rehabilitation professionals have much in common, and, although the accent of the work may be different, the principles of clinical practice and the environments in which they occur are remarkably similar.

References

Bayer, M.B., Brown, R.I., and Brown, P.M. 1988. Costs and benefits of alternative rehabilitation models. *Australia and New Zealand Journal of Developmental Disabilities* 14:271–81

Brown, R.I. 1992. Some challenges to counselling in the field of disabilities. In Sharon E. Robertson and Roy I. Brown (eds.), *Rehabilitation counselling: Approaches in the field of disability*. London: Chapman and Hall

Brown, R.I., Bayer, Max B., and MacFarlane, C. 1989. *Rehabilitation programmes: The performance and quality of life of adults with developmental handicaps*. Toronto: Lugus

Brown, R.I. and Hughson, E.A. 1987. *Behavioural and social rehabilitation and training*. New York: Wiley

Brown, R.I., Bayer, M.B., and Brown, P.M. 1992. *Quality of life: Impact of choice on programmes for adults with developmental handicaps*. Toronto/London: Caphes/Chapman & Hall)

Bronfenbrenner, U. 1979. *The ecology of human development*. Cambridge, MA: Harvard University Press

Clarke, A.D.B. and Clarke, A.M. 1954. Cognitive changes in the feeble-minded. *British Journal of Psychology*. 45:173–9

Close, D.W. and Foss, G. 1988. Approaches to training: The social skills needed for quality of life. In R.I. Brown (ed.), *Quality of life for handicapped people*. London:Croom Helm

Cobb, H.V. 1972. *The forecast of fulfillment*. New York: Teachers College Press

Csapo, M. and Goguen, L. 1989. *Special education across Canada: Issues and concerns for the 90's*. Vancouver: Centre for Human Development and Research.

Denholm, C.J. (ed.). 1991. *Adolescents with Down syndrome: Implications for parents, researchers and practitioners*. Victoria: University of Victoria

Feuerstein, R. 1979. *The dynamic assessment of retarded performers: The learning potential assessment device, theory, instruments, and techniques*. Baltimore: University Park Press

Fewster, G. and Curtis, J. 1989. Creating options: Designing a radical children's mental health program. In R.I. Brown and M. Chazan (eds.), *Learning difficulties and emotional problems*. Calgary: Detselig

Gunzburg, H.C. 1960. Social rehabilitation of the subnormal. London: Bailliere Tindall and Cox
–. 1968. *Social competence and mental handicap.* London: Tindall and Cassell
Halpern, A.S. 1991. *Quality of life for students with disabilities in transition from school to adulthood.* Calgary: Quality of Life
Hughson, E.A. and Brown, R.I. 1992. Learning difficulties in the context of social change: A challenge for professional action. In T. Thompson and P. Mathias (eds.), *Standard and mental handicap: Keys to competence.* London: Harcourt, Brace & Jovanovich
James, T. and Brown, R.I. 1992. *Prader Willi syndrome: Home, school and community.* London: Chapman and Hall
Marlett, N.J. 1976. *Adaptive functioning index.* Calgary: Vocational and Rehabilitation Research Institute
Martin, G. and Pear, J. 1978. *Behaviour modification: What it is and how to do it.* New Jersey: Prentice-Hall
Mitchell, D. 1986. A developmental systems approach to planning and evaluating services for persons with handicaps. In R.I. Brown (ed.), *Management and administration of rehabilitation programmes.* London: Croom Helm
Mitchell, D. and Singh, N. (eds.). 1987. *Exceptional children in New Zealand.* Palmerston North: Dunmore
Offord, D. 1986. *Ontario child health study: Summary of initial findings.* Ontario Ministry of Community and Social Services. Hamilton: Queen's Printer
Porter, G.L. and Richler, D. 1991. *Changing Canadian schools: Perspectives on disability and inclusion.* North York: Roeher Institute
Samuels, M. and Brown, R.I. 1989. (eds.). *Research and practice in learning difficulties: A demonstration model.* Toronto: Lugus
Segal, S.S. 1967. *No child is ineducable.* Special Education/Provision and Trends, London: Pergamon
Sobsey, R. and Varnhagen, C. 1989. Sexual abuse and exploitation. In Csapo, M., and Gougen L. (eds.), *Special education across Canada.* Vancouver: Vancouver Centre for Human Development and Research
Ward, J. 1989. Obtaining generalization outcome in developmentally disabled persons: A review of the current methodologies. In R.I. Brown and M. Chazan (eds.), *Learning difficulties and emotional problems.* Calgary: Detselig
Wolfensberger, W. 1972. *The principles of normalization in human services.* Toronto: National Institute on Mental Retardation
–. 1983. Social Role Valorization: A proposed new term for the Principle of Normalization. *Mental Retardation* 21:234–9

11
Parent Education and Support: An Emerging Field for Child and Youth Care Work

James Anglin and Robert Glossop

Background

Parent education and support is an area of child and youth care work that cuts across virtually all practice settings. The reason for this is that the vast majority of children and youth who are recipients of professional caregiving have parents who are important figures in their present and future development and functioning. In many cases, children continue to reside with their parents while receiving care or will be returning to live with their parents following a temporary substitute placement.

Thus, in most situations, there is an important role for child and youth care workers to play in (1) addressing the needs of parents *as* parents and (2) assisting parents to better understand and respond to the needs of their children. In the case of teenage parents, often single mothers, the worker may have to re-parent the parent before much change can be anticipated in the parent/child relationship (Miller 1983). In other situations, parents may be better able to discuss their own needs in the context of focusing on the needs of their children. In both cases, however, the needs, perceptions, and values of the parents are a critical dimension in the successful treatment of their children.

Overview

In this chapter, we will explore the role of parent education and support in the development of the child and youth care profession. Several key terms are critical to this discussion. *Parent education*, as used here, refers to a broad range of programs and strategies designed to assist parents, or parents-to-be, in fulfilling their child bearing and child rearing responsibilities through the enhancement of their knowledge of skills. Included within this term are individual, group, and mass media approaches which focus on information giving, skill development, and problem solving. Such approaches are usually designed and delivered by professionals. *Parent support*, on the other hand, encompasses formal and informal initiatives intended primarily to strengthen parents' emotional, social, or material resources. A wide spectrum of programs from mutual-aid groups to professional counselling has a common element in serving to provide a supportive environment for parents. Finally, *family support programs* provide direct services to families which have a preventive orientation. Such programs may involve parent education or parent support approaches or may focus on other modes of family-oriented intervention. Weiss (1983) has identified eight types of family support programs. These are: (1) prenatal and infant development; (2) child abuse and neglect prevention; (3) early childhood education; (4) parent education and support; (5) home, school, and community linkages; (6) families with special needs; (7) neighbourhood-based mutual help and informal support; and (8) family-oriented day care.

Child and youth care workers, although currently involved in a variety of family support programs, have not traditionally been employed in the provision of parent education and support. Prior to presenting some recent innovative programs involving child and youth care workers directly in parent education and support, several important themes evident in the current family support literature will be reviewed.

Changing Understandings of Family Life
In recent years it has become obvious that the contemporary family takes many forms: nuclear, extended, childless, single parent, blended, separated, communal, dual-residence, gay, tribal, and so on. In fact, at any moment, the number of Canadians living in the stereotypical model of 'mum at home, dad at work, and their own two biological children' represents the family reality of only 7 per cent of the population (Anglin 1983a:2). Even if this stereotypical family model is expanded to encompass *any* style or combination of two parents and two children, it represents the actual living situation of only one Canadian in five. It is clear that we need to talk and think about different *families* rather than the *family* — as if it were a single, monolithic entity. We must look beyond structure and form if we are truly to understand both the unique experiences and preferences as well as the common needs and aspirations of diverse family forms. In *Families in Canada Today*, Eichler (1983) suggests the need for a multidimensional view of

family to replace the traditional monolithic view. Specifically, Eichler identifies six dimensions: 'the procreative dimension; the socialization dimension; the sexual dimension; the residential dimension; the economic dimension; the emotional dimension' (1983:6). As she observes,

> If we free ourselves from the monolithic notion that families have a particular structure and instead operate on the assumption that the structure of families is (and always has been) fluid, there is no reason to concern ourselves with the thought of the 'death of the family' ... In short, then, families are currently in a process of transition that can be expected to continue for another generation since many of these changes at present involve the middle aged, and patterns of familial interactions for the young are still in the process of emerging. These changes are touching the very basis of our definitions of self and others. We have neither fully understood what the changes are, nor have we sufficiently tried to describe and analyse them and to try to look at some of their implications for individual members of families and policy makers. (pp. 25–6)

The implication for child and youth care workers is the necessity to remain open to learning from families themselves about what their family life is like, what it is becoming, and what they would like it to be.

The Social Ecological Perspective

An evolving awareness of the ecology of our social life (paralleling the concern with the ecology of our natural environment) has begun to sensitize human service professionals to the many and varied domains and levels of family functioning. It is no longer sufficient merely to view a family as a system. Each family, in a very real and significant way, is one system embedded in a series of overlapping systems. This realization of the complexity of family interactions within society requires a new set of conceptual categories to assist us to describe, analyze, and understand it. The father of the current movement in social ecology is Urie Bronfenbrenner, whose 1979 book, *The Ecology of Human Development*, has radically altered the direction of thinking, research, and practice in the fields of child development, social services, and social policy.

In Bronfenbrenner's terminology, the complex interrelations of persons within their immediate, face-to-face settings is referred to as the *microsystem*. The microsystem is the set of immediate, face-to-face relationships fanning out from a given individual in his or her immediate settings, such as family, school, church, peer group, and/or neighbourhood. One can then analyze a child's or parent's environment in terms of the range of microsystems in which he or she participates. The next level, the *mesosystem*, consists of the interrelationships between microsystems. Some important mesosystems for families include home/school, home/work, and home/neighbourhood. The extent and nature of a family's mesosystems constitute important variables affecting the functioning of family members.

Beyond the mesosystem lie the settings within which the person or family does not participate directly but which, nonetheless, have an impact on their lives: these settings form the *exosystem*. It is important to recognize that what may be an exosystem for one person may be a microsystem for another. A social ecological 'map' can be projected out from the particular person who is the focus of attention. Thus, the father's workplace may be an exosystem for the child while being a microsystem for the parent.

Last, the broad sociocultural and institutional patterns characteristic of a social group, or society at large, constitute the *macrosystem*. This level encompasses the basic assumptions and organizing frameworks that form the societal blueprints for how things work. Different views of human nature, an individualistic versus a cooperative ethic, democracy versus totalitarianism, all represent phenomena at the macrosystem level of society.

The social ecological perspective, once its 'high tech' sounding terminology is mastered, can provide important conceptual tools which can help make sense of what James Garbarino (1983:11) calls 'these swirling social forces' that surround all of us. For child and youth care workers to respond effectively to the needs of children, parents, and families, they must be able to understand and to be comfortable in assessing and intervening within all four of these ecological levels. Although an individual worker may be engaged primarily at the microsystem and mesosystem levels of a client's life, it is increasingly apparent that effective child and youth care practice requires a number of workers to enter into the exosystems of their client's worlds and that the child and youth care professional associations address themselves to issues at the macrosystem level of society (Ferguson and Anglin 1985).

Informal and Formal Helping

Our understanding of the social ecology of family life is still in its infancy. However, one of our earliest discoveries has been the daily fabric of family functioning relating to help-seeking and help-giving. A survey of helping relationships at the family level exposes a network of interwoven threads of helping, cutting across both informal forms of helping (helping provided by family members, friends, neighbours, and acquaintances) and formal helping (professional services). The range of helping sectors constituting the informal and formal domains are depicted in Figure 11.1.

Figure 11.1

Spectrum of informal and formal support

	INFORMAL			FORMAL	
Families	Friends & Acquaintances	Self-help Groups & Organizations	Semi-formal Helpers	Family Support Programs	Professional Helping Services
– Immediate and extended family members	– friends, neighbors, workmates, letter carriers, hairdressers, bartenders, and so forth	– group members	– teachers, clergy, physicians, lawyers, and so forth	– volunteers, paraprofessionals, counselors, social workers, child care workers, psychiatrists, and so forth	

Families

Different forms of information, social, emotional, and material resources are sought, provided, and exchanged in each of these sectors. For example, in the most informal sector, families, both nuclear and extended family members assist each other in a myriad of ways through exchanging goods and services (for example, purchasing of food and meal preparations), sharing experiences and advice (parent/child, parent/grandparent, and so on), gift-giving (birthdays, special events, spontaneously), and so forth.

Friends and Acquaintances

The web of personal relationships with friends and acquaintances that envelops families often provides important feedback and support to family members across a wide range of approaches to helping. When this network is weak, or largely non-existent, any family, no matter what its personal and economic resources, is more at risk of succumbing to stresses and strains that can spiral without such support.

Self-Help Groups

Increasingly, as a response to many of the changes in family life alluded to earlier, family members are moving beyond the sometimes fragile and limited sources of naturally occurring support networks and joining with those who share a common need or situation. Self-help groups represent one of the most powerful sources of experiential learning and social support available beyond the confines of the family itself (Katz and Bender 1976; Gottlieb 1983; Romeder 1989). Self-help groups consist of persons who intentionally, and without being controlled by a professional organization, come together to help each other to achieve a common purpose, whether it be of a personal, social, emotional, medical, intellectual, or political nature.

Semi-Formal Helpers

Beyond self-help groups and organizations can be found an important sector, consisting of what we call semi-formal helpers. These helpers include professionals, such as doctors, lawyers, clergy, police, and teachers, who have occasion to contact, or be contacted by, families at times of developmental or situational stress. As a secondary function of their work, they may be involved in a significant amount of counselling as well as referring clients to formal helping services. Being situated on the boundary between the informal and formal helping sectors provides such professionals with unique opportunities and responsibilities to facilitate the matching of families with the various resources of the formal and informal helping sectors.

Family Support Programs

As was noted in the introduction to this chapter, there exists a range of family support programs which have emerged over the past twenty years in North America. Although these programs differ widely in terms of their specific target groups, objectives, auspices, and modes of operation, they tend to be characterized by a preventive orientation which often incorporates principles of networking, peer support, and the empowerment of parents. Some of the most innovative parent education and support programs can be included in this category. As noted by Weiss (1983), such programs tend to be based on an awareness of the ecology of family functioning and a respect for informal and formal helping networks.

> One of the most striking things about the recent evolution of these programs is their emphasis on a more ecological approach. This approach is based on the ecological principle that while the family is the primary institution that determines a child's development, other institutions impinge on it and affect the family's capacity to nurture its children ... The movement towards more ecological intervention strategies is reflected in the shift from the focus on individuals, usually the child, to an emphasis on the relationship and interaction between the parent and child, and increasingly, on the relationship between the family and formal and informal sources of support for them within the community. (p. 3)

Professional Helping Services

Finally, we turn to the domain of the professional helping services. This sector includes all professionals primarily providing personal and family-oriented services, including counselling and therapeutic services as well as statutory interventions mandated by government legislation. These services can be provided under the auspices of public or private agencies and are increasingly focused on crisis-oriented forms of intervention. The role of professional helping services is currently being questioned by governments throughout the Western world; both the federal government and the various provincial governments across Canada are no exception. It is unlikely that we will witness further expansion of these services at anything like the rate experienced in the 1960s and 1970s. In the words of James Whittaker:

> Draconian budget cuts in child and family services, the continuing shortage of professionally trained child welfare staff, and the limits posed by energy shortages and by inflation all argue for the elevation of informal helping strategies to a first-order priority in child welfare ... It means adopting a state of mind that views strengthening the family and identifying social support networks as the primary goals and providing direct professional help as the secondary goal in service provision. (1983:179–80)

Professional child and youth care has come to be viewed as a temporary support service for the family, even when it involves placement in residential treatment centres (Maier 1981:59). Whatever the care or treatment modality, the guiding principle is to optimize the development of the child within the context of the family and community while seeking to minimize the intrusiveness and disruptiveness of the service.

With the preceding backdrop of discussion relating to contemporary family life, social ecology, and informal and formal helping networks, we will turn our attention briefly to a consideration of parenting in today's society.

A Perspective on Parenting

In line with the recent appreciation of family life and the nature of helping, a comprehensive study was undertaken by Rhona and Robert Rapoport and Ziona Strelitz (1980), which integrated findings from research in a variety of fields of inquiry. The study formulated a set of propositions that the researchers feel should guide our understanding of parenthood today. These propositions can assist child and youth care workers in assessing their responses to the needs and realities of parents with whom they work. These propositions include:

(1) Parents are people. Just as parents need to be reminded that their children are persons (Chess, Thomas, and Birch 1976), so do professionals need to be reminded that parents are persons too! As such, parents have a wide range of needs — emotional, intellectual, physical, financial, relational, familial, and spiritual — that require recognition and respect. A narrow focus solely on the needs and experiences of children, or even on the parent/child relationship, will ignore a large set of parenting issues equally important for the positive functioning of the child.

(2) There should be a balance of fulfilment within families and between family and other involvements. Parenthood involves responding to a continuous set of challenges which demand a balancing of the demands of friendships, work, leisure, community involvements and, frequently, spouse, as well as relations with children. One of the most difficult stresses on parents today results from changes to many traditional patterns in virtually all areas of family life, including sex roles, the division of labour, and child care. Each family is faced with the need to create and negotiate arrangements appropriate to itself and its members. It can draw from a wide range of socially acceptable alternatives. As such, there are no fixed formulas for today's parents or for child and youth care professionals regarding what will be best for any particular family.

(3) Parents' needs and children's needs are not always coterminous. Although parents' and children's needs sometimes coincide, compromises frequently must be worked out, preferably through arrangements of mutual accommodation rather than by unilateral use of force. Neither the total gratification of children nor the martyrdom of parents is realistic or desirable.

(4) Families vary in structure and culture. The pluralistic nature of society as a whole requires that professionals become sensitive to a range of values, beliefs, preferences, and customs. As noted earlier, the wide spectrum of contemporary family forms and structures calls for an appreciation of the dimensions of family life and the variety of ways in which these can be addressed.

(5) Biological parents are not the only people involved in parenting functions — nor should they be. In Canada, there is an ongoing debate concerning the proper role of government in relation to the care of children, particularly the care of young children of employed parents. The issue of the impact of a variety of caregiving arrangements, from family day care to long-term residential care, must be addressed by child and youth care workers if their expertise and experience are to play a significant part in the formation and evolution of public and institutional policies on parenting and child care.

(6) There is no 'right' way to parent; there are many ways to be a 'good parent.' The rich and complex interplay of such factors as parental character and style, children's needs and abilities, the family's stage of development, and community opportunities (to name but a few) provides a formidable challenge to workers seeking to assist families. It would appear that we know much more about what goes wrong in parenting than we do about creating conditions that are positive for particular families.

(7) Parents learn about themselves through parenting. Parenthood is now being seen as an important phase in adult development (Galinsky 1981). Child and youth care workers who are parents will well remember the dramatic changes in their perspectives on children, child care, and just about everything else that took place following the birth of their first child. Parenthood is a transforming experience, which must be understood not only in terms of the impact on the child's development but also in terms of the impact on the development of the parent.

Following this consideration of parenting, and informed by the previous discussions of family life, social ecology, and helping networks, it is now possible to set forth a framework for viewing the territory of parenting. Figure 11.2 outlines in graphic form the range of parenting concerns, utilizing the previously discussed ecological levels as outlined by Bronfenbrenner.

Figure 11.2

Ecology of parent functioning

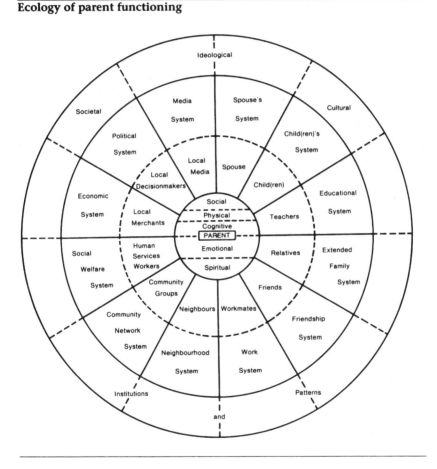

At the centre of the figure we have placed the parent, indicating that the parent has a variety of personal needs. Moving beyond the sphere of the parent as an individual person, we find a range of people in various settings, which constitute the parent's microsystem. Members characteristically include spouse or ex-spouse, children, relatives, teachers, friends, workmates, neighbours, human service workers (such as doctors or social workers), and local merchants and decision-makers. Included as well, in recognition of their important roles, are community groups (such as church, recreation, and social groups) and local media outlets (including radio, television, and newspapers). As noted earlier, it is the relationships between the persons in various microsystem settings that constitute the parent's mesosystem. Different parents, of course, will be characterized by different microsystem and mesosystem networks.

Beyond the circle of immediate personal contacts are depicted the broader exosystems, which extend beyond the microsystem level of the parent's direct experience. For example, there will likely be levels in the parent's work system (agency, company, corporation, and so forth) that lie beyond the parent's involvement. However, it is important to understand that the impact of decisions and organizational procedures at the exosystem level is continuously, and sometimes dramatically, experienced in the daily lives of parents and their families. Often this level of impact is not clearly acknowledged by families, and family members can blame themselves for the negative impact of the exosystem.

Finally, encompassing all of these subsystems — the individual parent, the microsystem, the mesosystem, and the exosystem — is the macrosystem, consisting of the overarching and all-pervasive ideological, cultural, and institutional patterns of our society as a whole. Fundamental beliefs and patterns related to childhood, child rearing, normal family functioning, and effective parenting differ considerably across cultures and throughout history within cultures.

With this understanding of the world of parenting, we will now turn to a consideration of some exciting and highly innovative responses to parents' needs for education and support involving child and youth care workers.

Parent Education and Support: The Child and Youth Care Response

As a basis for reviewing several programs in which child and youth care workers have addressed the needs of parents (as opposed to their children), a continuum of parent education needs and related professional responses, adapted from the work of Dokecki (Powell 1984), can provide a useful guide. The continuum consists of four levels, which are dynamic and overlapping. That is, most parent education or support programs will address more than one level of need or response.

This continuum identifies parents needs (from the need to anticipate future developments to the need for protection of the child) and professional responses (from provision of information to direct intervention). As the needs of the parents become more acute, professional services become more intensive. Four program approaches involving child and youth care workers in addressing different dimensions of the continuum of parent needs will be described.

The Primary Prevention Project
A notable program developed by child and youth care workers, which addresses the prospective and resource needs of parents, is the Primary Prevention Project carried out under the auspices of the Canadian Mental Health Association, Ontario Division. The project involved ten child and youth care workers participating in preparatory work with parents on the development of course content, with close collaboration by other professionals, including educators, psychiatrists, psychologists, and social workers. The project, true to the best principles of child and youth care work, went directly to the clients (in this case parents) to ascertain their needs. Feedback from over one thousand parents in more than eighteen cities in Ontario confirmed that parents had two fundamental needs: 'first, support in their role as parents and second, techniques that help them in their task' (Canadian Mental Health Association 1982:6). The authors stress in the project instructor's manual that

> certain qualities aid the development of good parenting skills ...
> parents who *understand* the importance of nurturing children, who
> have the ability to *communicate effectively* with their children, explore
> *flexible responses, empathize,* and who have acquired *insight* into their
> child's needs and their own behaviour, tend to parent well. (CMHA
> 1982:6 emphasis in original)

The delivery format for the program consists of weekly sessions held over a ten-week period facilitated by trained leaders, who have, according to the Ontario college DACUM classification, 'Child Care Worker Level III minimum or equivalency' and who have: '(a) demonstrated teaching ability with parents; (b) broad knowledge of basic child care skills; (c) broad knowledge of normal growth and development of children and adolescents; (d) familiarity with community resources'

(CMHA 1982:7). Others with three years of direct experience with children and a wide range of demonstrated abilities in group work, child and youth care skills, sensitivity to parental values and roles, knowledge of community resources, and respect for confidentiality could also be selected for leadership training in the project.

Parents are asked to examine their own feelings and experiences in relation to particular situations and to participate in role-playing. Situations are structured in order to provide an experiential basis ('grounding') not found in more traditional discussion formats. In addition to sessions, parents are provided with practice-oriented homework. Specific content includes: communication techniques; food (nutritional and emotional aspects); family routines; establishing limits and appropriate consequences; anchor points (aspects of the daily routine that represent primary interaction between the parent and child); play and family togetherness; the child, family, and school; and the child and the community.

Such features as the initial and extensive assessment of parents' needs, the emphasis on grounding, the practical orientation to daily routines and interactions provide a strong flavour of child and youth care work and serve to make this approach a flexible alternative to the more traditional and highly structured programs.

The ABC Project
A second approach, addressing parent needs primarily through the collaborative mode, was developed at the Clark Institute for Psychiatry in Toronto. Developing out of a day-treatment, operant conditioning program for autistic children, the ABC (A for Analysis; B for Behaviour; and C for Change) Project involves child and youth care workers in the provision of assessment and intervention services for families in the context of their own homes and community (Webster, Somjen, Sloman, Bradley, Mooney, and Mack 1979).

This project places a heavy emphasis on modelling and teaching behavioural techniques and involving parents as crucial members of the planning team. In conjunction with the home-based program, a Parent Education and Discussion (PED) program is also carried out. As the authors note, 'after some experimentation with "dynamic" approaches, we adopted a fairly didactic format in which one member more-or-less lectured for forty minutes and then led the group in discussion around the specific theme which had been introduced earlier' (Webster et al. 1979:16). The authors also observe that more personal matters generally emerge in the discussion, and that parents can sometimes make more effective presentations than can the child and youth care workers or other professionals. As well, the experience indicates that 'while family-centred child care work can offer plenty of satisfaction, it ... can be very wearing' (p. 17). The support of concerned and knowledgeable colleagues is deemed to be essential for the child and youth care workers involved in such intense and relatively autonomous functioning.

The authors conclude by recommending that 'child care training programs should teach students the skills needed for success in this kind of work since more child care programs will likely be centered on the family in future years' (p. 17). Prior to considering issues of education and training for parent education and support, two types of programs addressing parent needs through the protective mode will round out our discussion of child care program examples.

Special Services for Children Program
An important development in the child and youth care field has been the advent of community-based family support programs which assign responsibility to child and youth care workers for providing various forms of intensive parent education and support when a child is at risk. In British Columbia, for example, the Ministry of Social Services and Housing contracts on a yearly basis with private societies under the Special Services for Children Program to provide child and youth care workers to families identified by the ministry in an attempt to reduce the risk that a child may need to be taken into care. The special services society, in turn, contracts with individual workers to provide an agreed-upon number of hours of service to the family. Characteristically, this entails about five hours per week; contracts generally run for a three-month period, with the option of being renewed should circumstances warrant. Some agencies also offer parent groups provided on a similar basis. Such contract services can provide education and support for families requiring a protective orientation when removal of the child is not yet the intervention of choice.

Groups for Parents of Children in Residential Care
Traditionally, child and youth care intervention involved the removal of the child from the home and the provision of substitute care in a foster residence or institution. In more recent times, even this extreme response to inadequate family situations has come to be viewed as a

temporary supplementary service which needs to maintain ties with parents both to enhance the effectiveness of treatment while the child is in care and to prepare for the child's return home. Such strategies as home visits, brief and extended visits of family members to the program, and family counselling have been common elements in residential child and youth care work for some time (Littauer 1980). However, the development of parent groups offering education and support for parents of children in care does not appear to have been widely adopted as a key aspect of family involvement.

As has been demonstrated by a number of studies (Coates 1981; Delong and Boyer 1991; Grealish et al. l989; Mahoney 1981; Whittaker and Garbarino 1983), family support is both one of the best determiners of a child's success in residential treatment and the most important single factor in determining the child's post-discharge adaptation. Anglin (1985), in providing a framework for the development of education and support groups for parents of children in residential care, suggests a continuum of parent groups, which can complement the treatment program at all stages. At, or prior to, intake, parents could be invited to an orientation session, which could serve as a non-threatening introduction to the staff, program, and facilities. Such a session could set a tone for future involvement and initiate a supportive group process. During the child's stay in the residence, child and youth care workers could offer focused sessions relating to areas of strong parental concern, such as establishing routines, limit-setting, and discipline without force. As with the Parent Education and Discussion Program (PED), these sessions could be didactic and minimally threatening in the early stages, until parents are ready to share in a more personal manner. Following discharge of the child, sessions could be offered relating to the particular concerns of families with a returning child, such as school adjustment, the use of community resources, communicating with friends and extended family, and re-establishing some form of family equilibrium. For those willing and able to make use of an ongoing support group, child and youth care workers could either facilitate the initiation of such a group or refer parents to such groups in the community.

Assessing the Need for Education and Training
Although there is no comprehensive information on the types of programs involving child and youth care workers in parent education and support across Canada, data have been gathered in British Columbia

on the extent to which child and youth care workers in four types of programs are involved in 'parenting skills training' (Anglin 1983b). Parenting skills training was defined as 'assisting parents to learn and develop child-related skills.' Responses were gathered in structured interviews with 46 employers throughout the province, who, as a group, employed 576 workers. The two major urban centres (Vancouver and Victoria) and the northern and interior regions were sampled across four types of child and youth care programs: (1) residential care (225 workers); (2) education (64 workers); (3) family support[1] (government employed, community-based workers) (127 workers); and (4) special services (private agency, community-based contract workers) (160 workers). The family support workers were most frequently involved in parenting skills training (93.7 per cent of workers); residential care workers, perhaps surprisingly, were next (69.3 per cent), with the other two groups — educational and special services — the least involved (56.3 and 55 per cent). The overall percentage of child and youth care workers involved in parenting skill training was 68.6 per cent, which placed this job function in twelfth place in a ranking of all twenty-one direct service job functions. In terms of workers with a significant need for further education and training, parenting skills training was ranked seventh by employers, with 63.9 per cent of workers in need. Interestingly, when asked directly, 81.6 per cent of workers indicated that they had a high interest or need for further education and training in this area, representing a ranking of fourth in relation to all twenty-one job functions. A recent survey (Anglin 1989) indicates that the involvement of workers in parenting skills training increases directly with both years of experience and years of education.

Following completion of the survey, one of the authors offered workshops on parent education at regional and national child and youth care conferences and through community college extension programs. A strong response, indicated by both the number and enthusiasm of participants, appeared to confirm the high relevance of this area for child and youth care workers in general. A core course is now offered in the School of Child and Youth Care at the University of Victoria, combining an introduction to normative family development with a review of parent education and support approaches.

Strengths and Limitations of Child and Youth Care Workers

As more child and youth care workers are becoming involved in various approaches to parent education and support, a number of characteristic strengths and limitations are becoming apparent. Probably the greatest strength lies in the workers' direct experience of a variety of children, with a range of needs, across a number of settings. No other professional has such a broad perspective on the day-to-day functioning of children. Second, child and youth care workers characteristically possess a developmental (as opposed to pathological) orientation to child functioning. Parents, as much as professional workers, need such an understanding of normative child development. And third, child and youth care workers are generally able, as a result of their mandate and style of work, to participate with parents and children in their natural environments of home, school, and community. As such, they are in an excellent position both to observe and to provide feedback on daily routines and behaviours which form the essence of parent/child interaction.

Child and youth care workers also tend to have several limitations in relation to working with parents. One of the limiting factors, acutely perceived by many workers, is the fact that they tend to be relatively young and childless. This immediately raises doubts as to their credibility in the eyes of parents as well as a realization that, in spite of professional expertise, they are lacking relevant personal experience.

A second limitation which has to be addressed in relation to the traditional child and youth care role is the tendency of workers to over-identify with the child and to define themselves solely as advocates for her/him. Child and youth care workers are sometimes perceived, and often justifiably, as siding with the 'innocent' child against the 'hostile' or 'ignorant' parents. Child and youth care workers in general, not only those involved in parents education and support activities, need to ensure that in advocating for the child they do so in a manner congruent with a respect for the strengths and potentials of the parents and family as a whole.

A further aspect relating to parent group leadership pertains to the role of the leader. Parent groups vary in their emphasis on three major dimensions: knowledge, skills, and emotional support. Except for the relatively small number of groups emphasizing a high degree of knowledge dissemination, the most effective role for a group leader is as a facilitator rather than as an expert. As a facilitator, a child and youth care worker can utilize skills in group dynamics and interpersonal communication to assist parents in sharing their experiential expertise relating to parenting concerns. The parents themselves can contribute important information on norms relating to child development and parenting practices in the community. The worker with particular child- and family-related experience and training can offer another useful perspective as a resource rather than as 'the expert.'

Program Effectiveness: A Cautionary Note

Perhaps the major issue in the field of parent education and support is the evaluation of its effectiveness. Current enthusiasm for the various approaches tends to assume that all parent education and support efforts are indisputably good — the more the better! Two recent studies suggest that parent group approaches may not be benign but may, in fact, encourage some of the very behaviours they are seeking to reduce or eliminate.

Shain, Suurvali, and Kilty (1980) report on an evaluation of a parenting skills program which was implemented to assess the impact of enhancing parents' communication skills about their children's alcohol use. It is important to note that this program utilized trained group leaders who implemented a series of ten two-hour sessions over a period of ten weeks, which were based largely on Thomas Gordon's parent effectiveness training content supplemented by other sources.

The evaluation determined that if mom and dad smoked and drank it was *more* likely that their children would smoke and drink as communication improved. Further, in the evaluator's own words:

> There was some evidence ... that PCP (Parent Communication Project) could be *divisive* [emphasis in original] in families, e.g., where mother came against the wishes of father ... This divisiveness was reflected in children's perceptions of parents' behaviour — mothers becoming more accepting, fathers more rejecting. Clearly this sets up quite a bit of tension in the family. This effect was only formally observed in lower S.E.S. (socio-economic status) families but it was seen informally in middle-class families too where attendance at the course by women reportedly had at least a temporarily disruptive effect on marital harmony. Sometimes, it was permanent. Several divorces or separate household arrangements may have been stimulated by attendance at the course. (Anglin 1984:62–3)

Another researcher, referring to a different parenting program, has also noted that 'it is possible that the support groups had a negative effect on relationships with spouses' (Kagey, Vivace, and Lutz 1981:166). These observations ought to give us pause for reflection. With tens of thousands of parents, the vast majority mothers attending on their own, all subjected to parent group experiences, it is incumbent on those offering programs to ensure that they first do no harm. It may well be that some current approaches are, indeed, doing more harm than good to family life. However, few programs have even attempted to assess their effects in a manner that would bring forth such data. It is essential that, in addition to cost-benefit analyses, such data be sought out in future evaluation efforts.

It would appear that for both economic and theoretical reasons, the coming decade will see continued high interest in the area of parent education and support. Several trends will likely be important in this regard, including the continued questioning of professionalism, the retrenchment of government services, and the weakening of traditional economic structures. In seeking to contribute to the support of children and families, child and youth care workers will need to draw upon the literature of numerous disciplines and become involved in advocacy at the macrosystem level of society as well as in direct work with parents.

Summary
This chapter has introduced the reader to one of the most promising and challenging areas of child and youth care work. Much recent work has been done in developing the roles and methods of child and youth care workers in relation to parents (Birtsch 1990; Charles 1991; Lothian 1991). As we seek to intervene in the lives of children, parents, and families, we need to develop our understanding of the changes taking place in family life, the social ecology of human development, informal and formal helping, the realities of parenting, and the strengths and limitation of parent education and support programs.

As a profession, child and youth care is in a unique position to build on its considerable strengths and to shift its modes of operation to best suit the needs and realities of parents. A first step in this direction has been the acceptance of a new vision of the child and youth care profession and an unfailing commitment to the well-being of children *and* families.

Notes
1 The Family Support Worker Program originally established under the auspices of the BC Ministry of Human Resources (now Social Services and Housing) was terminated in October 1983. Data on the program are presented here because of

its innovative nature. For a detailed postmortem on the Family Support Worker Program, refer to Currie and Pishalski 1983.

References

Anglin, J.P. 1983a. The 7% solution: The myth of the 'normal,' 'typical' Canadian family. Unpublished manuscript, School of Child Care, University of Victoria

–. 1983b. Setting the sights: An assessment of child care job functions and training needs in British Columbia. In C. Denholm, A. Pence, and R.V. Ferguson (eds.), *The scope of professional child care in British Columbia*. Victoria: University of Victoria

–. (ed.). 1984. *Proceedings of education and support for parenting: An ecological perspective on primary prevention*. Symposium held at the University of Victoria, British Columbia, Health and Welfare Canada

–. 1985. Developing education and support groups for parents of children in residential care. *Residential Care and Treatment* 3:15–27

–. 1989. Child and youth care in British Columbia: A followup to the 1980 needs assessment survey. *Journal of Child and Youth Care* 4:97–117

Birtsch, V. 1990. Cooperation with parents in residential child care: Limits and perspectives. *FICE International Bulletin* 2:15–22

Brim, O.G., Jr. 1965. *Education for childrearing*. New York: Free Press

Bronfenbrenner, U. 1979. *The ecology of human development: Experiments by nature and design*. Cambridge: Harvard University Press

Canadian Mental Health Association. 1982. *The primary prevention project instructor's manual*. Toronto

Caplan, G. 1974. Support systems. In G. Caplan (ed.), *Support systems and community mental health*. New York: Basic Books

Charles, G. 1991. Suicide intervention and prevention among northern Native youth. *Journal of Child and Youth Care* 6:11–17

Chess, S., Thomas, A., and Birch, H.G. 1976. *Your child is a person: A psychological approach to parenthood without guilt*. Middlesex, England: Penguin

Coates, R. 1981. Community based services for juvenile delinquents: Concepts and implications for practice. *Journal of Social Issues* 37:87–101

Cochran, M. and Woolever, F. (eds.). 1983. Beyond the deficit model: The empowerment of parents with information and informal supports. In I.E. Sigel and L.M. Laosa (eds.), *Changing families*. New York: Plenum

Currie, J. and Pishalski, F. 1983. *Loosening the fabric: The termination of the family support program in British Columbia*. Victoria: Report of the Southern Vancouver Island Chapter of the British Columbia Association of Social Workers and The British Columbia Child Care Services Association

DeLong, L.A. and Boyer, M. 1991. Bringing them home: Community supports for the medically fragile child. *Journal of Child and Youth Care* 6:37–42

Eichler, M. 1983. *Families in Canada today: Recent changes and their policy consequences*. Toronto: Gage

Ferguson, R.V. and Anglin, J.P. 1985. The child care professional: A vision for the future. *Child Care Quarterly* 14:85–102

Galinsky, E. 1981. *Between generations: The six stages of parenthood*. New York: Berkeley Books

Garbarino, J. 1983. Social support networks: Rx for the helping professions. In J.K. Whittaker and J. Garbarino (eds.), *Social support networks: Informal helping in the human services*. New York: Aldine

Gottlieb, B.H. 1983. *Social support strategies: Guidelines for mental health practice*. Beverly Hills: Sage

Grealish, E.M., Hawkins, R.P., Meadowcroft, P., Weaver, P., Frost, S.S., and Lynch, P. 1989. A behavioural group procedure for parents of severely troubled and troubling youth in out-of-home care: Alternative to conventional parent training. *Child and Youth Care Quarterly* 18:49–61

Grubb, W.N. and Lazerson, M. 1982. *Broken promises: How Americans fail their children*. New York: Basic Books

Hobbs, N., Dokecki, P.R., Hoover-Dempsey, K.V., Thoroney, R.M., Shayne, M.W., and Weeks, K.H. 1984. *Strengthening families*. San Francisco: Jossey-Bass

Kagey, J.R., Vivace, J., and Lutz, W. 1981. Mental health primary prevention: The role of parent mutual support groups. *American Journal of Public Health* 71:166–7

Katz, A.H. and Bender, E.I. 1976. *The strength in us: Self-help groups in the modern world*. New York: New Viewpoints

Littauer, C. 1980. Working with families of children in residential treatment. *Child Welfare* 59:225–34

Lothian, D. 1991. Working with suicidal adolescents and their families. *Journal of Child and Youth Care* 6:1–9

Mahoney, A. 1981. Family participation for juvenile offenders in deinstitutionalization programs. *Journal of Social Issues* 37:133–4

Maier, H.W. 1981. Essential components in care and treatment for children. In F. Ainsworth, and L.C. Fulcher (eds.), *Group care for children: Concept and issues*. New York: Tavistock

Miller, S.M. 1983. *Children as parents: Final report on a study of child-bearing and child-rearing among 12–15-year-olds*. New York: Child Welfare League of America

Powell, D. 1984. Enhancing the effectiveness of parent education: An analysis of program assumptions. In L. Katz (ed.), *Current topics in early childhood education*. Vol. 5. Norwood, NJ: Ablex

Rapoport, R., Rapoport, R.N., and Strelitz, Z. 1980. *Fathers, mothers and society: Perspectives on parenting*. New York: Vintage Books

Romeder, J.M. 1989. *The self-help way: Mutual aid and health*. Ottawa: Canadian Council on Social Development

Schlossman, S.L. 1976. Before home start: Notes toward a history of parent education in America, 1897–1929. *Harvard Educational Review* 46:436–67

Shain, M., Suurvali, H., and Kilty, H.L. 1980. *Final report on the parent communication project*. Toronto: Addiction Research Foundation

Steere, G.H. 1964. *Changing values in child socialization: A study of United States child-rearing literature, 1865–1939*. Ann Arbor: University Microfilms

Strong-Boag, V. 1982. Intruders in the nursery: Child-care professionals reshape the years one to five. In J. Parr (ed.), *Childhood and family in Canadian history*. Toronto: McClelland & Stewart

Webster, C.D., Somjen, L., Sloman, L., Bradley, S., Mooney, S.A., and Mack, J.E. 1979. The child care worker in the family: Some case examples and implications for the design of family-centered programs. *Child Care Quarterly* 8:5–18

Weiss, H. 1983. Introduction. In *Programs to strengthen families: A resource guide.* Report of the Yale Bush Center in Child Development and Social Policy and the Family Resource Coalition. Chicago: Family Resource Coalition

Whittaker, J.K. 1983. Social support networks in child welfare. In J.K. Whittaker and J. Garbarino (eds.), *Social support networks: Informal helping in the human services.* New York: Aldine

Whittaker, J.K. and Garbarino, J. 1983. *Social support networks: Informal helping in the human services.* New York: Aldine

12
The Future of Child and Youth Care in Canada

Alan Pence, Roy Ferguson, and Carey Denholm

Previous chapters in this book have outlined selected segments of the umbrella model of child and youth care presented in the introduction. The variety of functions and settings depicted in these chapters indicates the degree to which the child and youth care field has developed from its early origins in day care and residential care. While the generic aspects of child and youth care (the essence of practice) will remain, the field will continue to evolve. The following is a sketch of some of the forces that will affect the future development of the child and youth care field.

New Directions

As has been noted with some consistency throughout this text, Canadian society continues to experience major and rapid transformations which impinge upon the entire human services structure and, thus, affect the evolution of professional child and youth care. These changes include shifts towards a greater emphasis on: information and information technologies, decentralized and down-sized human service structures, diversification of services and service approaches, private sector involvement in service delivery, multiple career options, and the need for innovative networking structures across and within the various human services both nationally and internationally. The 1990s have begun with an emphasis on immediacy of communication previously unknown, major international realignments that pose both great promises and threats to world stability, and a growing sense of shared ecological risk and responsibility for all humankind.

These changes and influences in our society have major implications for child and youth care professionals. For example, it is inevitable that greater emphasis will be placed on new and increasingly sophisticated forms of research in order to meet the demand for more and better professional information. New books, journals, and professional newsletters, which have developed at an unprecedented rate since the late 1980s, will continue to emerge at a rapid pace to disseminate the increased amount of information generated in the child and youth care field. Child and youth care professionals will need to balance interpersonal, clinical, and technical skills in order to function effectively within the new information-oriented society.

The movement towards more decentralized human service delivery structures means that services for children and families will increasingly develop from the 'ground up' rather than from the 'top down', resulting in greater diversification and the potential for increased responsiveness to individuals' and families' needs. The number of professional opportunities and choices will increase, as child and youth care personnel will have available a greater range of program approaches with regard to the development and delivery of human services.

Concomitant with the tendency of governments at all levels to decentralize and to down-size will be a continuation of the transfer of government services to the private sector as well as an increased emphasis on community-based, self-help mechanisms. As innovative services and programs develop at the community level, new roles and functions for child and youth care professionals, particularly those with an entrepreneurial orientation, will emerge.

The quest for multiple options has created a society in which there exists unprecedented choice and diversity regarding material goods as well as diversity in family structures, roles, and employment. Similarly, within the human service professions, a variety of therapeutic approaches are being used by multidisciplinary teams, who, characteristically, adopt a pragmatic and eclectic viewpoint when addressing the specific needs of their clients. Thus, child and youth care personnel can no longer rely primarily on intuition and extensive field-based experience or simply apply a single theoretical approach to all the situations they encounter. In the future, the skilled professional will need to possess a variety of skills, including networking with other professionals, and he or she will need to apply those various skills differentially according to the unique clinical needs of each client (Hills 1989).

As the ethnic population increases throughout Canada, human service delivery systems are recognizing the importance of providing more culturally sensitive programs. Providing care to children, youth, and families is a social process in which both the professional and the client interact on the basis of a set of beliefs, values, experiences, expectations, and practices. Ethnic membership often means differences from the predominant culture on perspectives relating to family structure and roles, extended family, children, gender issues, education, problem identification, and help-seeking behaviours.

To provide effective care throughout the broad multicultural mosaic that exists across Canada. it is necessary for practitioners to understand both inter- and intra-ethnic diversity in order to accommodate the client's viewpoint in negotiating appropriate care. In order to more effectively prepare caregivers to work in culturally diverse settings, innovations in education and training will be required (Pence, Kuehne, Greenwood-Church, Opekokew, and Mulligan 1992; Waxler-Morrison, Anderson, and Richardson 1990).

The above is a brief summary of some of the new directions evident in our society and some of their possible implications for the child and youth care professional. These various transformations are taking place against a complex backdrop of political and ecological uncertainty. Clearly, flexibility and adaptability will be key requirements of any health or human service professional in the years ahead. We will now turn our attention to the process of adaptation necessary if child and youth care professionals are to take advantage of the opportunities presented by these trends.

Adaptation: The Shifting Nature of Child and Youth Care

In order to adapt to the many trends evident throughout North American society, child and youth care workers must be prepared to demonstrate openness and flexibility while building upon those attributes which are unique and central to the field. The child and youth care professional will need to resist the temptation to hold on to restricting (though often comfortable) roles and definitions in the face of shifting social and governmental perceptions and demands. The ability of the professional to adapt and change must not be restricted by a rigid definition. Child and youth care will continue its need to be conceptualized as a professional field with a broad scope — a field which can expand its roles and functions in response to changing service needs and trends.

The Nature of Change

It is clear that we are in a time of enormous change within the human services. The child and youth care professional may feel threatened by this change and may deal with it by ignoring or denying it and becoming entrenched in old ways. On the other hand, change within the field and in society in general may be viewed as an opportunity for the child and youth care professional to develop new roles and functions which may not have been possible before.

The Change Cycle

Change is a continuous and ongoing process; the nature, type, and magnitude of the change may vary, but the responses are quite similar. Change usually creates stress, which, in turn, throws the individual, organization, or system into a state of disequilibrium. In response, one adapts to the changes, and a state of relative equilibrium returns, until the next major changes occur and the whole cycle repeats itself. This cyclical process is illustrated in Figure 12.1.

Figure 12.1

Change cycle

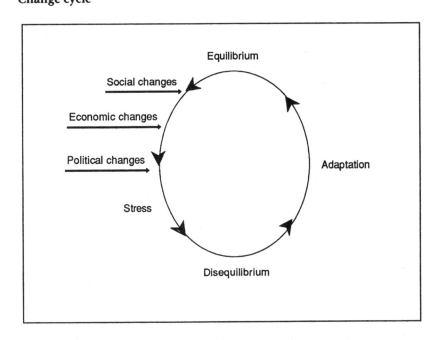

The change cycle depicts a process in which an adaptation is made to restore equilibrium in the system. However, if an adaptation is not made the system remains in a state of disequilibrium, which, if allowed to continue, can create more stress, resulting in still greater disequilibrium, and so on. The downward spiral which ensues can be a destructive process, ultimately leading to the disintegration of the system.

When applying this concept to child and youth care, it is clear that every effort must be made to adapt to the present changes in the field. The child and youth care professional cannot afford simply to sit back and wait for this crisis to pass, because, in view of the cyclical nature of the change process, other crises will undoubtedly follow. Adaptation is achieved through continual monitoring and assessment of the changing scene, seizing opportunities as they are presented.

A potential advantage for the child and youth care professional as he or she prepares to meet the challenges of the future is the historic lack of rigidity within the field. Largely because of its newness compared to many allied human service fields, child and youth care has, in large part, operated within a flexible organizational format. Child and youth care professionals have also been able to observe the experiences of other more established fields, identifying some of their structural problems and avoiding similar errors. The resulting flexibility is one of the attributes of the field which will make it easier to meet the challenges of the future.

One of the primary adaptations required within the field is the need for diversification. The scope of the field of child and youth care must continue to exhibit flexibility in order to meet changing societal trends. Every effort must be made to adopt an inclusive rather than an exclusive attitude in defining the scope of the field. The similarities among child and youth care professionals far exceed the differences, and the field of child and youth care must continue to be defined broadly. In Chapter 1, we depicted this broad scope through the use of an umbrella graphic, in which each of the sections of the umbrella represents a different specialized area of service and the handle indicates the range of educational and training opportunities.

In order to be actively involved in the development of such a continuum of care for children and families, the child and youth care field must also recognize the importance of a generalist orientation in its practitioners. It is interesting to observe that, after having focused on increasing specialization for the past two or three decades, some of the more established human service professions now emphasize general practice. While there certainly is a need for specialists in all of the professional areas, the greater need now is for generalists who are capable of creating and operating within a broad continuum of services. Such a trend was evident beginning in the 1980s, as noted by futurist John Naisbitt in his book *Megatrends*: 'we are moving from the specialist who is soon obsolete to the generalist who can adapt' (1984:32). Child and youth care will find these words appropriate in the 1990s as well.

The child and youth care field has avoided a high degree of specialization and, consequently, does not have to backtrack, as do some of the other professional fields trying to achieve a more generalized focus. Accordingly, child and youth care workers will find adaptation easier.

It is clear that the practice of child and youth care will continue to shift as the field adapts to the various social, political, and economic changes which impinge upon society. And just as change is a continuous process, so, too, is adaptation. An understanding of prevailing trends within society makes such shifts easier to accept, facilitating the process of adaptation. It can be said that the health, well-being, and future of the child and youth care field will be based upon its ability to adapt.

An Expanded Scope for Child Care: The Implications
A central theme throughout this book is the importance of recognizing the broad scope of the child and youth care field across the country. The first chapter outlined some of the prevailing trends existing in North America — trends which are having an impact upon the entire human service delivery system. It was suggested that, instead of becoming entrenched in old ways and restricting definitions, the child and youth care field should seize the opportunities provided by these trends and recognize its ability to respond proactively to changing service needs. An inclusive rather than exclusive perspective was presented as necessary to define the scope of the child and youth care field. The subsequent chapters focused on some of the more typical settings and functions constituting the broad child care service continuum.

It should be evident that across the settings and activities described in these chapters, the similarities in child and youth care function far exceed the differences. Similar descriptions of the major trends within society which directly affect allied areas (e.g., rehabilitation) have recently been published (Neufeldt 1992). It is clear that these trends impinge on all professional human service practices, yet, as the child and youth care field adapts to changing societal demands (largely through diversification of function and scope), there remain a number of implications to be considered.

Ecological Perspective

Throughout this discussion we have repeatedly observed the critical importance of the interplay of the child and youth care practitioner and the environmental context. Child and youth care is, above all, a field concerned with the social ecology of human development. Increasingly, practitioners, researchers, and policy-makers concerned with human development and care are adopting social ecological perspectives to help describe and explain more adequately the complexities of their concerns. As early as 1982, Powell called for the adoption of such a perspective by the field. In 1988, Pence provided the field with a collection of child and family research that had developed in response to Bronfenbrenner's earlier (1979) call for an ecological orientation. As described in capsule form by Bronfenbrenner:

> The ecology of human development involves the scientific study of the mutual accommodation between an active, growing human being and the changing human properties of the immediate settings in which the developing person lives, as this process is affected by relations between these settings, and by the larger contexts in which the settings are embedded. (1979:21)

It is our contention that an ecological perspective is central to the continuing development, understanding, and promotion of the field of child and youth care. Our consideration of the following various elements assumes the adoption of such an ecological perspective.

Education and Training

In order to function within a wide scope of roles and functions, child and youth care workers must receive broad-based professional training containing a core set of generic skills. Curriculum guidelines for such programs have now been well established and include required content areas such as life-span growth and development, program planning, case management, group dynamics, communication, and behavioural management. The call for a more educated, more politically astute, more cohesive and unified professional body of practitioners is regularly articulated at conferences and in the professional literature. Furthermore, attention to strengthening and further developing the *core* elements of knowledge, skills, and understanding of self, which can be applied to any setting in which a child and youth care worker would be employed, also continues to be made (Ricks 1989). Education and training programs for child and youth care workers remain limited in number across Canada and the United States. Jones and VanderVen (1990) suggest that this is due to factors such as lack of funding for universities and colleges, low wages for practitioners, and the inability of academic institutions to respond to the needs of adult learners who are not able to leave family and/or jobs to attend traditional, full-time, campus-based programs. On this last point it is interesting to note that a few colleges and universities are adapting to the needs of the adult, part-time learner by developing flexible, distance education programs that complement and augment existing on-campus programs (e.g., University of Victoria) or programs that are entirely built on a distance format (e.g., NOVA University). Ferguson (1990) suggests that flexible, distance programs and educational resource sharing are necessary ingredients, particularly in tight economic times, to meeting the enormous education and training needs of a new field such as child and youth care.

Gone are the days when the traditional clientele for university and college programs were exclusively students between eighteen and twenty-four years of age. This new influx of adult learners as both full- and part-time students has been referred to as 'the new majority' in higher education (Ferguson, Martin, and Wilson 1989). Thus, universities and colleges need to include flexible course offerings and utilize a range of delivery methods, including the establishment of direct partnerships with agencies which will support staff, if it is their wish, in upgrading their level of education. In order to keep pace with rapid changes in the field, the child and youth care professional must prepare to participate in training which continues over an extended period of time.

The basic education and training of child and youth care professionals is built around core, generic skills, which form a foundation upon which the more specialized knowledge and skills required for a particular practice setting can be added as required. This focus has direct implications for college and university-based educators in such programs. Greater emphasis is now being placed on educators, who, as well as having direct field experience, have a background in adult learning. The job description often includes curriculum design, development of off-campus learning packages, and theoretical perspectives on curriculum in relation to standards and needs within the field. Teaching at this level involves not simply talking about one's field-based experiences but principles of questioning, familiarity with adult learning theory and principles, knowledge of classroom management strategies, awareness of one's own competencies and strengths, clarity and practice with instructional approaches and techniques, understanding principles of assessment, giving feedback, grading strategies and well developed writing skills. (Denholm 1990:354)

Career Ladder

In the past, child and youth care services have been plagued with high staff turnover rates. This has usually been attributed to the existence of job-related stress in the worker compounded by limited career ladders (Krueger 1986). Too often the pay and authority given to child and youth care professionals were not commensurate with their responsibility. At the same time there tended to be an inherent avoidance of promotion within the field, as noted by Beker (1977): 'If we continue to maintain, as many of us have, that promotions somehow taint the "purity" of the child care worker, we will never attain professional stature' (p. 166).

Fortunately for the field, the issue of vertical advancement has become not whether to pursue but how best to pursue. As increasing numbers of child and youth care professionals assume non-front-line positions, the value of the unique perspective that our field brings to the human services at all levels of the career ladder becomes increasingly evident.

Increased vertical mobility, linked to broader horizontal mobility (as represented by the related ladders of the scope of child and youth care), creates a veritable lattice-work of professional opportunities. Rather than losing many of our most experienced practitioners to other professions and disciplines, we have an unexcelled opportunity to retain our most creative and forward-looking practitioners as they move horizontally, vertically, or diagonally across the lattice structure. Truly, expanded ladders and sets of ladders represent child and youth care's greatest potential for an exciting, creative future.

Integrated Education and Career Ladders

A major issue facing the field at present concerns establishing an integrated set of education and career ladders. Salaries and responsibilities for child and youth care practitioners need to be closely tied to educational preparation levels in a manner that creates both vertical and horizontal mobility options. This means that there must be some de-

gree of standardization in the curriculum content of educational programs. A good start on this task was made at the Conference-Research
Sequence in Child Care Education, where principles and guidelines for
child and youth care preparation programs (VanderVen, Mattingly,
and Morris 1982) were established. These guidelines shaped the structure and content of most of the college and university child and youth
care programs throughout the continent to a considerable degree. The
guidelines are in the process of being updated and will undoubtedly
contain more emphasis on topics such as child abuse, substance abuse,
and multiculturalism than existed a decade ago, when the original
ones were formulated.

In British Columbia, considerable effort is being invested in collaboration between university and college systems (Baines 1992). The
School of Child and Youth Care at the University of Victoria, in collaboration with a number of community colleges, is developing a child
and youth care curriculum blueprint that will integrate the content of
diploma, degree, and graduate level programs in such a way as to provide complete articulation and full transfer credit across all programs.
This will mean that students can move from one geographical location
to another in the province and find that college programs will be similar and fully linked with the university on- and off-campus programs.
Progress is also being made in cooperative course development, with
each program developing certain courses and sharing them with other
programs. Networking of resources significantly reduces the cost of curriculum development for each participant, since the same course is not
repeatedly developed in each institution. This cooperative curriculum
development also ensures greater standardization of content across
settings.

Another significant development that enhances the career ladder for
the field is the recent availability of graduate level programs for child
and youth care professionals in Canada. The first doctoral student in
child and youth care in Canada will soon be graduating from the University of Victoria, representing the final step in the development of a
complete educational career ladder.

Professional Stature

In order to meet the mandate created by a broader scope, child and
youth care must place greater emphasis on professionalism. It will be
necessary to establish a somewhat delicate balance between this increased desire and need for professionalism, while maintaining public

accountability. As previously noted, we must avoid the pitfalls experienced by some of the more established disciplines, which, in their zeal to professionalize, sometimes lost sight of the needs of the persons for whom they existed. The appearance of being self-serving created, in the general public, a basic distrust of professionals, as reflected in George Bernard Shaw's statement that 'every profession is a conspiracy against the layman.' However, we can learn from the experience of our colleagues and work towards developing a style of professionalism which places the needs of the client before those of the profession.

Practice standards must continue to be created to function as guidelines for professionals as they move out into a variety of new areas. While these collective standards need to be developed, they should not replace the individual standards already in existence. In an effort to enhance professional stature, child care must continue to create its own body of knowledge and professional literature and develop the ability to supervise its own practitioners. Child and youth care must adopt a universal code of ethics in addition to sanctions for misconduct and must operate under the auspices of a professional association. These are some of the basic characteristics of any professional field (Rose 1990).

Professional Communication/Organization
As the scope of the profession develops, the need for effective communication mechanisms for child and youth care professionals becomes greater. A method is required to connect professionals and provide them with a sense of their similarities, despite the variety of settings in which they practice. They must be able to identify the common issues and concerns which are inherent throughout the many areas of child and youth care practice. A broadened scope of child and youth care will significantly increase the numbers of persons within the field, so that efficient coordination and communication must become central issues.

There will be a need for small, decentralized organizational structures geared to regional issues and specific interests within different settings, such as day care, residential care, hospital care, and so forth. At the same time, there must also be national and international mechanisms able to function as an interface for this network of regional structures and specific interests. New mechanisms have developed in Canada that can assist in the coordination of the field. One such structure is the Council of Canadian Child and Youth Care Associations, which is a national body established to serve as a coordinating and networking organization for provincial and territorial child and youth care associations (Laliberté 1991).

As the roles and functions of child and youth care diversify, the need for information and support for individual practitioners and special interest groups will grow. As a result, professional networking becomes particularly important, and regional and central organizational structures can facilitate this networking process.

Professional Influence
To establish a higher professional profile, child and youth care will need to be more involved in public policy. This has, traditionally, been an area in which child and youth care professionals have not been very active, but political involvement is necessary when advocating for children and families. Responsible advocacy is an important function of the child and youth care field, particularly in a time when many governments do not consider human services to be a priority. Beker (1979) suggests that professionalism 'is a reality that imposes special responsibilities on all of us' (p. 245). Our responsibility is to assist the evolution of professionalism in child and youth care in a conscientious and thoughtful manner.

With a broad definition of the scope of child and youth care and an enhanced level of communications and organizational coordination within the broadly defined field, the potential for meaningful social and political action on behalf of children, youth, and families is greatly increased. Its greater size can contribute towards the establishment of a tremendous lobby power, which can then be utilized by the central organizational structures when advocating for children. The child and youth care field will have a larger role to play; rather than only responding to trends, it may, in fact, be capable of creating them.

In this chapter, we have emphasized the opportunities that are emerging from changes in human services and in the larger sociocultural context. It is certainly true that these changes also present dangers not only for the child and youth care field but also for children and families. The historical trend in society following the Second World War has been towards an increasing dependence upon formalized, bureaucratized, and professionalized forms of care and support. Our social and economic policies have served, in some cases, to erode the viability of family and community support networks. In this context, a context which has reinforced our dependency and weakened our capacities to care for ourselves and others, a simple withdrawal of government programs and support in the name of 'financial restraint' is both unrealistic and irresponsible.

Yet these changes and trends have created some potential opportunities for the child and youth care field. In order to adapt to the changes we are experiencing, child and youth care must recognize its scope while maintaining the concerns of children and families at the core of its professional identity. Roles, functions, and personal preferences must be adjusted in response to these opportunities in order that a continuum of care, which addresses the needs of children, families, and community life at all levels of society, can be established.

The current changes in society present the chance to construct within child and youth care a new vision for the future. We must seize these opportunities and bear in mind the observation attributed to the French philosopher and writer, Paul Valéry, that the problem with today is that the future isn't what it used to be.

References
Baines, C. 1992. College-university collaboration. *The Canadian Nurse* 88:17–19
Beker, J. 1977. On defining the child care profession. *Child Care Quarterly* 6:165–6
–. 1979. Professional frontiers in child care: Unfinished business and new priorities. *Child Care Quarterly* 8:245–53
British Columbia. Ministry of Health. 1990. *Foundations for the future.* Advisory Committee on Mental Health. Victoria
Bronfenbrenner, U. 1979. *The ecology of human development. Experiments by nature and design.* Cambridge: Harvard University Press
Denholm, C. 1990. 2000 and beyond: Future career directions for child and youth care professionals. In J. Anglin, C. Denholm, R. Ferguson, and A. Pence (eds.), *Perspectives in professional child and youth care.* New York: Haworth
Ferguson, R.V. 1990. Distance education: Catch the wave. In J. Anglin, C. Denholm, R. Ferguson, and A. Pence (eds.), *Perspectives in professional child and youth care.* New York: Haworth
Ferguson R.V., Martin, R., and Wilson, K. 1989. Distance education: The tip of the iceberg. *Journal of Child and Youth Care* 4:55–69
Goldberger, L. and Breznitz, S. (eds.). 1982. *Handbook of stress: Theoretical and clinical aspects.* New York: Free Press
Hills, W.D. 1989. The child and youth care student as an emerging professional practitioner. *Journal of Child and Youth Care* 4:17–31
Jones, H. and VanderVen, K. 1990. Education and training for child and youth care practice: The view from both sides of the Atlantic. *Child and Youth Care Quarterly* 19:105–22
Krueger, M. 1986. *Job satisfaction for child and youth care workers.* Washington: Child Welfare League

Laliberté, P. 1991. What is the Council of Canadian Child and Youth Care Associations? *Child and Youth Care in Canada* 1:1–2

Naisbitt, J. 1984. *Megatrends.* New York: Warner Books

Neufeldt, A. 1992. Major trends in rehabilitation: Implications for skill training. *Journal of Practical Approaches to Developmental Handicap* 16:5–10

Pence, A.R. 1988. *Ecological research with children and families.* New York: Teachers College Press

Pence, A., Kuehne, V., Mulligan V., Greenwood-Church, M., and Opekokew, M.R. 1992. First Nations early childhood care and education: The Meadow Lake Tribal Council — School of Child and Youth Care curriculum development project. *Multiculturalism Journal* 14:3

Powell, D.R. 1980. Towards a socio-ecological perspective of relations between parents and child care programs. In S. Klimer (ed.), *Advances in early education and day care.* Vol. I. Greenwich, CT: JAI Press

Ricks, R. 1989. Self awareness model for training and application in child and youth care. *Journal of Child and Youth Care* 4:33–41

Rose, L. 1990. Professionalization of child and youth care in British Columbia: A case study. M.A. thesis, University of Victoria

VanderVen, K., Mattingly, M., and Morris, M. 1982. Principles and guidelines for child care preparation programs. *Child Care Quarterly* 11:221–44

Waxler-Morrison, N., Anderson, J., and Richardson, E. 1990. *Cross-cultural caring: A handbook for health professionals in Western Canada.* Vancouver: UBC Press

Contributors

James P. Anglin, M.S.W. (University of British Columbia)
Director, School of Child and Youth Care, University of Victoria
James Anglin started teaching in the School of Child and Youth Care in 1979 and has been director of the school since 1989. He also serves as coordinator of the Child and Youth Care Education Consortium (CYCEC), as Canadian representative to the International Federation of Educative communities (FICE-UNESCO), as associate editor of the *Child and Youth Care Forum*, and as an editorial board member of the *Journal of Emotional and Behavioural Problems*. His major research and professional interests include parent education and family support, children's rights, and child and youth care education. Jim was the coordinating editor of the text *Perspectives in Professional Child and Youth Care* (New York: Haworth 1990) and edited a two-volume special issue of the *Child and Youth Care Forum* (New York: Human Sciences Press 1990) on international perspectives in child and youth care.

Roy I. Brown, Ph.D. (University of London)
Professor, Rehabilitation Studies, University of Calgary
Roy Brown came to the University of Calgary in 1968 where he was director of the Vocational Rehabilitation Research Institute. In the late 1970s he was instrumental in setting up unique bachelor's and master's specialization programs in Rehabilitation Education at the university for the education of personnel working with handicapped children and adults. Roy has consulted on a wide range of projects both here and abroad and continues to lecture around the world. He has published a broad spectrum of research and theoretical papers and books and is particularly interested in the application of research to practice and professional training. Recently he has finished the Rehabilitation Programmes Study which is concerned with quality of life and choice for persons with developmental handicaps. His most recent publication (with Max Bayer and Patricia M. Brown) is *Empowerment and Developmental Handicaps: Choices and Quality of Life* (Toronto/London: Captus University Publications/Chapman & Hall 1992).

Dana Brynelsen
Provincial Advisor, Infant Development Programme,
Vancouver, British Columbia
After teaching school in northern and coastal British Columbia, Dana Brynelsen was initially employed to supervise the Vancouver-Richmond Infant Development Programme (IDP) in 1973. As provincial advisor for infant development programs, she now assists communities in implementing and operating staff training programs and advises and supports IDP staff. Dana has provided consultation on the operation of IDPs throughout Canada and has spoken internationally on the IDP. She also coordinates the Institute on Infant Development at the University of British Columbia. Her particular interests relate to parent/professional relationships and she is editor of a news journal for parents that is circulating to 2,000 families in British Columbia.

Patricia M. Canning, Ph.D., C. Psych. (University of Windsor)
Associate Dean of Research and Development, Faculty of Education,
Memorial University of Newfoundland, St. John's, Newfoundland
Previous to her recent appointment as associate dean of research and development at Memorial University of Newfoundland, Patricia Canning was professor of child study at Mount Saint Vincent University in Halifax, Nova Scotia. She has had extensive experience developing teacher-training programs for early childhood educators in Canada and the Caribbean. She has published articles on the professionalization of child care, young children with special needs, program development, and cross-cultural education. Her current research focuses on the development of resource information for parents of young children with special needs and professionals working with them, the integration of children with special needs into preschool and school, and the relationship between children's developmental levels and characteristics of the child care environment.

Carey J. Denholm, Ph.D. (University of Victoria)
Senior Lecturer, Department of Education, University of Tasmania
(Hobart), Australia
Carey Denholm, after a period of twelve years in the School of Child and Youth Care at the University of Victoria, returned to his homeland, Australia. With a background in the Canadian and Australian education systems, he has concentrated on raising the profile of professional school-based child and youth care through a number of published articles and texts: *Canadian trends in school-based child care* (Victoria: Fotoprint 1981); *The scope of professional child care in British Columbia* (Victoria: University of Victoria 1983); *Canadian school-based child and youth care* (special edition of the *Journal of Child and Youth Care* 6 (1991). His research involves adolescents, stress, and the effects of hospitalization. He consults to various school systems and maintains a private practice with adolescents and families.

Roy V. Ferguson, Ph.D. (University of Alberta)
Extension Faculty Coordinator, School of Child and Youth Care,
University of Victoria
Roy Ferguson began his career in Edmonton, first working at the Alberta Guidance Clinic and then on the Unit for Emotionally Disturbed Children at Glenrose Hospital. In 1973, after completing his doctorate in clinical psychology, he moved to Calgary where he established the Department of Psychology and the Preschool Language and Behaviour Program at Alberta Children's Hospital. He continued as director of the Department of Psychology at Alberta Children's Hospital until 1979, when he moved to Victoria to be the director of the School of Child and Youth Care until 1984. Roy continues to teach and do research in the school and is responsible for coordinating distance education and collaboration activities with colleges and universities. He is involved in developing a curriculum blueprint for both early childhood education and child and youth care programs in the province and continues to consult to pediatric hospitals in Victoria and Vancouver. He is also an editorial board member for the *Journal of Child and Youth Care,* and his research interests include the study of environmental design for children, hospitalized children, and children with chronic disabilities.

Gerry Fewster, Ph.D. (University of Calgary)
Adjunct Professor, Educational Psychology, University of Calgary
Gerry Fewster is co-editor of the *Journal of Child and Youth Care* and adjunct associate professor of educational psychology at the University of Calgary. Until recently he was executive director of Hull Child and Family Services in Calgary, Alberta, a position he held for over twenty-three years. He is currently working in partnership with his wife, Judith, in the development of their program 'Options for the Well-Being.'

Peter Gabor, Ph.D. (Arizona State University)
Associate Professor and Division Head, Faculty of Social Work,
University of Calgary
Peter Gabor has been involved in the child and youth care field for over twenty years. He began his career as a front-line worker and has also held supervisory and management positions. Currently, Peter is active in teaching, research, and consultation. He is a frequent contributor to child and youth care journals and conferences and is co-author (with Richard Grinnell, Jr.) of the forthcoming text, *Evaluation in the Social Sciences* (Boston: Allyn & Bacon).

Thom Garfat, M.A. (Lakehead University)
Director of Treatment, Youth Horizons Reception Centre,
Montreal, Quebec
Thom Garfat began his professional career as a front-line child care worker and is actively involved in the child and youth care field in Canada and the United States as a speaker, trainer, and consultant. While teaching at the School of Child and Youth Care, he was chair of the first Canadian Child Care Workers

Conference, and he continues to be active in the planning of conferences at the national and international level. Thom is currently director of Treatment for Youth Horizons in Montreal and is co-editor of the *Journal of Child and Youth Care*.

Robert Glossop, Ph.D. (University of Birmingham)
Coordinator of Programs and Research, Vanier Institute of the Family,
Ottawa, Ontario
Robert Glossop is a sociologist and policy analyst whose research and writings have addressed such themes as: demographic change, adolescent motherhood, parent support programs, taxation policy, new life, and family policy. On behalf of the Vanier Institute, he advises a variety of government departments, both federally and provincially. He is also a regular commentator on family trends and social policy developments and a frequent interview subject for journalists writing on social issues.

Valerie Gonzales, M.Sc. (University of Victoria)
Valerie Gonzales is presently working on her doctoral program in psychology at the University of Victoria, where she is studying developmental changes in cognition, memory, and learning in children. She has worked as a pediatric occupational therapist in a rehabilitation facility for eight years before being the director of the Victoria Infant Development Program for fifteen years. As one of the founding members and first president of the British Columbia Association of Infant Development Consultants, she maintains active membership in the society as well as in professional occupational therapy societies in Canada and the United States.

Sandra Griffin, M.A. (University of Victoria)
Practica Coordinator, School of Child and Youth Care,
University of Victoria
Beginning with her own family day care home in the mid-seventies, Sandra Griffin has transformed a desire to provide the best environment for her daughter and other small children into an academic career focused on reshaping the caregiving field in Canada. Her experience includes working in a parent participation preschool and, later, directing a community-based day care centre. Her initial supervisor's training certificate eventually led to a bachelor's and master's degree in the School of Child and Youth Care at the University of Victoria, where she is a visiting assistant professor.

Valerie Kuehne, Ph.D. (Northwestern University)
Assistant Professor, School of Child and Youth Care,
University of Victoria
After practising pediatric nursing and teaching in a diploma nursing program, Valerie Kuehne completed her graduate studies in Chicago at the Erikson Institute at Northwestern University. Her areas of research interest include ecological perspectives on human development across the life course, inter-

generational relations in families and communities, and cross-cultural child and family issues. Since joining the School of Child and Youth Care in 1990, she has collaborated on the School of Child and Youth Care/Meadow Lake Tribal Council Child and Youth Care Career and Education Ladder Project. She is also involved in a number of intergenerational research initiatives in Canada and the United States.

Carolyn A. Larsen, M.A. (McGill University)
Lecturer, Education Department, Concordia University
Carolyn Larsen served as director of the Child Life Service and coordinator of School Services at Montreal Children's Hospital for many years. She also has taught university courses to nursing, and, currently, to education and child study students for several years. She has been actively involved in the multi-disciplinary Association for the Care of Children's Health, chairing its first conference in Canada in 1972 and serving as president and editorial board member. In 1989 she received the Child Life Council Certificate of Honour for outstanding service.

Barbara Maslowsky, M.A. (Sheffield University)
Barbara Maslowsky worked with young offenders for a period of six years before returning to work with female adult offenders. During the time that she worked as a probation officer with adolescents, she demonstrated her commitment and compassion for these youths and responded to them with integrity, respect, and humour. She was devoted to the ideas of fairness and justice, and her enthusiasm, professionalism, and passion for life touched everyone she worked with. Barbara died in February of 1992, but her light still shines.

Helen (Cummings) Norton, R.N., Dip. Public Health
Helen Norton has worked for ten years in community health nursing and for fourteen years in the rehabilitation field related to persons with disabilities. She was employed as a supervisor of the Calgary Early Intervention Program, which provided home-based support for families with developmentally delayed children from birth to three and one-half years old. Helen is now retired but remains active as a volunteer on several community boards and on committees of the Community Living Society.

Leigh Parish, M.A. (University of Toronto)
Director, Child Life Department, Hospital for Sick Children,
Toronto, Ontario
Leigh Parish has been involved with the child-life profession since 1977, both as a practitioner and as an administrator. She has served professionally as a member-at-large on the board of the Child Life Directors and is currently president-elect. She was president of the Canadian Association of Child Life Directors and was involved in the development of accreditation standards for child-life services through the Canadian Council of Health Facilities Accreditation.

Alan R. Pence, Ph.D. (Oregon)
Professor, School of Child and Youth Care, University of Victoria
Alan Pence has extensive experience in child day care, having worked for a ten-year period as a child and youth care worker, trainer, and program director before joining the School of Child and Youth Care in 1981. Since then, he has been primarily involved in the development of Canadian early childhood care and education research and was director of the School of Child and Youth Care from 1986 to 1989. Alan was co-principle investigator on the Victoria and Vancouver Day Care Research Projects, Canadian coordinator for the International Childhood as a Social Phenomenon Project, co-director of the Canadian National Child Care Study, and is presently coordinator of the First Nations Baccalaureate Degree Project for the School of Child and Youth Care. His most recent books include: *Ecological Research with Children and Families: From Concept to Methodology* (New York: Teachers College Press 1988) and (with Don Peters) *Family Day Care: Current Research for Informed Public Policy* (New York: Teachers College Press 1992).

R. Del Phillips, M.P.A. (University of Victoria)
Ombudsman Officer, Office of the Ombudsman, Province of British Columbia, Victoria
R. Del Phillips has managed institutions and programs for young offenders. In addition, he has been a sessional lecturer at the School of Child and Youth Care at University of Victoria and given presentations at conferences and public forums on child and youth issues. Del participated in the establishment of the Ombudsman's Institutional Team and is an original member of the Child and Youth Team. He investigates complaints involving persons under nineteen years of age and seeks resolutions to individual and systems issues through consultation with children and youth in British Columbia.

Kevin Pike, B.A. (University of Alberta)
Director of Parks and Recreation, Municipality of West Vancouver
Kevin Pike has been active in the parks and recreation movement for the past twenty-two years. Currently the director of Parks and Recreation for the municipality of West Vancouver, he was president of the British Columbia Recreation and Parks Association as well as a member of the board of directors of the Canadian Parks and Recreation Association. Kevin is a speaker on such subjects as community development, arts programming, job search skills, labour management relations, creativity, recreation commissioner effectiveness, and practical management. He is also an active member of several professional development organizations.

David Watkins, M.A. (Simon Fraser University)
Team Leader, Graduation Program Team, Ministry of Education, Victoria, British Columbia
Dave Watkins began his teaching career in the Kamloops School District and later taught in Dawson Creek, Langley, and Victoria, where he was principal of Spectrum and Victoria high schools. Dave has remained a strong child and

youth care advocate and has made numerous presentations in support of child and youth care services within the school system.

Gary Young, B.A. (York University)
Director of Recreation for City and District of North Vancouver,
Vancouver, British Columbia
Gary Young has worked in the parks and recreation field for the past twenty years and is currently director of Recreation for the City and District of North Vancouver. He has been an active member of several child and youth advocate organizations and has played a role in the development of the National Children's Play Policies and the Fair Play Codes. Gary is a past president of the British Columbia Recreation and Parks Association and a past member of the board of directors of the Canadian Parks and Recreation Association. He has also served as a community volunteer in both sports and arts organizations.

Editorial Board

Index

play, role of, 214–15;
professionals in, 213–14, 217,
219, 222, 225–7, 229; as
therapy, 224–5
Rehabilitation programs:
changes in approach, 234–7,
250, 251; and the disabled,
231–3, 234–44; future trends,
249–51; history of, 231–3,
239; and integration, 232,
233–4, 239; legal and ethical
issues in, 246–9; and
professionals, education of,
244–6; social and environmental factors in, 237–41,
251; structure of, 242–5
Residential care: and
community-based care, 197;
concept and issues in, 16–18,
27–36; current approaches,
22–3; future directions in,
36–40; history of, 15–16,
18–22; program models, 23–7,
39; treatment in, 30–6
Rogers, Rix, 61–2
Royal Commission on the
Status of Women, 142

Scanlan, D. 107–8
School-based care: influences
on education, 80–4; issues,
97–100; and professionals,

84–93, 99; program models,
84–8; and theoretical
applications, 93–7
Second National Day Care
Conference, 142
Shawbridge, 37
Status of Women Office, 143
Strelitz, Ziona, 261

Thistletown, 22, 37
Trieschman, Albert, 30

UN Convention on the Rights
of Children, 65–6
UN Declarations of Rights of
the Child, 66

VanderVen, K.D., 195–6, 283

Weiss, H., 255, 260
Whittaker, James, 260
Wilderspin, Samuel, 137
William Roper Hull Child and
Family Services, 22, 37
Wolfensberger, W., 3, 81, 165
Wollins, M., 17, 18
Wozner, Y., 17, 18

Young Offenders Act (YOA), 38,
44–5; description of 47–54,
64–6, 67
Youth Horizons, 22, 37

Printed on acid-free paper ∞

Set in Stone by The Typeworks

Printed and bound in Canada by
Friesens Corporation

Copy-editor: Joanne Richardson

Proofreader: Camilla Jenkins

Indexer: Perry Millar